RACE AND REPAST

FOOD AND FOODWAYS

SERIES EDITORS:
JENNIFER JENSEN WALLACH
AND MICHAEL WISE

OTHER TITLES IN THIS SERIES

Race and Repast

FOODSCAPES IN TWENTIETH-CENTURY SOUTHERN LITERATURE

URSZULA NIEWIADOMSKA-FLIS

The University of Arkansas Press
Fayetteville
2022

ISBN: 978-1-68226-219-1
eISBN: 978-1-61075-786-7

26 25 24 23 22   5 4 3 2 1

Manufactured in the United States of America

Untitled chapter artwork by Leszek Niewiadomski.

♾ The paper used in this publication meets the minimum requirements of the American National Standard for Permanence of Paper for Printed Library Materials Z39.48-1984.

Cataloging-in-Publication Data on file at the Library of Congress

CONTENTS

SERIES EDITORS' PREFACE

The University of Arkansas Press series on Food and Foodways explores historical and contemporary issues in global food studies. We are committed to representing a diverse set of voices that tell lesser-known food stories and to provoking new avenues of interdisciplinary research. Our strengths are works in the humanities and social sciences that use food as a critical lens to examine broader cultural, environmental, and ethical issues.

Feeding ourselves has long entangled human beings within complicated moral puzzles of social injustice and environmental destruction. When we eat, we consume not only the food on the plate but also the lives and labors of innumerable plants, animals, and people. This process distributes its costs unevenly across race, class, gender, and other social categories. The production and distribution of food often obscures these material and cultural connections, impeding honest assessments of our impacts on the world around us. By taking these relationships seriously, Food and Foodways provides critical studies that analyze the cultural and environmental relationships that have sustained human societies.

With the publication of *Race and Repast: Foodscapes in Twentieth-Century Southern Literature* by Urszula Niewiadomska-Flis, we have the exciting opportunity to bring the work of a talented literary scholar to a wider audience. This volume offers a fresh reorganization of *Live and Let Di(n)e: Food and Race in the Texts of the American South*, which was originally published in Poland in 2017 and garnered an American Studies Network Book Prize. Here, Niewiadomska-Flis revises and refocuses her earlier work, concentrating her analysis on "literary foodscapes" of the American South. These range from the Jim Crow-era kitchens where White and Black Southerners enacted and reacted against racial mores, the public dining spaces where Southerners performed and probed the limits of racial social roles, and the emblematic lunch counters that became central sites of the Black Freedom Struggle in the 1960s. In each chapter, Niewiadomska-Flis analyzes literary texts by iconic authors such as Ernest Gaines and Walker Percy, demonstrating that "fictional narratives possess great potential to probe the nuances and complexities of sociohistorical context."

Race and Repast compellingly mines literary texts to demonstrate that "food reflects and refracts power," making food studies an especially compelling lens through which to view a radically segregated society that was often on the cusp of violence. Furthermore, Niewiadomska-Flis also provides readers with a rich and succinct introduction to scholarship in Southern studies and food studies, not only elegantly situating her own work in these conversations but also taking the time to explain terms (such as *food voice*) and historical concepts (such as *de jure* and *de facto* segregation), the meanings of which are often taken for granted. This approach makes *Race and Repast* a compelling read both for readers new to these fields and for experts who will find scores of new insights conveyed in Niewiadomska-Flis's clear and graceful prose.

JENNIFER JENSEN WALLACH and MICHAEL WISE

ACKNOWLEDGMENTS

I have accumulated many debts as this project moved from inspiration to publication. I can barely indicate the extent of the kindness and time Robert Westerfelhaus (College of Charleston) has invested in this book project. With generosity of spirit and a "sympathetic eye," Robert has read every word of the manuscript. His editorial guidance steered me through the perils of immersing myself in Southern culture and foodways. His encouraging remarks led me to connections I did not imagine. I am indebted to him for encouragement, extensive and astute intellectual feedback, and most of all for his friendship. As the project unfolded, he also indulged me with some of the most delicious Southern treats: Charleston's Benne Wafers, pecans, BBQ sauces, Café Du Monde coffee, and other delicacies.

I also wish to thank Constante Gonzáles Groba (University of Santiago de Compostela, Spain), whose encyclopedic knowledge of Southern literature has been a source of constant inspiration. I have been spoiled by his friendly research assistance—while conducting his own research, Constante has always kept his eyes open for items that might interest me. A very special thank you for his thoughtful suggestions and intellectual generosity and for our extensive conversations.

The idea for this book was with me for quite a while, at least since when I was preparing for my first conference presentation about foodways in the American South. I had the privilege of presenting a talk entitled "The South through the Kitchen: Cooking and Dining Rituals in Southern Literature and Cinematography" at the Southern Studies Forum (of the European Association for American Studies), which was organized by Université Versailles Saint-Quentin-en-Yvelines and Université Paris IX in 2009. The essence of this book was verbalized during the following Southern Studies Forum symposium at the University of Santiago de Compostela in 2011. Since then, the idea of food reflecting and cocreating Southern culture and racialized identities has been marinating in my mind.

While researching this book, prompted by various conference discussions, I have pursued new research directions and expanded my original line of inquiry. Both formal and informal feedback moved me to broaden my analyses. I would like to thank my conference audiences for presenting useful criticism and introducing some new (positive) analytical complications. Robert Brinkmeyer (University of South Carolina), Elizabeth Hayes Turner (University of North Texas), Susana Jiménez Placer (University of Santiago de Compostela), and Beata Zawadka (University of Szczecin, Poland), all part of the Southern Studies Forum family, offered intellectual sustenance and challenging observations, for which I am truly grateful.

The major work on this book was made possible by the support of three institutions. My initial exploration of Southern foodways was facilitated by a research grant from the John Fitzgerald Kennedy Institute, Free University, Berlin (2009). An Eccles Centre Visiting European Fellowship in North American Studies (2014) provided me with access to the extensive holdings of the British Library in London and a wonderful intellectual environment in which to conduct my research. I also gratefully acknowledge the support of the Clifford and Mary Corbridge Trust of Robinson College (2013), whose scholarship allowed me to work on my project at the University of Cambridge, United Kingdom.

Last, I would like to thank my husband and my children for their support and encouragement, which have been all the more valuable because they have never been uncritical.

■ ■ ■

The present study had a prior life. After gestating for a couple of years, my research ideas finally crystallized as the book *Live and Let Di(n)e: Food and Race in the Texts of the American South* (Lublin, Poland: KUL Publishing House, 2017). The American Studies Network (ASN) of the European Association for American Studies recognized the book's critical significance by presenting it with the 2018 ASN Book Prize. The ASN praised the research project for offering "a carefully argued analysis of the cultural representations of race relations and black identity in the post-emancipation Dixie," exploring "racial interactions in a wide range of cultural artefacts to see how food production and consumption can signify the racial history of the South" and teasing out "the critical significance of food, both foodways and foodscape, in various texts of culture, demonstrating how it has served to enhance the meaning of the South."

With *Race and Repast*, my previous research project has received both a second life and an expanded audience. The present work is not merely the second edition of the original manuscript. While *Race and Repast* likewise spans the twentieth-century literary and cultural history of the American South, its framework is limited to the study of literary foodscapes. My decision to exclude discussions of African American foodways, which were present in the original publication, gives the project a more manageable scope and sharper focus. Even so, the thematic purview of *Race and Repast* still reflects the twentieth century's preoccupation with culinary performances of the color line.

Since the publication of *Live and Let Di(n)e*, other significant scholarly studies have explored the interconnectedness of food and race in the American South. On one hand, this continued research interest confirms that my theoretical assumptions were timely and relevant; on the other, it means that integrating the new research into the original manuscript would significantly alter the narrative. To maintain the integrity, clarity, and concision of that work, I have resisted the temptation to unwrite or rewrite the original manuscript. That is why the chapters themselves are published intact, although with revised titles. My only minor revisions have been to add footnotes to update the references.

In closing, I would like to acknowledge a debt to Elizabeth Hayes Turner for encouraging me to bring my research to a wider, international audience. It also gives me great pleasure to acknowledge Jennifer Jensen Wallach, who accepted my research project for inclusion in the Food and Foodways series of the University of Arkansas Press. And last, I thank the anonymous reviewer for their comments and suggestions for the manuscript.

Last, but no less enthusiastically, I wish to thank the University of Arkansas Press team for their professional handling of the publishing process. I am very grateful to Janet Foxman, the managing editor, for her expert care of the manuscript. I also wish to recognize the efforts put into this book by James Fraleigh, its copy editor. He did an amazing job shaping and refining this narrative. His attention to detail and diligent feedback helped greatly in designing changes for this edition. A great thank you to the whole dream team at the University of Arkansas Press. It was a sheer pleasure working with you all.

RACE AND REPAST

INTRODUCTION

> Eating, in fact, serves not only to maintain the biological
> machinery of the body, but to make concrete one of the
> specific modes of relation between a person and the world,
> thus forming one of the fundamental landmarks in space-time.
>
> —Michel De Certeau et al., *The Practice of Everyday Life*

Writing about Anthony Bourdain's second nonfiction book, *A Cook's Tour: Global Adventures in Extreme Cuisines* (2001), Susanne Freidberg remarks that "stories about eating something somewhere . . . are really stories about the place and the people there." She goes on to explain that "narratives about specific food commodities provide insights into the broader meanings attached, under particular political, economic and social conditions, to food and eating more generally. In other words, the reading of a food's story reveals, like any good biography or travelogue, a much bigger story—a cultural geography—of particular times and places" (3–4).

Food metonymically informs all aspects of human existence. It is a product of cultural and social experience while simultaneously performing that very culture. "Food is culture," Massimo Montanari claims.[1] By

---

1. Massimo Montanari further explains in his *Food Is Culture* that "food is culture when it is produced, even 'performed,' because man does not use only what is found in nature (as do all the other animal species) but seeks also to create his own food, a food specific unto himself, superimposing the action of production on that of predator or hunter. Food becomes culture when it is prepared because, once the basic products of his diet have been acquired, man transforms them by means of fire and a carefully wrought technology that is expressed in the practices of the kitchen. Food is culture when it is eaten because man, while able to eat anything, or precisely for this reason, does not in fact eat everything but rather chooses his own food, according to criteria linked either to the economic and nutritional dimensions of the gesture or to the symbolic values with which food itself is invested. Through such pathways food takes shape as a decisive element of human identity and as one of the most effective means of expressing and communicating that identity" (xi–xii).

offering a glimpse into the cultural geography of a place and its people, the study of food affords a deeper understanding of its producing culture. Carole Counihan observes that "rules about food consumption are an important means through which human beings construct reality. They are an allegory of social concerns, a way in which people give order to the physical, social, and symbolic world around them" (55). Food may be understood, then, as an embodied relationship with the social and cultural milieu. Identities, relations, and dependences are formed in social exchanges, and food is often used as the material and symbolic content of such negotiations. Food functions as a signifier;[2] Roland Barthes claims that "an entire 'world' (social environment) is present in and signified by food" (26). As such it is a diverse domain of everyday life that generates multiple cultural and social meanings. More than being just physical sustenance, food channels cultural positionings; as an element of material cultural practice, food is part of social processes involved in establishing relationships. People situate themselves and create their identities in social reality through their associations with food and its related practices. Their social and cultural positioning, which Rom Harré defines as a "cluster of short-term disputable rights, obligations and duties" (193), has implications for all engaged in social exchange. Food practices can be viewed as sites of complex social interactions; hence, the ideological potential of food to cocreate dominant and oppositional social orders cannot be underestimated.

Food can also be viewed as a locus of identity; thus, the relationship between food culture and socially imposed identity has the potential to reveal both covert and manifest beliefs, values, and rules in a given place and time. Identities are constantly being performed; they are never finished. One means by which identity is shaped is through performative acts related to the production and consumption of food for oneself and others, as well as social restrictions and inclusions

2. Roland Barthes sees food as a signifier: "When he buys an item of food, consumes it, or serves it, modern man does not manipulate a simple object in a purely transitive fashion; this item of food sums up and transmits a situation; it constitutes an information; it signifies. That is to say that it is not just an indicator of a set of more or less conscious motivations, but that it is real sign, perhaps the functional unit of a system of communication. By this I mean not only the elements of displaying food, such as foods involved in rites of hospitality, for all food serves as a sign among the members of a given society" (24).

associated with those performances. As an American studies scholar, I suggest that foodscape and foodways provide a lens through which we can productively analyze the cultural representations of race on the canvas of a cultural geography of the twentieth-century American South. Thus, following David Bell and Gill Valentine's advice/invitation to "think through food" (3), I intend to interrogate how regionally specific spaces and practices related to food preparation and consumption aid Southerners in imposing, negotiating, and contesting racial identity politics. I probe racialized meanings attached to particular spaces of food consumption, both private and public, as well as socially constructed notions of race as expressed in and through culinary culture. Therefore, I have situated this analysis at the intersection of Southern, critical race, and food studies while framing them through their cultural representations. Comprehensive insights into the asymmetrical racial positionings in the South can be afforded through the application of a range of sociological, anthropological, cultural, and historical perspectives. Indeed, various theories gathered under the umbrella term of *food studies* suggest a number of strategies with which one can interrogate the spaces of food preparation and consumption as well as Black Southern culinary culture as regional enactments of racial identity.

Southern food studies is not uncharted territory, as evident in multiple volumes of criticism; neither is African American studies. Fewer critical texts, however, address the intertwined issues of race and foodways in the context of the American South. Recent contributions to research that foregrounds the interconnectedness of race and food in the South include studies by John T. Edge (2017), Frederick Douglass Opie (2017), Jennifer Jensen Wallach (2015), Angela Cooley (2011), Psyche Williams-Forson (2006, 2010), Andrew Warnes (2004, 2008), and Doris Witt (2004). These researchers use ethnographic, historiographic, historical, and anthropological research methods to consider how Southerners situate themselves in relation to their social milieu. This book is partly a product of the trend inaugurated by African American food studies scholarship and undertaken by the aforementioned critics. My study contributes to this burgeoning field by demonstrating that literary writings are not simply illustrations or fictional recreations of aspects of social life, but also can offer a more nuanced perspective on social concerns, practices, and cultural ideals than those offered by historical documentaries or social science research. As sociologist Jon Frauley comments on the analytical power of fiction,

"Looking at fiction can help us understand more about our own social reality, as works of fiction are anchored, moored, or rooted in reality and deal with real issues such as racism, violence, or marginalization" (qtd. in Rosenblatt 2).[3] I also want to acknowledge in my research "the dialectical relationship between literary portrayal and lived experience," the very relationship that Koritha Mitchell used in her analysis of Bebe Moore Campbell's *Your Blues Ain't Like Mine* (1051).

I am not implying here that literature is simply a sum of realistic representations of historically observed reality. Even though "social science research arguably draws on some of the same imaginative well springs and often even speaks to the same events as fiction" (Rosenblatt 3), the latter should not be equated with the former.[4] Because fictional resources "possess a 'historicizing authority' that allows authors representational freedom . . . [and] an emotional or intellectual power that is different from documentary texts . . . fiction teaches things that history cannot" (Armstrong 87).[5] In other words, literature is more epistemologically advantageous than the standpoint of the social sciences and history. Even though "social research has the same cultural and experiential roots and subjectivities as fiction" (Rosenblatt 3), fictional narratives possess great potential to probe the nuances and complexities of sociohistorical context, which Douwe Draaisma dubbed "the implicit codes of daily interaction, the unspoken rules of behavior, all those protocols that set out what was proper or improper yet are not themselves set down anywhere" (179). This ability of fictional resources to offer "insightful and persuasive elements that link to and stimulate social science analysis and theoretical constructions" (Rosenblatt 2) has already been recognized in the context of Southern race studies by Trudier

---

3. Paul Rosenblatt subscribes to such reasoning, suggesting that "a novel can be rich in insightful and persuasive elements that link to and stimulate social science analysis and theoretical constructions" (2).

4. Wary of the subjectivity of artistic creations, possible autobiographical elements, and conventions, readers should not use novels in social research in an uncritical manner to build "confident and broadly applicable views of human social life" (Rosenblatt 2–3). Rosenblatt warns that fictional writings "deserve the same skepticism, disciplined scrutiny, and questioning as conventional social research" (2).

5. "Because literary language traffics in the difficult, the hard-to-express, and the ineffable, Jacqueline Goldsby observes, fiction and related storytelling forms possess a 'historicizing authority' that allows authors representational freedom they do not have with 'conventional histories'" (qtd. in Armstrong 87).

Harris and Psyche Williams-Forson.[6] With this research project I also intend to build on Christopher Metress's objective to explore "how literary representations of the [civil rights movement] are a valuable and untapped legacy for enriching our understanding of the black freedom struggle of the mid-twentieth century" (141). In doing so, my goal is to analyze various texts that capture the complex histories of Jim Crow segregation—the social drama of the civil rights movement. I further wish "to acknowledge the cognitive value of literary discourse in the production of social memory" (Metress 141) and of sociological and historical processes.

This study aims to examine how race relations are expressed through struggles over the meaning of food and access to food in Southern literature. Changes in racial relations across the twentieth century, as seen through the prism of foodscape, constitute the major narrative thread of this book. The texts chosen for analysis are arranged both diachronically and thematically. The progress of racial relations in the South is framed in the first two chapters, which explore the spaces shaping and shaped by racial encounters in the Jim Crow South, respectively the domestic and public spaces. It concludes in the third chapter with an analysis of the social drama of the civil rights movement.

An analysis of foodscape can illuminate our understanding of the South and "[provide] insight into the region's broader social, cultural, legal, and economic circumstances" (Cooley, *To Live* 3). The past and present are inscribed on Southern tables where commensality—defined by Kerner and Chou as "eating and drinking together in a common physical or social setting" (1)—has been performed and/or forbidden across class and color lines. The geography of food overlaps with the history of race in the South. Atkins-Sayre and Stokes similarly call attention to the fact that "Southern food, while defined by the physical region, is uniquely tied to its people. The cornerstones that make up Southern cuisine reflect the complex race and class history of the region" (78). Following a similar line of analysis of the meanings of

---

6. If "[George] Lipsitz (2011) used a single novel, Paule Marshall's *Brown Girl, Brownstones*, as an element in his analysis of how racism takes place" (Rosenblatt 5), and Trudier Harris based her research into domestics on African American literature, then the texts chosen for the analysis in the present project can possibly yield some insight into how social practices and behaviors connected with foodways both reflect on and perform racial relations in the American South.

food in the South, Marcie Cohen Ferris states a kindred sentiment: "In the South . . . a region scarred by war, slavery, and the aftermath of Reconstruction and segregation, food is especially important" ("Feeding the Jewish Soul" 54). Both foodways and foodscape facilitate a critical angle from which one can analyze the cultural practices Southerners use to locate themselves and others within the social hierarchy. In a similar vein, as Ferris points out, and most appropriately for the study at hand, "food is entangled in forces that have shaped southern history and culture for more than four centuries. . . . When we study food in the South, we unveil a web of social relations defined by race, class, ethnicity, gender, and shifting economic forces" ("The Edible South" 4).[7]

"Food Is Never Just Something to Eat"[8]

Food studies, as a scholarly discipline within the humanities and social sciences, is a still emerging field; for many years it was underrated and insufficiently researched.[9] The beginnings of food studies scholarship date back to the late 1980s. Since then, food studies has enjoyed popular attention[10] and "growing acceptance and legitimacy . . . as a discrete

---

7. On another occasion, Marcie Cohen Ferris explains that "when we examine the history of food in the American South, we encounter the tangled interactions of its people over time, a world of relationships fraught with conflict, yet bound by blood and attachment to place" ("History, Place" 3).

8. Visser, *Much Depends on Dinner* 12.

9. "The term 'foodways' survived a period in folklore studies, roughly from the mid-1950s into the early 1970s, when what is now generally referred to as 'material culture' in the United States did not rank as highly as the spoken word and the performed arts within the canon of folk expression" (Camp 30).

10. A number of food anthologies published in the last three decades reflect hedonistic interest in food. The following books, which satiate the appetite for food writings, are just a sample: *Food for Thought* (Digby and Digby, 1987), *Cooking by the Book* (Mary Anne Schofield, 1989), *Food: The Oxford Anthology* (Brigid Allen, 1995), *A Feast of Words: For Lovers of Food and Fiction* (Anna Shapiro, 1996), *Hungry for Home. Stories of Food from Across the Carolinas with More Than 200 Favorite Recipes* (Amy Rogers and John Egerton, 2004), and *Hunger and Thirst: Food Literature* (Nancy Cary, June Cressy, Ella de Castro Baron, 2008). More recently, two unique books inspired by food in literature were published. Dinah Fried's *Fictitious Dishes: An Album of Literature's Most Memorable Meals* (2014) offers a set of photographic interpretations of meals from classic and contemporary literature, supplemented by anecdotes about authors and interesting food facts. Gary Scharnhorst's *Literary Eats: Emily Dickinson's Gingerbread, Ernest Hemingway's*

field" (Berg et al. 17).[11] Scholars across many disciplines investigate the role of food in human life; these researchers have expanded the scope of food studies by cross-fertilization among and within anthropology, sociology, history, archeology, ethnography, semiotics, cultural studies, literary criticism, and communication studies.[12] Researchers in various academic disciplines within the humanities and social sciences "typically rely on ethnography, case studies, and historical investigations."[13] Adopting the foodways paradigm allows them to enrich debates about observed reality and human existence.

Anthropologists of every type position food as an interpretative tool, through the study of which they can explore how cultural and symbolic meanings are created, shared, maintained, and contested. In the twentieth century, anthropologists were engaged in debates regarding "whether culture is rooted in tangible and concrete artifacts . . . or in ideas and belief systems" (Berg et al. 17). These debates were framed through functionalist, structuralist, or developmentalist orientations as identified by Stephen Mennell and others in *The Sociology of Food: Eating, Diet, and Culture*. Structuralist anthropologists such as Claude Lévi-Strauss and Mary Douglas, and semiologists like Roland Barthes, try to decipher the universal language of food, which has homologous

---

Picadillo, Eudora Welty's Onion Pie and 400+ Other Recipes from American Authors Past and Present (2014) is the first "celebrity cookbook" consisting of authentic recipes of foods and drinks enjoyed by American authors.

11. The emergence of such organizations as the Association for the Study of Food and Society (ASFS) and the launching of such academic journals as *Food and Foodways* (1985), the *Journal for the Study of Food, Culture, and Society* (1997), and *Gastronomica* (2001) points to the rise of food studies as a scholarly discipline in American academia. Additionally, multiple panels devoted to the study of food have been chaired during conferences organized by the Modern Language Association, the American Studies Association, and the Cultural Studies Association.

12. Berg et al. comment on the interdisciplinary character of food studies: "By its very nature, food studies is interdisciplinary and must rely on methods, approaches, and themes derived from other disciplines. In this sense it is developing in much the same manner as other interdisciplinary fields, such as American studies. . . . Food studies may be unusual, however, in the breadth of the disciplines on which it draws. Economists, historians, psychologists, nutritionists, agronomists, geologists, geographers, archaeologists, environmental scientists, legal scholars, political scientists, and historians—culinary and otherwise—all bring distinct methods of research and analysis to bear on food themes" (17).

13. "Because food studies emerged from the humanities and social sciences, researchers typically rely on ethnography, case studies, and historical investigations" (Berg et al. 17).

counterparts in various cultures. In their analysis of how food generates and maintains cultural meanings, both Lévi-Strauss and Douglas
recognize that "'taste' is culturally shaped and socially controlled"
(Mennell 8). In "The Culinary Triangle," Claude Lévi-Strauss explains
that in attempts to define culture, cooking "has never been sufficiently
emphasized, [although cooking] is with language a truly universal form
of human activity: if there is no society without a language, nor is there
any which does not cook in some manner at least some of its food" (40).
Lévi-Strauss identifies food as a primal means of civilizing and defining
humans; indeed, he frames the shift from the savage to the civilized stage
of humanity "within a triangular semantic field whose three points correspond respectively to the categories of the raw, the cooked and the rot-
ted" (41). Likewise, Mary Douglas sees food as a language that translates
structures of human life. In her model, food acts as a code that conveys
messages about "different degrees of hierarchy, inclusion and exclusion,
boundaries and transactions across the boundaries" within a given culture ("Deciphering a Meal" 61). For Roland Barthes, food is also a sign,[14]
a signifier that transmits culturally loaded meanings. In his semiotically
oriented discussions, he views food as "a system of communication,
a body of images, a protocol of usages, situations, and behavior" (24).

Rather than seek stable meanings that could be universally
deciphered from activities associated with food across various cultures (which was the domain of structuralism), developmentalists
share, as Mennell reports, Sidney Mintz's opinion that the meaning
of food "arises from cultural applications" ("Food Enigmas" 17). Yet
developmentalists—from a range of disciplines such as history, sociology, and cultural studies—"do not at all deny the power of the symbolic
meanings of food in shaping and controlling social behavior" (Mennell
14). Historians of food adopt an anthropological approach; in doing so
they "investigate the ways in which foods have influenced world events
in the past and present" (Berg et al. 17). Historical research can also be
gender oriented. For instance, Psyche Williams-Forson examines the
material culture of food in order to explore the complexity of Black
women's culinary role in performing Blackness. Culinary historians,

---

14. Barthes reiterates that "food serves as a sign not only for themes, but also for
situations; and this, all told, means for a way of life that is emphasized, much more
than expressed, by it. To eat is a behavior that develops beyond its own ends,
replacing, summing up, and signalizing other behaviors, and it is precisely for these
reasons that it is a sign" (28).

on the other hand, employ historical research to study "recipes and cooking techniques, exploring when, where, and how specific foods or ingredients might have been grown, produced, prepared, and consumed in different periods" (Berg et al. 17).

Food has also emerged as an area of intensive sociological study. Unlike structuralists, sociologists interpret food habits and practices as a reflection of continuity or changes in social structures such as the family unit (e.g., division of labor); they study consumer behavior (social and historical conditioning that influence food choices); and they explore how class, race, gender, and ethnic identities are maintained through foodways. Marjorie DeVault, Claude Fischler, and Stephen Mennell, among others, analyze the social processes that shape taste and preference, cultural applications of food production and consumption, and creation of culinary rules and/or taboos.[15] The research of some cultural studies scholars illustrates how food studies and sociology can enrich each other; as Beth Latshaw explains, "the cultural approach sees food as a significant social construct imbued with symbolic meaning" (100). Some cultural studies researchers have adapted the theoretical framework drawn from sociology to explore how food mediates relations between people and reinforces social bonding, thus proving that the foodways paradigm supports cultural studies scholarship. Food simultaneously reflects and cocreates culture and identity. In performing this function, it can be, as Bell and Valentine describe, "a form of resistance, a form of discipline, of reward, a way of creating 'community' or a way of refusing or denying it" (100).

Cultural anthropologists, food historians, and sociologists share a belief that "amidst all these universals," which were the focus of the structuralist framework of Claude Lévi-Strauss, Mary Douglas, and Roland Barthes, "consumption of food has always been culturally constructed" (Diner 3). Each nationality, ethnic group, and society speaks with a different "food voice," which Annie Hauck-Lawson identifies as "the dynamic, creative, symbolic, and highly individualized ways that

---

15. Within health sociology, "food sociologists focus on issues of hunger, malnutrition, and inequities of the global food supply as well as on societal determinants of diet-related conditions, such as obesity or heart disease" (Berg et al. 17), which overlap with psychological research as well. "Psychologists often investigate how and why people make food choices or such matters as eating disorders, food phobias, and the psychological connections between eating and taste, pleasure, and disgust" (Berg et al. 17).

food serves as a channel of communication" (6).[16] A "food voice" can express both individual and collective cultural identities. These identities are at the same time self-imposed (how people perceive and define themselves) and ascribed by others (through the process of social "othering"). African Americans speak a different "food voice" than Southerners on the other side of the color line.[17] These different "food voices," reflected in both foodways and foodscape, are a tangible means of expressing racial identities.

Referring to more than physical food, the term *foodways* also encompasses activities associated with the procurement, preparation, serving, and consumption of food and drink. In doing so, the term denotes "the connection between food-related behavior and patterns of membership in cultural community, group, and society. In its most general usage, 'foodways' refers to the systems of knowledge and expression related to food that vary with culture" (Camp 29). In this sense, foodways, as part of a cultural system, reflect that system's changing social and historical circumstances and co-construct the sociocultural identities of those who operate within it. Thus, as Charles Camp explains, foodways stand at "the intersection of food and culture" (625). The term *foodways* originated within folklife research[18] "to describe the entire range of food habits, behaviors, customs, and cultural practices associated with food consumption" (Berg et al. 16)

---

16. Remarking about her research on Polish American foodways in New York, Annie Hauck-Lawson comments: "For me, this *food voice* emerged as a term that crystallized the dynamic, creative, symbolic, and highly individualized ways that food serves as a channel of communication. Listening to the *food voice* provided a window onto the ways that the individuals . . . used food to express their views about themselves and their culture. The food voice became a category through which I interpreted each participant's perspectives about community, economics, gender, nutrition, ethnic identity, and traditions" (6).

17. Hasia Diner offers a general observation that "while we can talk in general about the history of food habits in particular places, food differences existed within each individual society" (4).

18. Taylor and Edge name Jay Anderson as a pioneer of foodways within folklife research (8). However, Berg et al. credit the folklorist Don Yoder for popularizing the term *foodways* (16), whereas Charles Camp credits Don Yoder and Warren Roberts with bringing out the study of foodways "from a period of relative low American academic interest into the current state of broad, heightened engagement" (30). Charles Camp wrote two separate articles under the same title— "Foodways"—which were published in two encyclopedias, *Encyclopedia of Food and Culture* and *American Folklore: An Encyclopedia.*

as well as to embrace "the whole interrelated system of food concep-
tualization and evaluation, procurement, preservation, preparation,
consumption, and nutrition shared by all the members of a particular society" (Anderson, qtd. in Taylor and Edge 8–9). Similarly, Camp
notes that the term *foodways* "refers to those food-related behaviors
that are believed to identify the primary cultural attributes of an individual or group of individuals" (29). Extrapolating from Camp, I would
argue that social customs connected with food, food-related traditions,
food beliefs, and nutritional choices sustain and reinforce the various
and diverse identities that comprise the complex culture of the United
States.[19] Susan Kalcik notes the same symbolical potential of foodways
to define identities: "Foodways provide a whole area of performance in
which statements of identity can be made—in preparing, eating, serving, forbidding, and talking about food" (54). This hews very closely
to Camp's description of foodways as "a 'performed' tradition whose
'texts' are activities that can be observed, and perhaps sampled, but are
as emblematic of the people who produce those texts as the more con-
ventionally recognized folk expressions that comprise collections and
anthologies of published folklore" (30).

While foodways reflect and co-create culture and identity, the
term *foodscape* relates foodways by places endowing them with specific meanings. In her analysis of a festive foodscape, Pauline Adema
demonstrates that "foodscape implicates the multiple informative historic and contemporary personal, social, political, cultural, and economic forces that inform how people think about and use (or eschew)
food in various spaces they inhabit" (5). Foodscape is more than just
the sum of its parts (landscape + food). Foodscape, as a physical space
connected with food-related activities (foodways), is thus a geographically situated reminder of the social interactions framed through foodways. Adema observes that "foodscape incorporates the geographic
notion of landscape as a physical space and the sociocultural forces that
inform how people deliberately or unselfconsciously use that space"
(5). Thus, foodscapes become an expression not only of identities, but
also of the power structure of a given society within a particular place;
they "are personal, social, cultural, political, economic, or historical
landscapes that, in one way or another, are about food. . . . [They] are

---

19. Charles Camp observes that "in modern America, foodways continue to represent cultural diversity within an increasingly interwoven society" (29).

symbolic of real and desired identities and of power, social, and spatial relations articulated through food" (Adema 7). My research into domestic and public foodscapes will remain mindful of the implications of adopting the "interpretive framework of foodscape [that] reads physical landscapes . . . that have been transformed ideologically and/or literally into food-centered spaces while necessarily attending to human interaction with the physical spaces that constitute the foodscape" (6).

The history of Southern food reflects the history of racial relations; hence, the evolution of race relations can be traced through the (re)invention of foodways and negotiations of one's place within the Southern foodscape. Because food and race relations define the South, and also define each other, they constitute a Möbius strip of sorts; given this intimately interwoven relationship, it is difficult not to consider one without the other. Food reinforces racial identity, which in turn shapes foodways and foodscape. Any analysis of Southern foodways that ignores the issue of race offers an inadequate, reductive portrayal of the Southern cultural and social landscape. Similarly, because racial relations are inscribed on the Southern foodscape (both domestic and public), a critical analysis neglecting this inscription omits a core comment on the South's complex history and culture, resulting in a simplistic and distorted understanding of the region and its peoples.

"Race Matters"[20]

Race still matters in the United States, despite high-sounding efforts to create a colorblind society (as a legacy of Martin Luther King Jr.'s meritorious call to judge people based on the content of their character, not on the color of their skin). However noble the intentions behind the façade of "deracialized ideology"—expressed in the "I don't see color, I see people" standpoint—colorblindness prevents people from acknowledging the racial wound that still afflicts American society and recognizing privileges resulting from Whiteness.[21] It is impossible to solve a problem if one does not recognize its existence; thus, if one does not acknowledge the impact of race on social inequalities, committing to

20. West, *Race Matters*.
21. The existence of invisible "colorblind racism" is comprehensively addressed in Eduardo Bonilla-Silva's *Racism without Racists: Color-Blind Racism and the Persistence of Racial Inequality in America*.

colorblindness will facilitate complacency. In the ostensibly postracial America at the end of the twentieth century, racial prejudice, discord, and discrimination supposedly no longer exist.[22] Disparities therefore cannot be redressed because they remain stubbornly unrecognized, even if the privileged themselves were to cease abusing their advantageous position through the oppression and exploitation of those lacking their privilege and the attendant benefits of same. Such a state of affairs reflects how racial ideologies have evolved over the years.

Before concerted and ongoing efforts were made to dispel the concept of race as a supposedly scientific category warranting social injustice, it had reigned for decades in intellectual and political circles as a means of justifying chattel slavery. The concept served an ideology that viewed people possessing physical characteristics deemed undesirable (e.g., an excess of melanin) as inherently inferior. The social implications of categorizing human beings this way were devastating: "In the context of slavery and imperial colonialism, race was a useful construct, both for classifying human variation and for providing an apparent scientific justification for the exploitation of groups that were regarded as inferior" (Williams, "African-American Health" 304). Proponents of scientific racism[23] used "biological characteristics to scout for racial hierarchies in social life, levels of civilization, even language" in order not to prove that "biology determined culture. . . . but that race, understood as an indivisible essence that included not only biology but also culture, morality, and intelligence, was a compellingly significant factor in history and society" (Pascoe 47–48).

Efforts to discredit such an essentialist perspective on race began in the 1920s, led by scientists who determined that "the extant racial categories do not represent biological distinctiveness. There is more genetic variation within races than between them. Irrespective of geographic

---

22. Instead of a race-conscious debate, a colorblind denial of reality underlies such phenomena as disparities in education and employment, and the American system of mass incarceration (which Michelle Alexander calls "the New Jim Crow").
23. Useful sources probing the issue of scientific racism include Thomas F. Gossett, *Race: The History of an Idea in America* (Southern Methodist University Press, 1963); George M. Fredrickson, *The Black Image in the White Mind: The Debate on Afro-American Character and Destiny, 1817–1914* (Harper and Row, 1971); Elazar Barkan, *Retreat of Scientific Racism: Changing Concepts of Race in Britain and the United States between the World Wars* (Cambridge University Press, 1992), and Audrey and Brian Smedley, *Race in North America: Origin and Evolution of a Worldview* (Avalon Publishing, 2011).

origin or race, all human beings are identical for 75 percent of known genetic factors, with some 95 percent of human genetic variation existing within racial groups" (Williams, "African-American Health" 304–5).[24] Social scientists and cultural anthropologists joined the chorus of voices refuting scientific racism because, as Peggy Pascoe explains, "when modern social science emerges, racism runs out of intellectual steam. In the absence of any other narrative, this forms the basis for a commonly held but rarely examined intellectual trickle-down theory in which the attack on scientific racism emerges in universities in the 1920s and eventually, if belatedly, spreads to courts in the 1940s and 1950s and to government policy in the 1960s and 1970s" (47).

No longer perceived as a set of primordial, genetically assigned characteristics, race began to be seen as a social and cultural construction.[25] Race, as a sociological concept, is dynamic in nature rather than stable or given.[26] Mary Waters explains that identity is a combination of

---

24. Williams goes on to explain that "there are patterns to the distribution of genetic characteristics across human population groups, but our racial categories do not capture them. Most physical anthropologists have abandoned the concept of race and use the construct of clines instead" ("African-American Health" 305). Julian Huxley, a British biologist, introduced the concept of clines in 1938, defining them as "gradation in measurable characters" (219)—in other words, a form of continuous variation that can be based on directly observable external biological traits (phenotypes) or derived from genes (genotypes). Expanding on Huxley's proposal, Frank Livingstone, an American biological anthropologist, suggested that "there are no races, there are only clines" (279).

25. Historian Evelyn Brooks Higginbotham acknowledges that "race must be seen as a social construction predicated upon the recognition of difference and signifying the simultaneous distinguishing and positioning of groups vis-à-vis one another. More than this, race is a highly contested representation of relations of power between social categories by which individuals are identified and identify themselves" (253).

26. Mary Waters explains that "the widely held societal definitions of race and ethnicity take the categories and classifications in place at any one time for granted, and hence do not generally see them as socially created or dynamic in nature" (17). Moreover, Stuart Hall explains that the outdated view of cultural identity identifies race "in terms of one, shared culture, a sort of collective 'one true self,' hiding inside the many other, more superficial or artificially imposed 'selves,' which people with a shared history and ancestry hold in common. Within the terms of this definition, our cultural identities reflect the common historical experiences and shared cultural codes which provide us, as 'one people,' with stable, unchanging and continuous frames of reference and meaning, beneath the shifting divisions and vicissitudes of our actual history" (223).

"self-ascription and ascription of others" (17); hence, Blackness is both the product of social creation and self-creation.

Mary Waters's observation resonates with an epistemological paradigm shift of race studies within the humanities and social sciences. So does cultural theorist Stuart Hall's assertion about cultural identities. He shrewdly observes that cultural identities "are the points of identification, the unstable points of identification or suture, which are made, within the discourses of history and culture. Not an essence but a *positioning*" (226). The instability of constructs of race, which need to be renegotiated daily, conveys divagations about racial identity from the aforementioned positioning theory. Cultural identity is not the finished product of a finite process, but rather is in a state of becoming. The process of identity formation, which involves what Joan Scott calls "redefinition, resistance and change," is an ongoing, dynamic process[27] that not only stresses what we are, but what we become:

> Cultural identity . . . is a matter of "becoming" as well as of "being." It belongs to the future as much as to the past. It is not something which already exists, transcending place, time, history and culture. Cultural identities come from somewhere, have histories. . . . Far from being eternally fixed in some essentialised past, they are subject to the continuous "play" of history, culture and power. . . . Identities are the names we give to the different ways we are positioned by, and position ourselves within, the narratives of the past. (Hall 235)

Race as a social construct embodies the dialogue of past and future, being and becoming, power and resistance, and denial and recognition. Cultural identities, be they racial or ethnic,[28] position people

---

27. Joan Scott argues that in the symbolic process of identification, "subjects are produced through multiple identifications, some of which become politically salient for a time in certain contexts, and. . . . the project of history is not to reify identity but to understand its production as an ongoing process of differentiation, relentless in its repetition, but also . . . subject to redefinition, resistance and change" (11).

28. In his article "Paradigm Lost: Race, Ethnicity, and the Search for a New Population Taxonomy" Gerald Oppenheimer discusses the US National Institutes of Health recommendation to "use a different population classification, that of 'ethnic group,' instead of 'race'" (1049). The implication is that the term "'ethnic group' would turn research attention away from biological determinism and toward a focus on culture and behavior"; however, "ethnicity" and "ethnic group" are "not neutral terms; instead, they carry their own burden of political, social, and ideological meaning" (1049). Oppenheimer's arguments for maintaining both forms of identity in social science research might be instructive for the epistemological framework of the humanities.

in agreement with or in opposition to the practical and symbolic work-ings of "Whiteness." According to Rachel Slocum, race exists "as a dis-cursive category, the result of societal norms privileging paler skin and the practices of bourgeois whiteness that became salient through colo-nialism's engagement with non-white and poor white groups" (304). Hence, Whiteness becomes a yardstick against which other races are judged as wanting or defective. Hoelscher similarly asserts that

> race and ethnicity are salient features in Southern identity. Because of the region's racial history, race in the South has a dis-tinctive flavor.
>
> Whiteness's contradictory, simultaneous need for race to be both recognized (blackness) and unacknowledged (whiteness) has been more apparent and well defined in the South than in any other American region. Precisely because its "color line" had been drawn so clearly, because its dramas have been so violent and so graphic, and because—ultimately and tragically—it has pro-foundly shaped national conceptions of cultural difference, it is the place where one must look to understand the historical geog-raphy of this most modern and deeply entrenched aspect of racial-ization. (Hoelscher 662–63)

The legacy of institutionalized racism—a.k.a. the "color line"—is crys-tallized by Southerners through repetitive performances and nego-tiations of their racialized positioning. Rachel Slocum refreshingly integrates food into the construction of race when she calls attention to the fact that "bodies are shaped in racial terms through their labor, what they eat and where they live" (318). If race is performed and produced daily, then Blackness is socially shaped as the negation of Whiteness; as Joel Williamson claims, "whites are made white by blacks" (497).[29]

---

29. Interestingly enough, if racial identity is performed and produced, then any perceived biological distinctiveness between and among races can be used to justify social inequality based on the supposedly less-than-desirable morality of the racial Other. In this sense, as Williamson explains, "blackness and whiteness became a matter not just of color or even blood, but of inner morality reflected by outward performance" (497). "A white person could cross over to blackness" due to unthink-able behavior (497); thus the genetically curious, but morally explainable, existence of "white niggers" came into existence in the postbellum South. Williamson explains this phenomenon: "Whites who sided too closely with blacks, were, as the phrase went, 'white niggers.' One could be perfectly white genetically and yet be black morally" (495).

An interrogation of interactions connected with negotiating a person's position in a society (in relation both to people and objects) can facilitate an understanding of "how race is made and how it constitutes society" (Slocum 318).[30] One of the ways to produce race and reinforce racism is through foodscape (Slocum 313). Similarly, race can be inscribed on the body through its position on the foodscape and its relation to foodways. When an analysis of racial relations in the American South adopts the study of food as another prism offering an additional layer of examination, the analyst can achieve a more comprehensive and nuanced image of the inherent interrelatedness of power and race. Thus, one of the aims of the present study is also to answer Slocum's question, "What does food become when we consider race and, conversely, how might we view race differently through food practices?" (303). This approach embraces "two methodological schools of thought when talking about African American foodways" (Williams-Forson, "More than Just" 108). Williams-Forson explains that the food itself and its relation to the material culture of the African Diaspora form the axis around which African American scholars, historians, and food scholars perform their analyses (108).[31]

Although my study profits from the research just referenced, with its specific focus on the material culture of African American foodways, I join the chorus of voices that, as Psyche Williams-Forson puts it, "focus[es] generally on the intersections of food and identity, representation, and/or contestation" ("More than Just" 108). In common with other literary critics and cultural studies scholars, I "understand food preparation and consumption as central to the development and

30. Rachel Slocum adopts Mary Weismantel's interpretation of race as "a 'constant physical process of interaction between living things' [that] had to be understood as the 'interactions between bodies and the substances they ingest, the possessions they accumulate and the tools they use to act on the world'" (318).
31. The scholarship that investigates African American foodways as a social form of creating relations with the physical world includes Jessica Harris's *High on the Hog* (2001), Andrew Warnes's *Savage Barbecue: Race, Culture and the Invention of America's First Food* (2008), Frederick Douglass Opie's *Hog and Hominy: Soul Food from Africa to America* (2008), Rebecca Sharpless's *Cooking in Other Women's Kitchens: Domestic Workers in the South, 1865–1960* (2010), and Adrian Miller's *Soul Food: The Surprising Story of an American Cuisine* (2013). A more comprehensive list is offered by Psyche Williams-Forson in "More than Just the 'Big Piece of Chicken': The Power of Race, Class, and Food in American Consciousness" (108).

preservation of racialized identity" (Slocum 305).[32] The present study attempts to add another perspective to how racialized identities are produced through their positioning within foodscape as depicted in such literary and cultural food studies projects as Doris Witt's pioneering *Black Hunger: Food and the Politics of U.S. Identity* (1999), Andrew Warnes's *Hunger Overcome? Food and Resistance in Twentieth-Century African American Literature* (2004), Psyche Williams-Forson's *Building Houses Out of Chicken Legs: Black Women, Food, and Power* (2006), Anne Bower's *African American Foodways: Explorations of History and Culture* (2007), Kyla Wazana Tompkins's *Racial Indigestion* (2012), Jennifer Jensen Wallach's *Dethroning the Deceitful Pork Chop: Rethinking African American Foodways from Slavery to Obama* (2015), Toni Tipton-Martin's *The Jemima Code: Two Centuries of African American Cookbooks* (2015), and more recently in John Edge's *The Potlikker Papers: A Food History of the Modern South* (2017) and Frederick Douglass Opie's *Southern Food and Civil Rights: Feeding the Revolution* (2017).[33] This book owes a great deal to Psyche Williams-Forson's research, which is a model of the kind of rhetorically and historically informed work I find stimulating. I take a cue for my study's line of analysis from the works of such historians as Grace Elizabeth Hale, Rebecca Sharpless, Elizabeth Abel, and Angela Cooley, whose scholarly rigor generates greater understanding of and insight into overlapping areas of race and food. My research builds on these studies to tease out the ways in which foodscape can be interpreted in the light of what racial positioning in twentieth-century Southern literature has to tell us about the conflict between structures of power and resistance, and the collision between racial self-designation and classifications.

No aspect of Southern studies triggers more ideologically charged responses than the issue of race. Wary of the dangers that Rachel Slocum indicates regarding writing about race in food research,[34] I

---

32. Such analyses ask "how food histories of marginalized people are ignored, appropriated or maligned by dominant groups and how racialized groups discursively resist these oppressions" (Slocum 306).

33. See Psyche Williams-Forson's aforementioned list of literary and cultural food analyses that reframe African American studies ("More than Just" 108).

34. In her article "Race in the Study of Food," Rachel Slocum warns that "it is politically important to be explicit about race in food research and dangerous to write about the concept without a commitment to its theorization. The dangers are, first, that racist analyses might be authorized. Second, race may be tucked away

have decided to capitalize *White* and *Black* when used with reference to peoples and their associated cultures. Moreover, motivated by "a number of studies conducted in the United States that [which] have found that *Black* and *African American* are the preferred labels for ethnic/racial self-designation by Blacks" (Boatswain and Lalonde 216), I have decided to use *African American* and *Black* interchangeably as racial labels and racial designations.[35]

Race and Repast

The preceding discussion of food and critical race studies foregrounds theoretical perspectives from a variety of research areas addressing themes and issues discussed in the following chapters in the context of racial relations in the South. The chapters focus on the spaces of food procurement, preparation, and consumption. To contain my analysis (I do not intend to offer a panoramic, Balzacian social observation on Southern states—a never-ending project), I have concentrated on snapshots of interracial contacts that accentuate and intensify the potential conflicts and negotiations of boundaries of inclusion and exclusion in Southern society. I frame my analysis of how African Americans actively reconfigure their racialized identities and overtly and covertly challenge the confining social scripts they are expected to follow through historical events such as the rise and demise of Jim Crow, the Great Migration, and the civil rights movement, which determines the

---

under the theorization of a more important process. Third, authors might think that to discuss a racialized group is to write about race, but this leaves its theorization implicit or absent. Rather than assume that social construction is the only means by which one can ethically write about race, more engagement with the other lines of thought outlined here would be welcome" (320).

35. Jeremy Zilber and David Niven offer a rich discussion of racial labels. They explain that the terms *African American* and *Black* are not interchangeable for some. They support their observation that the "African American term connotes ethnicity and pride, while black connotes otherness" (655) with Jesse Jackson's comment that "just as we were called colored, but were not that, and then Negro, but were not that, to be called black is just as baseless. . . . To be called African-American has cultural integrity. It puts us in our proper historical context" (655). The changes in racial (self-)designation are also analyzed in Tom Smith, "Changing Racial Labels: From 'Colored' to 'Negro' to 'Black' to 'African American,'" and Ben Martin, "From Negro to Black to African American: The Power of Names and Naming."

chronological arrangement of the texts chosen for analysis in individual chapters and the book in general. Although my project is not a work of historiography, it supplements literary and cultural criticism with methodology used by historians and sociologists to explore how foodways mediate relations between people on both sides of the color line. The conclusions drawn are not meant to be comprehensive of social changes in the American South; rather, they concretely and discretely demonstrate the relation among foodways, foodscape, identity formation, and other social processes that can be abstracted from the texts under analysis.

The first chapter, "The Domestic Contact Zones of Racial Encounters in White Households," presents an analytical expedition into the domestic foodscape of Walker Percy's *The Last Gentleman* (1966), Ellen Douglas's *Can't Quit You, Baby* (1989), and *Driving Miss Daisy*—the latter both as the Alfred Uhry play (1986) and its film adaptation by Bruce Beresford (1989). The chapter probes the racial relations in the "contact zones" of the South during Jim Crow and the civil rights movement between White employers and their Black helpers, be they servants, cooks, or chauffeurs. The social structure of the South during those times was sustained through racialized social "positions"[36] associated with performance of food/identity and its display—forced servitude, benign paternalism, divided loyalty, denial of access to particular goods, and stigmatizing food practices. Exploring the everyday spatiality of food preparation and consumption reveals the complicated reality behind the official, whitewashed version of racial relations (e.g., the saccharine-sweet legacy of *Gone with the Wind*). My analysis of the spaces of pantry, kitchen, and dining and living rooms affords the "fresh insights on race and class in the South" that historian John Egerton was hoping to find in explorations of that region and era's dining room, kitchen, garden, and field.[37]

---

36. Rom Harré defined *positioning theory* as being "based on the principle that not everyone involved in a social episode has equal access to rights and duties to perform particular kinds of meaningful actions at *that moment* and with *those people*. In many interesting cases, the rights and duties determine who can use a certain discourse mode. . . . A cluster of short-term disputable rights, obligations and duties is called a 'position'" (193).

37. John Egerton explains, "I was looking for fresh insights on race and class in the South, and I was hoping I could find them by exploring the dining room, kitchen,

These domestic spaces of racial encounters metonymically refer to the uneven relationship between Blacks and Whites in the South.

An analysis of racial relations in the public foodscape offers a more encompassing view of society. Hence, the second chapter, "Consuming Public Spaces: Performance of the Color Lines in Jim Crow Dining Cars, Stores, and Cafes," interrogates how racial roles are played out in the public foodscape of the American South. Flannery O'Connor's "The Artificial Nigger" (1971), Ernest Gaines's "The Sky Is Gray" (1963), and Fannie Flagg's *Fried Green Tomatoes at the Whistle Stop Cafe* (1987) serve as illustrative examples of the capacity of foodscapes to establish relations, cocreate identities, and express social power relations. Bell and Valentine rightly contend that food is "one way in which boundaries get drawn, and insiders and outsiders distinguished" (91). Sharpless similarly explains that "food delineates a culture, demonstrating who is and who is not a part of that culture and expressing status and prestige" (xii). Carole Counihan corroborates this observation: "Rules about food consumption are an important means through which human beings construct reality. They are an allegory of social concerns, a way in which people give order to the physical, social, and symbolic world around them" (55). Thus, food is an instrument of power in a Foucaultian sense.[38] Food reflects and refracts power, unevenly ascribing agency to the privileged and the oppressed. The control of public spaces of food procurement and consumption communicates denigration and subjugation of the racial Other by the ruling class. Only on the surface, however, do Black Southerners meekly accept these power

---

garden, and field. . . . When I did, I learned that the study has the same mission of many narrative social histories: a telling of the way we were and how it shapes the way we are" (qtd. in Ferris, "The Edible South" 21).

38. Michel Foucault explains that power produces reality: "Power is everywhere; not because it embraces everything, but because it comes from everywhere. And 'Power,' insofar as it is permanent, repetitious, inert, and self-reproducing, is simply the over-all effect that emerges from all these mobilities" (*The Will to Knowledge* 93). Foucault understands power as "the process which, through ceaseless struggles and confrontations, transforms, strengthens, or reverses them; as the support which these force relations find in one another, thus forming a chain or a system, or on the contrary, the disjunctions and contradictions which isolate them from one another; and lastly, as the strategies in which they take effect, whose general design or institutional crystallization is embodied in the state apparatus, in the formulation of the law, in the various social hegemonies" (*The Will to Knowledge* 92–93).

relations; beneath their ostensibly servile exteriors, anger, frustration, and outrage seethe. This subterranean defiance corresponds with Foucault's observation that "where there is power, there is resistance, and yet, or rather consequently, this resistance is never in a position of exteriority in relation to power"; or rather, "there is a plurality of resistances, each of them a special case: resistances that are possible, necessary, improbable; other that are spontaneous, savage, solitary, concerted, rampant, or violent; still others that are quick to compromise, interested, or sacrificial" (*The Will to Knowledge* 95, 96).

Because accommodation to the Jim Crow system, of the kind expressed in the saying "live and let live," was unattainable without structural disadvantages on one side of the color line, a reconfiguration of racial relations was inevitable. The civil rights movement overwrote the original metaphor with "live and let die," a sadly appropriate ruling metaphor for the racial status quo in the American South desired by those Whites who possessed political power and enjoyed its associated economic benefits. The existence and eventual dismantling of the Jim Crow system both were partly enabled by connecting race and food.

White Southerners' defense of segregated eating establishments as "the enclave and embryo of a racially pure nation" (Abel 177)—which gained momentum during the turbulent 1960s—is the subject of the third chapter, "A Sweet Taste of Victory: Food and Social Drama at the Lunch Counter." Historian Donna Gabaccia insists that in order to "understand changing American identities, we must explore also the symbolic power of food to reflect cultural or social affinities in moments of change or transition" (9). Anthony Grooms's "Food that Pleases, Food to Take Home" (1995) is one such potentially productive model for studying the moment of social crisis and change that civil rights activists enacted at lunch counters. The symbolical importance of this space cannot be underestimated, as the wave of protests organized by the Southern Christian Leadership Conference "did not start at the kitchen tables or the black restaurants where King and his followers had planned the Montgomery bus boycott. Rather, it started at the lunch counter of a five-and-dime store" (Harris, *High on the Hog*). A close reading of Grooms's short story reveals the complexities of the racial situation in the American South. The image of White violence during these lunch-counter confrontations over civil rights—as recorded, for instance, by Anne Moody in her memoir, *Coming of Age in Mississippi* (1968)—is problematized in "Food that Pleases, Food to

Take Home"; so is Black nonviolence. To complicate even further the image of "the social drama" at the lunch counter,[39] Grooms challenges not only White closed-mindedness about and complacency with segregation but also the issue of nonviolence as the gold standard for civil rights demonstrators. With the mainline White oppressor–Black oppressed polarity dislodged, Grooms creates an opportunity for the sit-in protestors to break the cycle of exploitation and misunderstanding, to use the vantage point of the oppressed in order to share power rather than usurp it through an act of social repositioning.

The texts chosen for analysis in *Race and Repast* reflect social changes in the foodscape of the twentieth-century South. The narratives focusing on domestic contact zones, which I interrogate in the first chapter, are all penned by White authors. Two novelists and a playwright provide insights into the social relations between White and Black Southerners in the space that made Blacks "invisible" yet indispensable. These White authors do not usurp the Black voice, nor do they adopt John Howard Griffin's strategy in *Black Like Me* (1961) of White–Black passing for the sake of uncovering White Americans' racist complicity. The refusal of most Southern Whites to see and acknowledge the racial Other was present both in the domestic and public foodscapes. However, in the public space, both the visibility and voice of Blacks were more conspicuous and more difficult to ignore. Thus, my selection of texts for analysis in the second chapter—two offering a White perspective (Flannery O'Connor's and Fannie Flagg's narratives) and one giving voice to Blacks (Ernest Gaines's short story)— was motivated by a desire to examine representations of this enhanced presence of African Americans in public spaces. Last, because I could not ignore the hypervisibility that the "problematic" presence of Blacks at public lunch counters constituted during the civil rights movement, I concentrate in the final chapter on a single short story written by Anthony Grooms, a contemporary African American author.

---

39. Victor Turner's theory of "social drama," explicated in *From Ritual to Theatre*, will be my theoretical touchstone in analyzing Anthony Grooms's "Food that Pleases, Food to Take Home."

CHAPTER 1

The Domestic Contact Zones of Racial Encounters in White Households[1]

To eat and drink with someone was at the same time a
symbol and a confirmation of social community and of the
assumption of mutual obligations.

—Sigmund Freud, *Totem and Taboo*

[A relationship of power is] a mode of action which does
not act directly and immediately on others. Instead it acts
upon their actions: an action upon an action, on existing
actions or on those which may arise in the present or the
future.

—Foucault, "Afterword: The Subject and the Power"

Racism, or as they say now, tradition, is passed down like
recipes. The trick is, you got to know what to eat, and what
to leave on the plate.

—*Mississippi Masala* (1991)

---

1. The chapter "The Domestic Contact Zones of Racial Encounters in White
Households" offers a much extended and revised analysis originally carried out in
the article "A Culinary Journey across the Color Line: Foodways and Race in
Southern Literature and Motion Pictures," *Unsteadily Marching On: The US South
in Motion,* edited by Constante Gonzáles Groba, Publicacions de la Universitat de
València, 2013, pp. 101–10. Although the "nucleus" of the original analysis is
reproduced more or less verbatim, this chapter offers a more thorough explanation and an extensive exploration of the domestic contact zones.

In 1960s Jackson, Mississippi, Eugenia "Skeeter" Phelan—a graduate of the University of Mississippi who returned to her family's plantation—undertook a book project to reveal the truth about Black women's domestic service in White upper-class homes. To communicate the assumptions informing her book project (called *The Help*) to her editor-to-be, Skeeter, with a telephone in her hand, locked herself away in the pantry. Of all the places in the home that provide privacy, peace, and quiet, she chose the pantry.[2] It was the natural breeding ground for her daring project, which would most certainly upset the racial status quo of her community.[3] In light of the explosive charge of her book, the connotative value of the pantry as the "contact zone" of the two races adds symbolism to Skeeter's project. Quite interestingly, other spaces connected with the discourse of food and domesticity—such as kitchens and dining rooms—can be seen as *contact zones*, the term Mary Louise Pratt coined in her critique of colonialist discourse, which she defined as "the space of colonial encounters, the space in which peoples geographically and historically separated come into contact with each other and establish ongoing relations, usually involving conditions of coercion, radical inequality and intractable conflict" (8). Although most Southern historians and literary critics researching the culinary negotiations of the racial status quo concentrate on the kitchen, in this chapter I intend to shift the focus to those other domestic contact zones where "disparate cultures meet, clash, and grapple with each other, often in highly asymmetrical relations of domination and subordination" (Pratt 7).

Representing patriarchal ideology, the Southern plantation home is without doubt a contact zone between two races. How those two races are individually constituted is the direct result of their "co-presence, interaction, interlocking understandings and practices" (Pratt 8). The racial divide, along with the lack of understanding and general mistrust by each race of the other, are the logical consequences

---

2. The cool and quiet of the pantry seems to transcend regional division lines. The pantry also appealed to Emily Dickinson's most emphatic creativity; this is where she composed and read her poems aloud to her relatives (Scharnhorst, 485, as qtd. in *Woman's Journal* 1904).

3. Harper Lee's *To Kill a Mockingbird*, which Skeeter had been rereading, immediately suggests her racial sensitivity. The foundation of her daring book project will give voice to the unacknowledged Black perspective, and as such it will reflect and adhere to Atticus Finch's model of *noblesse oblige*.

of racial domination in the Southern states. There, the White race has been manipulated by its own racist ideology into not seeing African Americans as humans or individuals. As the racial Other, African Americans "have been ignored, rendered invisible" in Southern states (hooks, *Black Looks* 51). Ralph Ellison gave this idea memorable expression in *Invisible Man*. The novel's titular character sees invisibility as the defining trope of Blackness: "I am invisible, understand, simply because people refuse to see me. . . . When they approach me they only see my surroundings, themselves or figments of their imagination—indeed, everything and anything except me" (3). In White consciousness, Black identity is malleable; "dehumanizing oppressive forces," according to bell hooks, render African Americans invisible and deny their recognition (*Black Looks* 65). In supposedly more benevolent cases, the White race patronizes its "less civilized" household workers. In her study, *Black Hunger: Food and the Politics of U.S. Identity*, historian Doris Witt perceptively comments on the function of Black people in the consciousness of White Southerners. She observes that a stereotypical and nostalgic image of African Americans expressed "individual and collective fears about threats to white patriarchal power in a volatile social order" (57). Further, as Sharpless demonstrates, stereotypes in a paternalistic system served to keep Blacks subordinate: "Stereotypes were among the means that white Southerners developed and expanded in the hope of controlling African Americans. Powerful white people created images of African American women as subservient and jolly, images designated to persuade both whites and African Americans of the truth of such a description" (xiv).[4]

At least one of the forty interviews in Judith Rollins's *Between Women: Domestics and Their Employers* provides a recollection of the dehumanizing potential of treating a household worker as if they were invisible. The practice of denying Blacks their subjectivity was rightly perceived by household workers as disconcerting and objectifying. Rollins herself confessed, "I felt I was treated as though I were not really there. . . . On one occasion, while sitting in a kitchen having my lunch . . . a couple walked and talked around me, my sense of being invisible

---

4. In his *Seven Days a Week: Women and Domestic Service in Industrializing America*, Katzman makes a similar observation that "racial stereotypes buttressed and justified the subordination of black women in the South" (186).

was so great that I took out paper and started writing field notes" (209). Such "conspicuous invisibility" implied African American domestic workers were lowly, if not worthless, and as such, it was the source of great indignity; again Rollins shares her sentiment: "It was this aspect of servitude I found to be one of the strongest affronts to my dignity as a human being. To Mrs. Thomas and her son, I became invisible; their conversation was private with me, the black servant, in the room as it would have been with no one in the room" (209). The White practice of ignoring the presence of Black servants functions ideologically to support racial hierarchy and is vividly expressed in a multitude of the texts of the American South. For instance, *The Long Walk Home* (1990), directed by Richard Pearce, depicts the case of Mr. Thompson's highly discourteous, audacious comments about African Americans participating in a bus boycott in the presence of their family's guests as well as Odessa Cotter, his family's Black maid, and other Black servants. Mr. Thompson's wanton disregard for his employees' feelings seems to be justified on the grounds of the assumed racial superiority of the family and their guests. However, Rollins's impression and understanding of the erasure of her own subjectivity and agency through the rude dismissal of her physical presence seems to explain and soften White insolence: "These gestures of ignoring my presence were not, I think, intended as insults; they were expressions of the employer's ability to annihilate the humanness and even, at times, the very existence of me, a servant and a black woman" (209).

"Blacks, I realized, were simply invisible to most white people, except as a pair of hands offering a drink on a silver tray." With these words, Sallie Bingham, in her autobiography *Passion and Prejudice*, reveals the extent of Whites' denial of Black people's subjectivity.[5] Similarly, Williston Barrett, the hero of *The Last Gentleman*, Walker Percy's second novel, comments on the conspicuous general invisibility of African Americans in White Southerners' lives: "A Southerner looks at a Negro twice: once when he is a child and sees his nurse for the first time; second, when he is dying and there is a Negro with him to change his bedclothes. But he does not look at him during the sixty

---

5. Qtd. in hooks, *Black Looks* 255. As a "mark of oppression," the strategy of making Black lives invisible attempted "to erase all traces of their subjectivity during slavery and the long years of racial apartheid, so that they could be better, less threatening servants" (hooks, *Black Looks* 254).

years in between. And so he knows as little about Negroes as he knows about Martians, less, because he knows that he does not know about Martians" (195).

It appears that in the American South African Americans are only registered in the "White mentality" when they can perform some social function for Whites. Thus, African Americans become merely social types on which racial ignorance feeds. "It is true in the South that whites and blacks live side by side," explains William Alexander Percy in his memoir, "exchange affection liberally, and believe they have an innate and miraculous understanding of one another. But the sober fact is we understand one another not at all" (299). This blissful racial ignorance reveals itself most in the fact that up until the civil rights movement, White Southerners tended to see African Americans through the prism of the role the other race had to play (as a collective workforce and a threat to White hegemony—that is, a collective enemy that had been pressed into service). Only in cases when White Southerners (in both the actual and fictionalized South) look past preconceived racial assumptions and engage in personal contacts with individuals, regardless of their skin color, can they attempt to understand Blacks and consequently communicate across the color line. Interestingly enough, the spaces of the pantry, kitchen, and dining room have the potential to assist Southerners in their attempts to understand both themselves and the racial Other.

Pantry and Kitchen as Contact Zones

In *The Last Gentleman*, Will Barrett inherits his grandfather's and father's paternalistic attitude toward African Americans.[6] This young gentleman, without conviction or understanding, extrapolates from the misconceived versions of White–Black relations passed down to him

---

6. Joel Williamson observes that "paternalism toward neo-Sambo was its [the conservatism's] heaviest burden, and that burden was light, almost a pleasure to carry, hardly more than a miniature flag on one's lapel. Anybody who thought about black people at all in these years was able to find some black person to patronize—the cook, the laundress, the janitor at the office. Southern whites drifted into a racial dream world in which there really were no problems—that is, if Yankees, Germans, and Communists would simply leave the blacks alone. As Southerners saw it, they were married to their black people, and they took care of them—in sickness and in jail" (479).

and tries to act on the inherited racial beliefs inscribed in Southern White supremacy. Will for some years has had

> a nervous condition and as a consequence he did not know how to live his life. . . . It was *déjà vu*, at least he reckoned it was. What happened anyhow was that even when he was a child and was sitting in the kitchen watching D'lo snap beans and make beaten biscuits, there came over him . . . the strongest sense that it had all happened before and that something else was going to happen and when it did he would know the secret of his own life. (Percy, *The Last Gentleman* 10–11)

Since his childhood, Will has had an eerie feeling that he is unwittingly reenacting scripted racial relations. The simple performative acts he observes in the space of the kitchen refer to the routine, everyday experiences that one takes for granted. In his adulthood, Will, at this point amnesiac and baffled, rightly recognizes African Americans as the key to understanding himself—the racial Other is the negative image of oneself, so knowing the Other conditions knowing oneself. Unfortunately for him, Will knows as much about himself as he knows about the racial Other.

During his journey back to the South to understand his legacy, the troubled engineer finds temporary shelter in the Vaughts' castle, one of the higher-status servant-keeping establishments that ineffectually attempts to evoke the grandeur of "heroic ages" (Percy, *The Last Gentleman* 189). There, Will instinctively gravitates toward the pantry—a room that "conveys a sense of order and 'a place for everything and everything in its place'" (Pond, *The Pantry* 11). In this room Will comes into contact with Black domestics. They feel intimidated and confused by this young White man because he is so unlike the rest of his race. But his willingness to look at and listen to them is what baffles them most: "this strange young man . . . transmitted no signal at all but . . . rather, like them, was all ears and eyes and antennae. He *actually* looked at them" (Percy, *The Last Gentleman* 195, emphasis added). These Black domestics are astonished because Will does not treat them as a collective Other, and hence he does not uphold a tradition-honored rule demanding, as one of Faulkner's characters puts it, "the nigger acting like a nigger and the white folks acting like white folks and no real hard feelings on either side" (*Intruder in the Dust* 34). Faulkner's novel depicts the fate of Lucas Beauchamp, a Black farmer accused of murdering a White man, who carries himself with unabashed pride and unapologetic dignity. Lucas behaves "not black nor white either, not arrogant at all and not even scornful: just intolerant, inflexible and composed" (*Intruder in the Dust* 12). He shows more self-respect than was thought appropriate in Black people. This deportment catalyzes the frustration and fear of White Southerners who believe Lucas does not know his "place." Trying to see another human being in African Americans, which is a prerequisite of understanding and respecting them, contradicts the traditional Southern White attitude that—again as formulated by Faulkner—"All he [a White man] requires is that they [African Americans] act like niggers" (*Intruder in the Dust* 34).

By contrast, Will, unlike other White Southerners, has an exceptional ability and willingness to read between the lines. He can understand the surface message (transmitted for the benefit of Whites) as well as the coded message (intended for the insiders—the Black audience). Will's ability to tune in to the wavelengths of both races seems to be the result of his prolonged exposure to a space that was traditionally the domain of Black women—the kitchen. Homes in general and kitchens in particular are the "spaces where food and power intersect in the performance of identity negotiation, formation, and reformation" (Williams-Forson, "Other Women" 437). Because the kitchen was Will's favorite room in the house, the young gentleman's identity was shaped by the exposure to the Other race. Described as "a white child . . . who [grew] up in the kitchen" (Percy, *The Last Gentleman* 195), Williston is naturally sensitive to both races. As an adult he feels most comfortable in the interstice, which, according to Homi Bhabha, "prevents identities at either end of it from settling into primordial polarities. This interstitial passage between fixed identities opens up the possibility of a cultural hybridity that entertains difference without an assumed or imposed hierarchy" (qtd. in Costello 29). The pantry—which functions as such an intermediate passage—prevents Will from complacently accepting racial identities and keeps him open to possibilities beyond preconceived notions of racial relations.

For a person trying to understand his legacy, the space of the pantry—which is "symbolic of a plentiful simplicity dependent on what we 'put up' from our own place and not what we purchased at a store" (Pond, *The Pantry* 11)—affords personal and private, if not intimate, contact with real people, not the types his deceased father's stoical inheritance offered. Because pantries, according to Pond, "harbor a nostalgic whiff of our domestic past" (*The Pantry* 10), Will instinctively feels most comfortable in one, where he likes to sit while watching and talking to the servants (Percy, *The Last Gentleman* 195). The pantry can evoke "all manner of pleasant things—visual delights, memories of taste and smell, perhaps even security and comfort" (Pond, *The Pantry* 12). Even though people tend to "store their foodstuffs, dishes, unusual collections, and memories of their own making" (Pond, *The Pantry* 12), Will does not simply want to anchor his estranged soul in reminiscences of a happy childhood.[7] He wants to have spontaneous contact with real people; thus he chooses the informal intimacy of the pantry, an auxiliary kitchen space that holds "the staples and extra things from our kitchens and dining rooms" (Pond, *The Pantry* 11), rather than the stuffy dining room filled with the Vaughts and their pretentious guests.

The location of the pantry in the Vaughts' household seems to replicate the historical location of "a butler's pantry during the Victorian era [which] was a buffer between the domestic service arena of the kitchen and the murmur of a full-course dinner party" (Pond, *The Pantry* 10). The Vaughts' pantry is "a large irregular room with a single bay window. . . . It fell out somehow or other that both Negro and white could sit in the pantry, perhaps because it was an intermediate room between dining room and kitchen" (Percy, *The Last Gentleman* 195–96). This interstitial location turns the pantry into a liminal space for the transcultural interaction to which Will is predisposed (Costello 29). In other words, the pantry is a contact zone between two different worlds.

One more element of the design and location of the pantry in the Vaughts' household, which Costello overlooks in his analysis of Williston's identity quest, needs to be mentioned. The fact that the pantry "was not properly a room at all but rather the space left over in the center of the house when the necessary rooms had been built" (Percy, *The Last Gentleman* 195) symbolically points to the simultaneous centrality and marginality of racial relations in White identity. The centrality of the pantry in the household signifies that the domination over the allegedly inferior race is at the core of White identity, since the function of the pantry is to provide "practical ancillary space for prep,

---

7. Pond contends that "pantries can be a part of our longings for Grandmother's kitchen or a place of memories. Nearly everyone has a pantry memory or reference to share" (*The Pantry* 11).

cleanup, or storage" (Pond, "Storage and Nostalgia")—all activities done by "ubiquitous and invisible" Black helpers, servants, and cooks (Davis, "Invisible in the Kitchen" 143).[8] However, the concurrent dependence on Black domestic service, like hushed guilt about slavery, is pushed aside into the margins of the White mentality and consciousness:[9] the pantry literally and symbolically is not a proper room but leftover space—one whose importance is crucial, but rarely acknowledged.[10]

The location of the kitchen in plantation households, like that of the pantry, corresponds to the self-representation of aristocratic living: "The separation of kitchen from dining room, and the symbolic separation or 'ritual break' between black food preparation and white consumption which that distance expressed, made the kitchen a marginalized location in the white household" (Titus 247). This division, according to Charles Camp, "between those who prepare the food and those who will enjoy the fruits of their labors," had a spatial dimension (qtd. in Sharpless 77). The spatial hierarchy of house and outbuildings "relegate[d] food preparation as well as disposal of wastes to buildings separate from the main house and [made] them invisible" (Titus 246). From colonial times, through the Jim Crow era, and up until the civil rights movement, the kitchen of Southern homes was a battleground.

---

8. Moreover, referring to philosopher Lisa Heldke, Sharpless remarks that "many of the daily chores of a domestic worker . . . are virtually invisible to those who benefit from them, or are regarded by beneficiaries as beneath attention or comment" (2). She also concludes that "in most societies, domestic work is assigned the least value of all occupations and given to members of society who are most oppressed and paid the worst" (Sharpless 2).

9. Rarely and reluctantly did White Southerners admit their utter dependence on Black domestic service. Demonstrating this argument, Booker T. Washington writes, "It is sometimes said that the destiny of the Negro is in the hands of the white people of the South. I say that the destiny of the white people of the South is, to a large degree, in the hands of the Negro cook! The majority of our prosperous Southern white people have their food prepared and served three times a day by a Negro woman or girl" (qtd. in Spivey 285).

10. The metamorphoses of American kitchen design and the consequent resignification of the pantry throughout the twentieth century reflect historical and economic changes: from the centrality of the pantry and Hoosier cabinets during the World Wars, with the emphasis on "canning from the home kitchen as a patriotic duty," through the 1950s, with the pantry almost sinking into oblivion due to the increase of prepared foods and refrigeration, till the 1990s—when "a pantry revival in American homes [was] driven by a preference for separate food or dish storage and an emergent nostalgic appreciation of this valuable kitchen space" (Pond, "Brief History of Pantries").

White women attempted to wield their power first over enslaved Black people and then over domestic servants, while Black women reciprocated with covert acts of resistance against White domination. Mary Titus further explains that, ironically, "the kitchen became a place where black authority could be established and could threaten the household at its very center—in the dining room and its rituals" (246).

Even more importantly, screening off the cooking and cleaning activities performed by the servants in Whites' kitchens could never eradicate from White consciousness the knowledge that Southern traditional hospitality could not be achieved without African American women doing the actual preparations in the kitchen:

> Social relations of this sort not only fit with their conceptions of a natural racial hierarchy and of themselves as benevolent superiors but were also necessary, since whites depended on blacks to work for them as servants, cooking their food, caring for their children, and performing many other physically intimate tasks. As historian Tera Hunter has written of turn-of-the-century Atlanta, segregation and domestic service "represented contradictory desires among urban whites striving to distance themselves from an 'inferior race,' but dependent on the very same people they despised to perform the most intimate labor in their homes." (Ritterhouse 14–15)

Thus, by making the presence of Black domestics "invisible" in the dining room, White Southerners, intentionally or not, reveal the hypocrisy of their racial etiquette—they gladly consume food prepared by the supposedly inferior Black help, but they consider their servants too dirty,[11] inferior, or primitive to sit with at the table. Commensality, as "undeniably one of the most important articulations of human

---

11. The motif of dirt and illness associated with Black servants recurs in various texts of the American South. For instance, in Langston Hughes's *Not Without Laughter*, Aunt Hager discloses her White employers' attitude to their Black help: "You oughter hear de way white folks talks 'bout niggers. Says dey's lazy, an' says dey stinks, an' all. Huh! Dey ought to smell deyselves!" (103). The fear of bacteria and dirt spread by Black servants also becomes a pretext for Whites not to fraternize with their servants. Aware of the strict rules of hygienic conduct, Minny's mother trains her daughter to be a servant with such instructions: "When you're cooking white people's food, you taste it with a different spoon. You put that spoon to your mouth, think nobody's looking, put it back in the pot, might as well throw it out . . . You use the same cup, same fork, same plate every day. Keep it in a

sociality" (Kerner and Chou 1), would be perceived as a breach of racial etiquette and hierarchy, which were the legacy of the antebellum South.[12]

Doreen Massey observes that "a large component of the identity of that place called home derived precisely from the fact that it had always in one way or another been open, constructed out of movement, communication, social relations which always stretched beyond it" (14). Thus, a hegemonic relationship between the White employer and Black servant synecdochally reflects the racial status quo in Southern society. In *Seven Days a Week: Women and Domestic Service in Industrializing America*, Katzman notes the same dependence: "Subordination within the household mirrored the white/black relationship prevalent in the South" (185). Thus, to maintain "the white family's position in the hierarchical order of the plantation," which symbolized the patriarchal South (Titus 245), the White family disassociated themselves from the other race through the rituals of food consumption. The inconvenient proximity of the domestics was solved by segregating the spaces of consumption—the dining room belonged to the White family, while the domestics were consigned to the kitchen.[13] Alice Childress memorably evoked such a spatial division in *Like One of the Family*. In the novel, Mildred responds to her employer's arrogant bragging that she, as a paid servant, is part of the family:

> I am not just like one of the family at all! The family eats in the dining room and I eat in the kitchen. Your mama borrows your lace tablecloth for her company and your son entertains his friends in your parlour, your daughter takes her afternoon nap on the living room couch and the puppy sleeps on your satin spread . . . so you can see I am not just like one of the family. (Childress 2)

---

separate cupboard and tell that white woman that's the one you'll use from here on out . . . you eat in the kitchen" (Stockett 39). Such advice may be the historic legacy of training for perfect domestic servants offered at the Hampton and Tuskegee Institutes (Spivey 284–85).

12. Jennifer Ritterhouse remarks that "the separation of blacks and whites at mealtime, however minimal or artificial, was among the most strictly enforced rules of racial etiquette in the antebellum period" (31).

13. This spatial arrangement is true of all master–servant relations in upper-class households. However, in the Northern states, or England for that matter, the domestics ate in the kitchen because of social stratification based on class membership, while in the American South this symbolic interaction in the culinary domain was representative of race relations, rather than class membership.

The primacy of the White family is reflected in the central location of the dining room in the household, while the rear location of the kitchen naturally echoed the peripheral position of Black help.[14] As such the spatial relation between the kitchen and the dining room in architectural design manifests a hierarchy of status in a segregated South. If we see the dining room as the frame through which we can gain access into the self-projected image of the patriarchal South, then what is left out of the "culinary" picture—the kitchen—offers a view of what White Southerners wanted to remove from their consciousness. According to Entman, "frames select and call attention to particular aspects of the reality described, which logically means that frames simultaneously direct attention away from other aspects. Most frames are defined by what they omit as well as include" (54). Thus, an analysis of what is outside the frame—the kitchen and the pantry—may enrich our understanding of racial relations in the domestic space, and, by extension, the South.

Kitchen versus Dining Room[15]

There are too many examples in Southern literature and cinematography to list here in which the division of labor in food production and participation in the consumption of food highlights racial divisions. However, Alfred Uhry's *Driving Miss Daisy*, winner of the 1988 Pulitzer Prize and later adapted into an Oscar-winning film, is an interesting case in this context.[16] The play unfolds from 1948 to 1973, mostly in

---

14. Another observation that further underscores this spatial arrangement of White households has already been mentioned. The act of screening off the cooking and cleaning activities performed in the kitchen was motivated by both ideological and practical reasons. Locating the kitchen in the middle of the house would also cause problems with heat, ventilation, and cooking smells.

15. This section of chapter 1 appeared in print in slightly modified form as "Come Dine with Me, or Not: Performing Racial Relations in the Domestic Sphere in Alfred Uhry's *Driving Miss Daisy*" in *Performing South: The U.S. South as Medium/Message*, edited by Beata Zawadka, Wydawnictwo Naukowe Uniwersytetu Szczecińskiego, 2015, pp. 185–203.

16. *Driving Miss Daisy* was directed by Bruce Beresford and produced by Richard D. and Lili Fini Zanuck in 1989. The next March, at the 62nd Academy Awards, the film received four Oscars (out of nine nominations), including Best Picture, Best Adapted Screenplay (written by Alfred Uhry), and Best Actress (Jessica Tandy as Daisy Werthan). While adapting his play for film, Alfred Uhry accentuated the significance of the culinary spaces that reveal the power structure

Atlanta, Georgia, in the Werthan family home. Dining rituals and culinary spaces reveal the power structure in a house inhabited by an affluent elderly Jewish matron, Mrs. Daisy Werthan, a widow who employs Idella, a Black cook, but who is initially reluctant to be driven by Hoke Coleburn, an elderly Black chauffeur. Daisy's stereotypical stinginess (she is economical with money and thinks hiring a chauffeur is a needless expense)[17] coupled with her feistiness (she attempts to be fiercely independent till the end) is balanced by her family's great ability to function and thrive within the social status quo of the segregated South (the Werthans keep servants). The domestic space is one of the last vestiges of Mrs. Werthan's control over her sovereignty. In a conversation with her son Boolie, Daisy expresses her indignation:

> I am seventy-two years old as you so gallantly reminded me and I am a widow, but unless they rewrote the Constitution and didn't tell me, I still have rights. And one of my rights is the right to invite who I want—not who you want—into my house. You do accept the fact that this is my house? What I do not want—and absolutely will not have is some—(*She gropes for a bad-enough word*) some chauffeur sitting in my kitchen, gobbling my food, running up my phone bill. Oh, I hate all that in my house! (Uhry 3–4)

Daisy understands that employing domestic help is a necessary and convenient measure, but considers the personal price tag for having a chauffeur too high.[18] Her interactions with her servants inspire intense emotions and controversies. The image of a chauffeur gobbling food in her kitchen is a reverse projection of Daisy's unconscious self-image as a more sophisticated, polite and—in other words—superior

---

in Daisy's house and traced the trajectory of the Daisy–Hoke relationship present in the source play. Thus, to buttress my case, I will consult both the literary original and its adaptation.

17. Hoke presents such an opinion as well. When Daisy's son Boolie interviews him for a job, Hoke reveals that he thinks Jews are infamous for being cheap and stingy (Uhry 6). However, Hoke knows how to avoid conflicts with employers. When a job turns out to be financially disadvantageous, he simply terminates his employment rather than agree to humiliating conditions.

18. Daisy's car seems to be the other vestige of control over her sovereignty. This would explain her great reluctance to hire Hoke (implying dependence on the service of another, whom one has to pay) and subsequent compulsive need to have the final word in any matter concerning her trips (e.g., the one to the Piggly Wiggly; pp. 12–13).

person. Even though the potential chauffeur's skin color is never mentioned, his race is made implicit through such a projection of greedy, impolite, quick, and noisy food consumption. Clearly this projection is based on Daisy's own sense of racial superiority, which she is unwilling to admit.

Mrs. Werthan can put up with the presence of a Black female helper occupying her kitchen and eating her food; her agreement to this presence is based on the convenient invisibility of the help. The domestic servant was required to be invisible; the "ideal servant," Katzman observes, "would be invisible and silent, responsive to demands but deaf to gossip, household chatter, and conflicts, attentive to the needs of mistress and master but blind to their faults, sensitive to the moods and whims of those around them but undemanding of family warmth, love, or security. Only blacks could be invisible people in white homes" (188). Mrs. Werthan has learned to treat Idella as invisible, as Daisy explains to Boolie: "Idella is different. She's been coming to me three times a week since you were in the eighth grade." Addressing Boolie again, she maintains that "we know how to *stay out of each other's way*. And even so there are nicks and chips in most of my wedding china and I've seen her throw silver forks in the garbage more than once" (Uhry 4; emphasis mine). Even though Mrs. Werthan tolerates Idella's presence[19] and her sporadic ineffectiveness, she forbids Hoke from talking to her cook. Daisy wants to retain control over the work process: "Don't talk to Idella. She has work to do" (Uhry 10).

Daisy's actual prohibition of conversation and the reasons for it—be it fear of collusion against her or reduced efficiency—is not as important as the space where the ban is imposed. The movie seems to make a stronger statement in this particular case. In the play Daisy forbids Hoke from fraternizing with Idella when they engage in a

---

19. Idella is not a live-in servant; she has a nonresidential part-time job. Not living on the premises of her employer's house, or "living out" as this arrangement was called, gives the servant a sense of autonomy, while offering her employer more privacy. Katzman rightly observes that "for blacks, emancipation and live-out service had become linked" (198). For more on the differences between live-in and day work, see Elizabeth Clark-Lewis, "'This Work Had a' End': The Transition from Live-In to Day Work. Southern Women: The Intersection of Race, Class and Gender. Working Paper #2."

casual conversation in the living room, the very space of the household that is without a doubt recognized as White. In the movie adaptation Daisy intrudes into the kitchen space to give the order, much like other fictitious Southern matrons in the idealized plantation narratives who made "occasional ceremonial passage into the kitchen" (Titus 251). Daisy encroaches on territory that was never an unambiguous space. About the kitchen, Trudier Harris remarks that it is "the one room in the house where the White woman can give up spatial ownership without compromising herself . . . passing that particular space on the domestic is a royal decree of her subservience and inferiority" (*From Mammies* 15). Thus, the kitchen—a White woman's property—became a Black woman's domain to the point that the employers were uncertain as to whether they were permitted access to that room. This is not a case in the Werthan household, though. The worried widow voices her concern about the loss of control over kitchen-space: "Is that what you and Idella talk about in the kitchen? Oh, I hate this! I hate being discussed behind my back in my own house!" (Uhry 10–11). Clearly Daisy is afraid of Idella and Hoke banding together for understanding and support that potentially position them against their employer.

White Southern employers expected their domestic workers to display respectful submissiveness, "obedience, meekness, deference and competence. . . . Through superiority of wealth, social position and often age, they could demand those qualities and punish those who failed them" (Sharpless 129). Racial etiquette demanded that "blacks display not only civil but often servile behavior, to be manifested in a wide array of verbal and physical cues" (Ritterhouse 25). Much like legions of real-life domestics, Hoke[20] and Idella observe daily rituals of cautious deference. Their daily physical reminders of the deferential relationship include entering the house through the back door,[21]

---

20. In their review of the movie adaptation of *Driving Miss Daisy*, Helene Vann and Jane Caputi introduce Hoke as a "good natured, unflappable, subservient, and folksy [chauffeur], . . . [who] is a White dream, the 'Uncle Tom' who unfailingly knows his place and genuinely worships those who boss him around while consistently neglecting to notice his humanity" (80).

21. "Barred from the front doors of Southern white homes, all blacks regardless of calling used the back- or side-door servant's entrance" (Katzman 185).

wearing uniforms,[22] eating their meals in the kitchen, and acknowledging Daisy's orders with "Yessum."[23] In the play Idella is a marginal
character who is never given a voice or surname. The fact that she is
identified only by her first name underscores, in contacts with the
White mistress, how replaceable she is. Like many other historical
counterparts, Idella performs a socially useful task, but in accord with
social convention is ideally invisible when doing so. She may be a
beloved cook, but she is just a cook nonetheless. Her usefulness extends
only to the kitchen, so her identity is circumscribed by that very space.
Her hypothetical presence in the dining room is tolerated only when
she is serving, and even then, she would be reminded of her inferior
status "by her dress, her role as servant, and her exclusion from the
pleasantries of the white people's table" (Sharpless 142).

To underscore the invisibility of Idella's role in the Werthan household, readers learn about Idella's death from a remark made in passing when Hoke brings Daisy coffee during an ice storm: "We ain'
had good coffee roun' heah since Idella pass" (Uhry 35). The secret of
Idella's coffee seems to illustrate Doris Smith's claim about withholding
recipes: "Knowledge of a recipe, and the power to withhold that knowledge, perhaps has been one of the ways in which African-American
slaves and servants have exerted control (albeit limited) over mistresses
and employers. And this knowledge was not to be given away" (qtd. in
Sharpless xxi). Not sharing a recipe could well be perceived as a form of
leverage in the power struggle in the kitchen, and as such it might help

---

22. Elizabeth Clark-Lewis interviewed live-in and day work servants who unanimously expressed their disapproval of uniforms: "The use of the uniform objecti-
fied the live-in servant, determined her fate in the workplace, and reinforced the
belief that the staff was only an audience working in appreciation of the wife's
power displays. The home was the White mistress' stage and major realm of influence, and the uniform legitimized her power. Ophilia Simpson felt, 'them uniforms
just seemed to make them know you was theirs'" (21). Similarly, Rebecca Sharpless
recollected the cooks' and servants' opinions about uniforms as "signs of attempted
subordination" that "negated a woman's individuality" (144).

23. About the performance of racial etiquette, which "jealously guarded the titles
'Mr.,' 'Mrs.,' and 'Miss' for white people," Ritterhouse explained that "demanding
deference and using racial keywords to distance and subordinate blacks inscribed
white southerners' fundamental lesson of white supremacy" (45, 18). Even though
acknowledging employer's orders with "Yes, Ma'am" would be perceived as a ritual
of deference, it carried a subversive potential. According to Sharpless, "under her
mild 'Yes, Ma'am,' and 'No, Ma'am,' there is often a comprehension which is unsus-
pected and far from mutual" (157).

Black domestics redress the power structure of the White household. On the other hand, the appropriation of a recipe by a White woman signals her power over the African American cook/servant. Marjorie Kinnan Rawlings's expropriation of the recipes belonging to Idella Parker, her Black maid, is the most infamous example of usurping culinary expertise in Southern history.[24]

In the movie version, Idella's death of a heart attack while shelling peas in the kitchen for Daisy's dinner underscores the degree of her servitude, loyalty, and commitment. What is interesting is the fact that shortly before the cook's death, Daisy is seen again entering the kitchen—this time without the impression of intrusion or trespassing. The matron seems finally to accept Hoke and Idella eating and chatting together while working. Her remark about a television program they are watching shows a degree of attachment and sentiment toward them. Even though Daisy talks with affection, she still perpetuates a hierarchical relationship between herself and her "colored" help. No longer are they seen as the collective, antagonistic *they*; instead, she accepts them as individuals. This certainly does not mean that Daisy lays down her arms. Her comment, "Don't make a mess with those peas, Idella," carries the residue of control she is so unwilling to relinquish. However, the way Daisy makes her comment reveals a mixture of authority and sentiment.

Daisy and Hoke fondly bring back the memory of Idella's presence through culinary favorites in which she specialized. Daisy affectionately remarks to her Black chauffeur, "You're right. I can fix her biscuits and you can fry her chicken, but nobody can make Idella's coffee" (Uhry 35). Daisy's praise for Idella's coffee and biscuits alludes to the cook's culinary excellence and her special position in the White household.[25] A sense of empowerment that comes from Idella's expertise in making

---

24. More about Marjorie Kinnan Rawlings's appropriation of Idella's recipes can be found in Idella Parker and Marjorie Keating, *Idella: Marjorie Rawlings' "Perfect Maid"* 69. The expropriation of Parker's recipes has been also analyzed by Williams-Forson, *Building Houses* 166–67.
25. Referring to the culinary repertoire of Black cooks, Sharpless contends that "among the most highly prized southern quick breads were biscuits" (41). Idella's undisputed culinary expertise, echoed in Daisy's claims, may also be substantiated by both Charles Reagan Wilson's observation that "biscuits on Sunday helped to make that a special day in the South" (123) and Ellen Woodward's claim that "making good biscuits was more important for a domestic's success than learning to make many dishes in an overall mediocre meal" (qtd. in Palmer 108).

coffee is illustrative of what John T. Edge perceptively acknowledged: "Jim Crow laws may have dictated where blacks could go to school and with whom they could consort, but in the kitchen the black cook was able to express a sort of subversive creativity. . . . In the kitchen, freedom of expression was tolerated, even encouraged" (*A Gracious Plenty* 209). In the context of this "subversive creativity" John Egerton's claim about Black female cooks who "could work culinary miracles day in and day out, but couldn't for the life of them tell anyone how they did it" (*Southern Food* 16) seems only partially accurate. The implied inability to tell the recipe (reflected in the choice of the second modal verb), which might be the consequence of their illiteracy, deprives Black women of agency, the very agency that is evident in the deliberate act of withholding the culinary knowledge.

Daisy's reference to Idella's biscuits, chicken, and coffee (35) attests to the fact that by making and consuming Idella's culinary specialties, the lady of the house may establish an emotional connection with the deceased cook, and by extension other Black domestics. Instead of affectionate reminiscences of Idella's presence via food references, the movie makes a much more evocative case for a qualified interpersonal connection by depicting Hoke and Daisy cooking together. As mentioned, in Southern households the kitchen is never an unambiguous space; apart from being a battleground for White or Black rule, it may also present an opportunity to bond and transcend social norms. The kitchen in the Werthan household also becomes such a site of a possible breach of racial barriers: "Just after Idella's funeral, upon returning home, Daisy and Hoke . . . together cook a supper of fried chicken" (Fischer 182). "Fried chicken, a largely southern food that emerged out of social institutions shaped by racial complexities, is," according to Psyche Williams-Forson, "one of many foods that blurs the lines between the 'symbolic separations [of] those who prepare the food and those who consume it'" ("More than Just" 113). Capitalizing on the symbolic meaning of fried chicken, director Bruce Beresford uses this dish to create a bond of companionship through references to Idella's culinary abilities. In the interstice of the kitchen Hoke bears an air of authority (after all, he has insider's information) and warns Daisy that she is going to ruin the chicken unless she cooks it like Idella. As a White matron, Daisy has to hold on to the vestiges of control so she cannot openly follow the instructions. Her sharp retort, "Mind your own business," is the only logical response of a White woman trying to regain control of her kitchen. She pretends to disregard the instructions coming from her servant, and as such her position in the house is not undermined or impaired. Yet, aware of the fact that Idella excelled at preparing this dish, she does exactly as Hoke has instructed her to do— once he leaves the kitchen.

In terms of racial relations, the making of this particular dish is a highly symbolic, if ambiguous, gesture. Were it not for the fact that it was Idella's specialty dish, the choice of fried chicken could be construed as Daisy's patronizing, condescending, if not racist gesture.[26] Even if we disregard the derogatory image of fried chicken (like watermelon) as the stereotypical food of choice of African Americans,[27] still the dish, the origins of which are not ideologically neutral, is haunted by the past. Historian Williams-Forson reveals its connotative charge: "From a semiotic point of view, fried chicken becomes a contested social marker of the 'Old South,' southern mores, and ways of being" (*Building Houses* 78). However, because it is Idella's signature dish (along with two other specialties of hers: coffee and biscuits), the act of preparing and serving it also becomes Daisy's and Hoke's commemoration of sorts of a cook/friend.

The subversive potential of the dish is wasted, however. Hoke serves Daisy fried chicken in the dining room only to retire to eat the

---

26. Even though fried chicken as a dish is not racist in and of itself, its derogatory, stereotypical connotation with African Americans was already popularized by Griffith's *The Birth of a Nation* (1915). In Griffith's now-classic film, one of the scenes portrays Black legislative officials engaging in offensive, primitive behavior: greedily drinking, ostentatiously eating fried chicken, and putting their feet on their desks. Such an image both capitalized on and perpetuated racist stereotypes.

27. The position of fried chicken as a quintessential Southern dish is indisputable. Historians commonly claim that "the sine qua non of southern cooking has long been fried chicken" (Sharpless 51), and "Southern fried chicken is probably the single most popular and universally consumed food ever to come from this region of the country" (Egerton, "Fried Chicken" 142). However, there are voices that question African Americans' affinity for the dish, and there are others, such as John Edge, director of the Southern Foodways Alliance, who "[decline] to determine the origins of fried chicken" (qtd. in Sharpless 207, f.117). Following a similar line of analysis, John Egerton remarks: "The standard explanation for the origins of fried chicken suggests that the wide availability of fowl in the colonial era and the cooking techniques of African slaves combined to produce 'fried' chicken, and cooks of African descent have long been recognized as among the region's best fryers. But rarely do southerners reach consensus on a definitive version of the dish" ("Fried Chicken" 141–42).

dish alone in the equally empty kitchen. Both Daisy and Hoke "are grieving; both really need the companionship of a friend" (Fischer 182). The division into "White" dining room and "Black" kitchen defines inside/outside demarcations in Southern households. Hoke knows only too well not to impose his companionship—or rather, he has been taught not to. Hoke seems to have internalized the unwritten rule that "no black could demand to use the front door or eat with the family; Southern racial etiquette ruled these out as areas of legitimate conflict" (Katzman 195). What Williams-Forson remarked about African American women eating in White women's presence can be extended to apply to both female and male domestic workers: "to share in the consumption of the food, especially in the presence of whites, meant that culinary (and social) boundaries would have to be broken" (*Building Houses* 77). Analogously, Mrs. Werthan is not ready to dine with Hoke in the dining room, the very room that was "part of the ideal Christian family home . . . , a sacred space where the family could commune together" (Clark 151). The dining room makes an explicit connection with family values and connotes familial harmony, sharing and togetherness.

Commensality, as "an important principle of expressions of friendship and hospitality" (Chee-Beng 25), implies social equality between the races. For Daisy to invite Hoke to join her at the dinner table would mean accepting him as her social equal, friend, or family member. Sociologist Charles Spurgeon Johnson explains that "the taboo against eating together was so strong that it was 'rarely broken.' Eating together was 'thoroughly prohibited and severely punished' because it suggested 'social intimacy which is universally banned'" (qtd. in Sharpless 143).[28] Tolerating Hoke's presence in the house is one thing, but fraternizing with him is another. Daisy's decision resonates with Gil Valentine's observation that "eating together at home is therefore a particularly important way of incorporating new members and fostering a sense of unity amongst reconstituted families" (493). Moreover, following this line of argumentation, commensality is seen to

---

28. Similarly, Jennifer Ritterhouse observes that "taboos against eating and drinking with blacks remained strong in the post-emancipation South and, for many white southerners, became deeply ingrained. 'If anything would make me kill my children, it would be the possibility that niggers might sometime eat at the same table and associate with them as equals,' one woman told Clifton Johnson in 1904" (42).

cultivate solidarity or feelings of acceptance. This human experience is easily extended to persons outside the family or friends to show friendship or solidarity. Inviting a non-family member to eat with the family is the highest expression of friendship, and an invitation to share one's food or to eat with one's group, which can be one's family or a kin group or circle of friends, is at the minimum a friendly gesture. (Chee-Beng 25)

Mrs. Werthan understands that eating with Hoke in her dining room would imply she has incorporated him as a guest into her social sphere. That gesture would be worth a thousand words. Therefore, if she

> picked up her plate and joined Hoke at the kitchen table, she would have simply been conforming to an old southern tradition of the kitchen as common ground for both races, the one integrated room in a segregated household. Such a gesture . . . would have made a more convincing affirmation of racial reconciliation than any dialogue imaginable. (Fischer 182)

Such a transgression of spaces of consumption—Daisy eating dinner with Hoke in the kitchen—would bespeak her desire to breach dining etiquette in order to reach domestic détente and end the principles of de facto segregation in her household.

Their journey to remedy what Davis calls "asymmetrical intimacy" ("Invisible in the Kitchen" 153) is a bumpy one, if the goal can be said to have been attained at all. The trajectory of their relationship is again framed in the spaces connected with food: a kitchen, a pantry, and dining rooms. Daisy initially perceives Hoke, and Idella for that matter, through the prism of the collective "Other":

Daisy: . . . I was brought up to do for myself. On Forsyth Street we could not afford *them* and we did for ourselves. That's still the best way, if you ask me.

Boolie: Them! You sound like Governor Talmadge.

Daisy: Why, Boolie! What a thing to say! I'm not prejudiced! Aren't you ashamed? (Uhry 4; emphasis mine)

The equation of "them" with the domestic help clearly indicates the racialization of household employees. The Black help, be it a cook or chauffeur, seems to be a necessary evil in Mrs. Werthan's house. The racial divide does not make communication and understanding between the matron and her employees any easier.

As a White matron of the house, Daisy has to adapt to the role of gatekeeper, the function sociologists ascribe to women whose task is "control of the flow of goods, specially food, into the household" (Sharpless 35).[29] As "food created the most friction" in Southern households (Sharpless 154), a diligent housewife's role was not only to supervise the flow of food but also to prevent its illicit outflow from the household. Early accounts of planters' diaries documented cases of the "sticky fingers" of enslaved people. A major assumption was that theft lay in their nature:

> Plantation owners lived by a credo of order and control that they had established. Knowing that their slaves were able to skillfully (at times) pilfer and steal under their roof disturbed this sense of order. By attributing stealing by slaves to an inherent nature rather than a condition of their circumstances, slave owners were able to deflect attention from their own participation in this aspect of slave victimization. Morally, it was much better to believe that slaves were natural thieves than to believe that the institution of enslavement contributed to this condition. So there is some truth to slaves engaging in thievery, but much of this belief is rooted in planter ideology. (Williams-Forson, *Building Houses* 23)

By denouncing the genes of enslaved Blacks, rather than the system that subjugated them, White Southerners exploited the prevailing ideological conceptions of racial inferiority to whitewash their guilt from holding fellow humans in bondage. There were other, less common voices that claimed that "no amount of moral instruction or provisioning would curb slaves' propensity to steal . . . the bondman was not motivated by 'the advantage of obtaining a desired object . . . but rather the excitement produced by the very act of stealing'" (Hillard 106). Whether blamed on inborn proclivity, vengeance,[30] or wicked excitement,[31] stealing from their masters/employers alluded to African

---

29. The historian refers here to McIntosh and Zey's sociological study "Women as Gatekeepers," 317–19.

30. "Inadequate rations were a tacit license for theft. . . . Slaves quickly mastered scrounging, scavenging for food and hiding the evidence" (Yentsch).

31. Degradation or wickedness, not just simply hunger, seem to have been major incentives for the theft of food. Eugene Genovese's historical study of the antebellum South reveals that "for many slaves, stealing from their own or other masters became a science and an art, employed as much for the satisfaction of outwitting Ole' Massa as anything else" (606).

Americans' supposedly inferior,[32] "morally bankrupt," and degenerate nature.[33] Over the years, White Southerners' accusations turned into a stereotypical image of stealing and pilfering African Americans. Katzman remarks that "aspects of the employer/employee relationship came to be touted as racial characteristics of the servant group itself. Employer suspicion and employee theft were translated into a racial characteristic" (222). With systemic abuse and discrimination applied to keep the Black help at a subsistence level right up until the civil rights movement, "one of the most constant sources of tension between housewives and cooks was theft, whether real, imagined, intentional, accidental, or through misunderstanding" (Sharpless 154). Black people were aware that their White employers, and most White Southerners by extension, saw them as inherently dishonest and believed them to be thieves.[34]

While discussing reasons for enslaved people to commit theft, such as jealousy, hunger, or vindication, historian Psyche Williams-Forson remarks that "theft by blacks was less common than believed but was used as a convenient tool of control" (*Building Houses* 26). With "this notion of black people's 'disposition to theft'" (26), White Southerners absolved themselves from whatever responsibility for the situation they

---

32. In the 1930s, social anthropologist John Dollard perceptively captured the social divisiveness of colors in the Southern states: "Whiteness represents full personal dignity and full participation in American society [whereas] Blackness or darkness represents limitation and inferiority; and sometimes even animal character is imputed into it" (70).

33. Sharpless quotes from Cecilia M. Rio's doctoral dissertation, in which Rio observes that "the practice of employees removing food from the home 'reinforced the stereotype of African Americans as morally bankrupt and shifty characters and reinforced the notions of black inferiority and dependency and white paternalism'" ("From Feudal Serfs to Independent Contractors: Class and African American Women's Paid Domestic Labor, 1863–1980," 56–57, qtd. in Sharpless 154).

34. Williams-Forson, *Building Houses* 29, and Fleming 17. Rebecca Sharpless claims that "stealing food was an extension of the widely sanctioned practice known as 'toting,' in which cooks received leftover food as part of their pay, in lieu of cash" (154). Discussing "the servant problem," Fleming mentions two foodways-related aspects of employing Black household workers: White men agreed to toting and knew about pilfering. In face of a strike or too-great demands, "the housekeeper can protect herself against pilfering or privileges, and this would require almost a reorganization of the Southern social system. . . . Then the employer will be forced to demand better work, will cut off privileges and donations, and will stop 'toting' and pilfering" (16).

might have felt. "Treating an employee as a potential thief would create a cloud of suspicion that would shadow her every move" (Sharpless 154) while justifying the White employer's constant surveillance. To supervise the planning or execution of food consumption, a gatekeeper might even limit unsupervised access to the food supplies, as was the case in Katherine Du Pre Lumpkin's upper-class White home:

> We often spoke of the peculiar inborn traits of this so peculiar race. For instance, the Negro's "thieving propensities." White men stole too, but not "as a race." We verily believed that a Negro could not help but steal. So we acted accordingly. We must lock up our valuables. We children should never leave the key in the food pantry door, but turn it and put it back in its hiding place. Let something be missing; we suspected the cook, unless it was found; maybe even then, for she could have 'got scared' and returned it. It was not serious with us; just a disability of the race, we said, that only we Southerners understood and took charitably. (153)

White children internalized benevolent paternalism when dealing with Black domestics who were "'innately irresponsible,' . . . 'not to be trusted,' 'slovenly,' and [imbued with] a dozen more [undesirable traits]." With disarming honesty Lumpkin repeats racist comments: "The inner traits, we said, applied to the race" (153).

Guilty of conventional racial prejudice and consequently a lack of trust in her servants, Daisy is suspicious of Hoke's behavior and intentions. Internalizing the belief that thievery runs in Black blood, Mrs. Werthan suspects Hoke. At the crack of dawn Daisy summons her son to show how she employed her great detective skills in a compulsive attempt to find the culprit of a crime against her. Of course she does not make empty accusations:

> He's stealing from me! . . . I have proof! . . . This! (*She triumphantly pulls an empty can of salmon out of her robe pocket*) I caught him red-handed! I found this hidden in the garbage pail under some coffee grounds. . . . Here it is! Oh I knew. I knew something was funny. They all take things, you know. So I counted. . . . The silverware first and the linen dinner napkins and then I went into the pantry. I turned on the light and the first thing that caught my eye was a hole behind the corned beef. And I knew right away. There were only eight cans of salmon. I had nine. Three for a dollar on sale. (Uhry 17)

Pilfering from the workplace is no small matter for the employer; however, the circumstances of this case challenge the sanity of Daisy's crusade against Hoke.

Once Boolie offers to reimburse his mother for the purloined can of salmon, Daisy explains what the can represents:

> Why, Boolie! The idea! Waving money at me like I don't know what! I don't want the money. I want my things! . . . It was mine. I bought it and I put it there and he went into my pantry and took it and he never said a word. I leave him plenty of food every day and I always tell him exactly what it is. They are like having little *children* in the house. They want something so they just take it. Not a smidgin [*sic*] of manners. No conscience. He'll never admit to this. . . . I don't like it! I don't like living this way! I have no privacy. (Uhry 18, emphasis added)

The shift from a singular to plural personal pronoun (from "he" to "they") showcases Daisy's prejudice against the racial Other. Her including Hoke in the collective Other ("they") exposes her antagonistic mistrust and displeasure at the company of the "colored" help in the house. The disappearance of one food product results in an emotional outburst because Mrs. Werthan, rather than stowing away a few foodstuffs, is hoarding. By comparing Hoke to a young pantry raider, Daisy wants to restore her home's power structure: she likens him to a naughty child in need of correction and defines herself as the one who wields uncontested power in her house. Daisy does not have to punish Hoke for disobedience by having him whitewash her picket fence.[35] A verbal reprimand is enough. Taking Hoke to task serves to underscore Daisy's control over the household.

Hoke manages to take the wind out of her sails, however. Upon greeting Mrs. Daisy in the early hours of the morning, he says: "Yestiddy when you out with yo' sister I ate a can o' your salmon. I know you say eat the leff-over pork chops, but they stiff. Here, I done buy you another can. You want me to put it in the pantry fo' you?" (Uhry 19). Hoke's confession reveals the reason behind his disrespectful intrusion into Daisy's pantry: he was motivated by hunger resulting from inadequate, if not inedible, leftover food. His comment may not

---

35. Tom Sawyer's Aunt Polly chose whitewashing a picket fence as a form of punishment for Tom's raiding her pantry for jam (Twain, *The Adventures of Tom Sawyer*).

be construed as directly offensive. However, if one takes into account enslaved Blacks' practice of "toting,"[36] then Daisy's gesture carries patronizing and condescending undertones.[37] Hoke's unwillingness to consent to such treatment, which reflects badly on Daisy, leaves her *"trying for dignity"* (Uhry 19, stage direction).

Daisy's relationship with Hoke moves from mistrust arising from stereotypical antagonism (accusation of pilfering from her pantry), through benevolent tolerance (acceptance of Hoke and Idella eating and chatting together in the kitchen), to fondness in old age. Despite Daisy's declaration of friendship ("You are my best friend"; Uhry 47) made during one of the lucid moments of her progressing dementia, they try to bond but they are not quite there yet. Some gestures that Daisy makes out of good intentions, such as inviting Hoke to a banquet honoring Martin Luther King Jr., prove patronizing and backfire.[38] Their bond, Fischer claims, is "a relationship perpetually in a

---

36. Eating arrangements in the kitchens of Southern households had many variations. In some, "domestic workers received food on site but were not allowed to take it home" (Sharpless 155). In others, toting—"taking leftovers from one's employer in lieu of cash wages" (Sharpless 102)—was practiced. About households' in-kind payments supplementing paid wages, Salmon observed: "Many employees received several types of in-kind payment in lieu of cash wages, including board, lodging, leftover food, and castoff household goods and clothing" (*Domestic Service* 89; qtd. in Sharpless 74).

37. Similarly, Daisy's offer to Hoke—"Eat anything you want out of the icebox. It's all going to spoil anyway" (Uhry 36)—made during the ice storm may as well be construed as a patronizing gesture. By not accepting an offer of otherwise soon-to-be spoiled food, Hoke realizes that, by causing Daisy's displeasure at revealing her faulty paternalism, he risks future (not-so-) hypothetical retaliation. Talking about the servant–served relationship, Evelyn Nakano Glenn arrives at the same conclusion: "Employees learned to accept employers' 'noblesse oblige' even when they didn't want the goods to keep from seeming 'too proud' an tempting their employers to withhold future gifts and bonuses'" ("Dialectics of Wage Work" 455, qtd. in Sharpless 77).

38. Daisy invites Hoke to a United Jewish Appeal banquet honoring King only because her son refuses to attend it with her because of his business interests (being hailed a civil rights supporter would be frowned upon in certain Atlanta business circles). For all her good intentions, Hoke proves that the gesture is paternalistic:

> Hoke: What you think I am, Miz Daisy? . . . You think I some somethin' sittin' up here doan' know nothin' 'bout how to do? . . . Invitation to disheah dinner come in the mail a mont' ago. Did be you want me to go wid you, how come you wait till we are in the car on the way to ask me? . . .

stage of becoming" (182). The final stop on their journey to a relationship based on integrity and fondness ironically happens to be on Thanksgiving Day, a feast expressing gratitude and connection—through the sharing of food—for and with family and other people with whom one has important relationships. Not bound by an employment contract, Hoke decides to visit his friend during a holiday that celebrates the virtues of gratitude, family joy and reunions, and prosperity (Muir 198–99, 204–5). In the final scene, when Daisy and Hoke at last sit together in the dining room to talk, their conversation and gestures reveal an atmosphere of cordiality, kindness, and warmth. Even though Daisy seems preoccupied with herself and it is she who controls the conversation,[39] Hoke gives her a friendly helping hand as she eats a Thanksgiving pie, which she seems to accept with gratitude. Hoke's instinctive reaction "Looka here. You ain' eat yo' Thanksgiving pie. Lemme hep you wid this" (Uhry 51) reveals his genuine concern and deep-rooted affection. Rather than being a patronizing sexist gesture, Hoke's gently feeding Daisy one small piece of pie after another has reconciliatory potential, as it happens in the dining room of a nursing home for White people. In that place both Hoke and Daisy are visitors, not on their own ground. Paradoxically, the very place that seems to allow for such a friendly gesture may simultaneously undermine its frankness. If it were not for the colorblind space of the nursing home dining room, which allows for a meeting of two equals, would they be able to subvert the Black chauffeur–White lady dichotomy?

Daisy: You know you're welcome to come, Hoke.

Hoke: Mmmm-hmmm. . . . Nevermind baby, next time you ask me someplace ask me regular. . . . . Things changin', but they ain't change all dat much. (Uhry 44)

Working for White people for so many years has trained Hoke to sense a condescending attitude. Hoke maintains dignity and self-worth by refusing the invitation. His refusal embodies what Elizabeth Janeway named the "powers of the weak." According to Janeway, the most significant form of power held by the weak is "the refusal to accept the definition of oneself that is put forward by the powerful" (*Powers of the Weak* 167). Hoke understands that he cannot expect others to respect him if he does not respect himself.

39. My interpretation of this scene diverges from that of Fischer, who claims that "even in the nursing home finale, as Daisy chats amiably with Hoke and for once inquires into his family, her thoughts and words betray a consuming preoccupation with herself" (182).

From a White Kitchen to a Black Living Room[40]

The subversion of the housekeeper–lady-of-the-house dynamic that appears in Ellen Douglas's *Can't Quit You, Baby* takes on a spatial dimension. It is visible in the meeting grounds of Cornelia O'Kelly and her Black maid, Julia "Tweet" Carrier. The trajectory of Cornelia and Julia's racial reconciliation spans the whole novel, beginning in a White woman's kitchen and ending in a Black woman's living room. The story begins in 1960s Mississippi in the only space where these two women could be in each other's company without feeling socially awkward[41]— Cornelia's kitchen:

> There would have been no way in that time and place . . . for them to get acquainted, except across the kitchen table from each other, shelling peas, peeling apples, polishing silver. True, other black and white women became friends under other circumstances, but such friendships . . . were rare.[42] In this house the white woman had to choose to sit down to set the tone of their conversation. (Douglas, *Can't Quit* 4–5)

Cornelia's casual complicity with de jure or de facto racial domination[43] complies with and serves to support the segregationist laws

---

40. This section of chapter 1 was originally published under the title "From a White Woman's Kitchen into a Black Woman's Living Room: A Reconfiguration of the Servant/Served Paradigm in Ellen Douglas's *Can't Quit You, Baby*" in *Annales Universitatis Mariae Curie-Skłodowska*, Sec. FF, vol. 34 (2016), pp. 95–106.
41. Sharpless claims that "domestic work, including cooking, almost always took place in the employer's home, bringing the African American woman into a white family's intimate physical space" (141). While discussing the difference between Northern and Southern domestic relations, Katzman reveals that "the thread of woman-to-woman interaction that interwove the pattern of service in the North and West was almost nonexistent in the South" (201). The personal and intimate sphere of the relationship between mistress of the house and her servant was missing in the Southern states.
42. Sharpless observes that "bonds of mutual affection did exist, particularly in situations where the employer and employee knew each other for many years. As sociologist Mary Romero observed, 'In general, the longer the period of employment, the more informal the employer-employee relationship tends to be, as well as the more likely it is that a personal relationship will emerge'" (Romero, "Sisterhood and Domestic Service" 327–28; qtd. in Sharpless 162–63).
43. Glenn observes that "power and domination, conflict and struggle all occur in people's lives. In an association such as that between a housewife and a domestic

of subservience that exploit African American women. The complicated entanglement of race relations, added to an already uneven employer–employee dependence, does not render Mrs. O'Kelly and Julia's relationship any easier. In the O'Kelly household, the relationship between the employer and her domestic has retained the traditional racial asymmetry. In a relationship of the putatively superior to the supposedly inferior, Julia has to attune herself to the feelings and moods of the mistress of the house. The employer–housekeeper relationship is clearly complicated by what Davidoff et al. identify as the mixture of "power, dependence, deference, care, gift-giving. . . . love and hate" (qtd. in Sharpless 129), and as such the kitchen space in segregated homes in the South hindered the formation of sisterhood across the color line.[44]

Cornelia and Julia's seating arrangement is highly symbolic: "The two women are sitting at right angles to each other at the kitchen table" (Douglas, *Can't Quit* 3). Their spatial awareness (the proper angle) reflects both the emotional and ideological distance that yawns between their lives. The kitchen is Cornelia's haven of peace and order. As such, it is a space where everything and everybody is in the right place, where "she can be sure that order prevails" (146). There is no room for misinterpretation. Everything is either black or white. Even though over the years African American women have, as Clark-Lewis reported, "developed the determination to transform a master-servant relationship into an employer-employee relationship" (qtd. in Sharpless 71), Cornelia and Julia's harks back to a complex servant–served

---

worker, everyday actions both control and oppose" (*Unequal Freedom* 16; qtd. in Sharpless 129). It is not amiss to mention that in the Southern context, it was the mistress of the house who gave orders to the domestics, and hence she participated in the racist system designed to subdue Blacks. "In most accounts of domestic service written by servants, the male figures were generally distant, shadowy figures. They seemed to intrude into the household rather than to be part of it. Or they seemed to be relatively powerless in the household" (Katzman 215). Removing her husband from the oppressor–oppressed equation in the household, a White woman reveals her complicity in upholding laws and customs that exploit other women.

44. For more information about women's difficulty in bonding across the color line in the kitchen space, see Anne E. Goldman, "'I Yam What I Yam': Cooking, Culture, and Colonialism," esp. 171–73.

paradigm.[45] Theoretically, the aura of servant keeping as a feudal institution has faded[46] and Douglas's women share their domestic duties—housework is Tweet's domain, whereas cooking is Cornelia's forte. Yet, when Julia, like many of her real-life counterparts, "enters the white woman's kitchen, she moves into a culture which is at least apart from her own, if not alien or openly hostile" (Harris, *From Mammies* 14). Because there is no doubt that "the ultimate ownership of the space [of the kitchen] and authority remained with the housewife/employer" (15), Cornelia presides in hers as though it were her "throne room" (Douglas, *Can't Quit* 6).

Even though no open and intense antagonism seems to exist between the lady of the house and her employee, Cornelia's less than enthusiastic response to Julia's sharing her songs and stories reveals her superior social status. Julia's gifts, be they flowers or stories, are supposed to render their relationship more personal and any awkward silence more tolerable. Cornelia listens to Tweet's stories "with a distant courtesy—condescension, even," sometimes with revulsion and reluctance (Douglas, *Can't Quit* 7, 47):

> Cornelia over the years has considered herself a listener. Another woman might not have time for Tweet's gifts—for the tales of childhood, the snatches of song, the handful of ragged robins. But from the beginning Cornelia, kneading dough, fluting a piecrust, cutting carrot curls or radish rosettes, has never by a word or gesture betrayed the boredom, the condescension she sometimes feels, her rejection of the moral code that Tweet's stories sometimes imply, her doubts about the verity of some outlandish set of events. She accepts the tales like the flowers that she sticks in a

---

45. Minrose Gwin explores "the volatile, often violent connection between Black and White women of the Old South" in the texts of the American South (*Black and White Women* 4). Having analyzed many interracial relationships between women, the critic points out their conflicted nature: "in its paradox and conflict, in its connective tissue of race, gender, and power, the relationship between black and white women in the nineteenth-century South may be seen as paradigmatic of the central ambiguity of southern racial experience: its antipathy, bitterness, and guilt on the one hand, its very real bonding through common suffering on the other" (*Black and White Women* 4).

46. Only theoretically is the aura of servant keeping as a feudal institution gone. In Southern households "throughout much of the twentieth century, patterns of 'domination and deference prevailed even as they had in the late nineteenth century'" (Ritterhouse, "Etiquette" 21, 25, qtd. in Sharpless 135).

jelly glass and sets in the window by the kitchen sink and forgets. (13–14)

Cornelia's disregard and lack of sympathy for Julia is visible in her abandonment of "both listening and appearing to listen" (15). Her deceptive self-image as a listener points to her fundamental lack of self-criticism and self-analysis. Her maintenance of emotional distance—"expressionless, absentminded, Cornelia listened and did not listen" (36)—is a sign of presumed moral superiority, White domination, and lack of interest. If it were not for Cornelia's lack of empathy, Julia's stories might have precipitated their bonding. "Cornelia's personality delays the development of the relationship that"—according to Theresa James—"might result from years of their close proximity and her intimate knowledge of Tweet's life" (81–82).

In imposing her stories on an ungrateful Cornelia, Julia is the only person in the household who "raises her voice and tells Cornelia what is really going on" (Douglas, *Can't Quit* 129). In doing so she attempts to push the emotional and physical boundaries (represented both literally and symbolically by Cornelia's hearing impairment) the mistress of the house has erected. Critical race theorist Patricia Williams's comments are particularly revealing in this context. She claims that for White people, "racial denial tends to engender a profoundly invested disingenuousness, an innocence that amounts to the transgressive refusal to know" (27). For various reasons, Cornelia, like many "sheltered women" of the upper-class South (Douglas, *Can't Quit* 11), prefers evasion to truth. Tweet's situation is like that of legions of real-life domestic workers who "were uniquely positioned to see human nature at its worst, and they were exposed up close to their employers' unhappiness" (Sharpless 159).[47] Tweet, aware of her employer's strained relations with her own family (Cornelia's love for her family seems conditional), can speak up because their relationship is fueled not by her need of acceptance or love, but by Julia's antagonism.

Even though the housekeeper and her employer never talk about the race issue, "*they* weren't absentminded about these ludicrous and dreadful [racial] matters. To them race sounded the endlessly repeated ground bass above and entwined with which they danced

---

47. "Blacks acquired encyclopedic knowledge of white communities and knew the intimate details of white lives, while whites remained ignorant of black lives" (Katzman 200–201).

the passacaglia . . . of their lives" (Douglas, *Can't Quit* 5).[48] This code of silence suggests that both "have other, more complex business with each other" (240). As such, silence and silencing others underscores the transition of White power—from human chattel to domestic servants. Still, the racial component of their relationship is like an elephant in the living room, which mask-wearing and avoiding the topic make even bigger. The end result of this silence is that Cornelia, who has perfectly internalized the conventions of behavior befitting a White matron, adopts a patronizing attitude toward Julia. She subconsciously reveals her condescension by turning off her hearing aid when Julia starts sharing her stories. Theresa James perceptively remarks that Cornelia "does not want to hear any part of the story that will offend her or make her think about unpleasantness" (81). She may be "alone in a cocoon of dead silence" (127),[49] but she never seems to be interested in being more than a White matron.[50]

Cornelia's turning off her hearing aid clearly refers to the racial imbalance in the employer's kitchen and serves as an evocative symbol of the code of silence. Such a workplace asymmetry, complicated by the race issue in the kitchen, may delay, if not prevent, women from forming sisterhood across the color line. The White mistress attempts to cross that line when she visits Tweet in her house after the assassination of Martin Luther King Jr.[51] Because her servant does not come to work, Cornelia pays Julia "a bereavement call" (98), which the narrator retrospectively misidentifies as "a gesture of sympathy" giving "substance to her courage and generosity of spirit" (240). However, her gesture might be motivated by fear of losing her help—after all she

48. Sharpless comments that the "connections between employees and employers, intrinsically vexed, became even more tangled when old expectations clashed with current realities and race remained an overriding consideration" (129).

49. Cornelia has been avoiding reality for a long time, to the point that Andrew, her son, accusingly asks her, "Where do you *live*? . . . Where *are* you?" (Douglas, *Can't Quit* 137; original emphasis).

50. Being a White housewife defines Cornelia's identity: she "became mistress of her household, purveyor of génoises, fig preserves, and homemade pasta" (Douglas, *Can't Quit* 40).

51. "Few whites knew much about their black servants except for the stereotyped views which they held about the nature of all blacks. Many black servants spent most of their lives in white homes, while mistresses never entered their servants' homes" (Katzman 200). In such a social context, Cornelia's visit to Tweet's home, regardless of her interior motives, is highly unconventional.

already noticed "garbage not collected, chickens not picked, trucks not loaded" (98), or perhaps it reflects a patronizing pity. Her naiveté and lack of perspective—Cornelia "puts her hand on the doorknob, moves the door gently back against the pressure of Tweet's presence, steps in" (98–99)—might imply that her patronizing feeling of moral obligation and inherent generosity of spirit are fighting for dominance in her personality.[52] The physical distance between the women is a metaphor of the two separate worlds they inhabit over the White–Black dividing line. Cornelia's inability to empathetically reach out to Tweet is evident in the polite phrase "I am sorry," which does not correspond to her gestures: "she dares not reach out, dares not cross the two paces that separate them" (99). Yet, the incongruity of Cornelia's words and gestures suggests that Mrs. O'Kelly might have good intentions, however ineffective at this point, of breaking the mistress/servant paradigm and treating Tweet as another human being instead of as her servant (Jacobsen 29).

Not until Cornelia's mental breakdown and Julia's stroke[53] will the former, while visiting her servant, who now relies on a wheelchair, set "the volume of her hearing aid higher than she used to" (Douglas, *Can't Quit* 231).[54] It is Cornelia who takes care of Tweet "slumped in the wheelchair, her right hand and right leg swathed in bandages, her left arm in her lap, fingers trembling against her thigh" (232). It is Cornelia who "nurse[s] her back to health by refusing to give up on her when all of Tweet's family has written her off as a vegetable who will never be able to speak again" (Bomberger). At this point Cornelia subverts

---

52. Davis opines that Cornelia's decision to visit Julia proves their uneven relationship: "the fact that she came there to console Tweet over the death of Dr. King, the symbolic end of the civil rights movement, yet still asserts authority over Tweet's home indicates the rigid nature of asymmetrical intimacy" ("Invisible in the Kitchen" 151).

53. The lives of the two women get complicated within a relatively short time. After her husband's death, Cornelia suffers an emotional paralysis. First, she stays at her son's for six months, then sojourns in New York. Cynthia, Tweet's stepdaughter, calls Cornelia in the metropolis to inform her that Julia has suffered from "a seizure of some sort . . . passed out standing over the stove stirring a pot of greens . . . she must have fallen forward onto the stove and . . . got scalded pretty badly on her arm and leg" (Douglas, *Can't Quit* 221).

54. This scene marks Cornelia's recognition of the end of her sheltered life and the beginning of truthful and receptive existence: "Acutely aware of sound, unable to assign every vibration its proper place in an aural order, she is like a woman long blind and suddenly seeing again" (Douglas, *Can't Quit* 232).

the servant–served dichotomy by recognizing Julia as a sovereign equal and treating her as such, by "touching with loving hands, asking permission to visit Tweet in her living room, serving Tweet by bringing in the groceries" (Bomberger). Companionship and truthfulness are what finally bind the two women together. Cornelia reciprocates Julia's earlier gifts by bringing flowers, a dress, and guests—the visit of her own step-grandchildren (Douglas, *Can't Quit* 243). More importantly, though, Cornelia is ready to talk while Julia "as usual appeared not to be listening" (241). The tables have clearly turned—Cornelia's initial revulsion at and reluctance toward establishing a genuine relationship with her servant resonates in Tweet's lack of receptiveness (she just sits and hums to herself; she cannot talk and only gospel music and blues calm her down; 233 and 235). This does not discourage Cornelia in her efforts to share stories with Tweet and formulate her own openly expressed opinions. In her own kitchen Cornelia does not wish to share her intimate stories with Tweet because "to her it is almost unthinkable to speak to anyone, even herself, of her feelings, her childhood, her intimate life with her husband, even her children's lives. Such confidences are not simply trashy, dishonorable . . . for her they are scarcely formulable" (66).[55] Revealing her inner secrets and thoughts is supposed to have therapeutic value in Tweet's recovery rather than simply function as Cornelia's act of unburdening herself and thus requiring Julia to provide "emotional labor."[56]

Historian Rebecca Sharpless claims that a "relationship [that is] 'inherently asymmetrical' can never be made equal"[57]—that is, one feels

---

55. Although a discussion of narrative voice in the novel falls outside the purview of this chapter, it is not amiss to mention here that Tweet speaks for herself while Cornelia's thoughts and life story are presented through the perspective of the omnipresent narrator, who probes the White–Black relations with great intensity.

56. Sharpless remarked that "employers sometimes expected their cooks to provide 'emotional labor,' to provide listening ears and sympathetic words whenever their employers were having a rough time. . . . Adults also turned to their domestic workers as confidantes, regardless of whether the African American women wanted to hear them unburden themselves. Sociologist Mary Romero observes that class differences make domestic workers safe listeners, 'giving the middle-class mistress little fear of rebuttal, retaliation, or disparagement.' Emotional relationships developed, furthermore, because the domestic worker was a regular presence in the employer's life" (Sharpless 158, quoting Romero, "Sisterhood and Domestic Service" 329–30).

57. Ritterhouse, "Etiquette" 25, qtd. in Sharpless 129.

compelled to add, unless one changes its circumstances and location. Cornelia's visits in Tweet's living room demonstrate that their recognition of "a mutual need for each other's company and aid" (James 81) depends not only on Cornelia finally being able to listen to and hear Tweet but also on Cornelia's saving herself from emotional misery and estrangement by reaching out and saving her companion. It is in Julia's living room that Cornelia draws or provokes Tweet's response and helps the stroke patient regain her voice—the very same voice she was deaf to when they were together in her own kitchen. When Cornelia confesses that Julia was with her in New York,[58] Tweet responds to verbal stimuli for the first time after the accident. The language of her body is quite telling: a look of rage and hatred lights in Tweet's otherwise blank eyes and she even manages to pull her hand away and turn her head to the side (Douglas, *Can't Quit* 238). As Cornelia keeps on talking, Tweet, to the accompaniment of gospel music, is able to say her first words, and so their verbal exchange begins with chanting and swearing, a merging of the sacred and the vulgar.

Being on her own premises boosts Julia's confidence and strength to vent the accumulating frustration and anger (her enunciation consists of the word "SHIT"; 247). No longer bound by an asymmetrical employer–housekeeper contract, Julia verbalizes her intense antagonism and resentment toward Cornelia: "You ain't got *sense* enough to know I hated you. I hate you all my life, before I ever know you" (254).[59] Julia's deep antipathy toward Cornelia results from her employer's Whiteness (her employer's collective identity as the racial Other) rather than from her personality flaws, although the latter do not make the situation any easier. The longevity of their arrangement does not help either. Even though Julia was shielded in her employer's kitchen by Cornelia's deafness and unwillingness to participate in her maid's life, Julia employed a tactic developed by many an African American woman as a means of managing her relationships with White employers, referred to by Rebecca Sharpless as "cultivating dissemblance." This

---

58. It is while sojourning in New York that Julia's words finally reach Cornelia's consciousness: "Despite Cornelia's efforts to downplay Tweet's importance, Tweet's stories have penetrated to such a degree that Cornelia relives them when she is grieving for her husband, alone in New York City" (James 83).

59. It would be difficult to disagree with Donaldson's opinion that "*Can't Quit You, Baby* focuses on the layers of habit, antipathy, resentment, suspicion, attachment, and silence linking white employer and black employee" (40).

strategy was "a careful concealment of what she [a domestic] actually thought and felt" (Sharpless 145). Melanie Benson cogently argues that "texts by southern African Americans may approximate white methods and personas subversively in ways that betray a self-effacing, narcissistic desire to embody whichever identity will garner the greatest success and 'self-aggrandizement' in the twentieth-century South" (63). Extrapolating from Melanie Benson's argument, I would like to argue that on a personal level, the act of dissemblance subversively works as a "hidden transcript." The ideological resistance of a subordinate group of African American servants through the act of dissembling is a means of expressing their subversive social dissent. The informative charge of what was said and unsaid was neutral, but what a perceptive observer can intuit from gestures, body language, or tone of voice resembles what David Goldfield referred to as a theatre of Southern personal relations.[60] Therefore, Julia's honest disclosure of the hatred she has felt for Cornelia could only be voiced in Julia's own living room, and as such it constitutes a breach in the fine art of cultivating dissemblance.

The cathartic value of revealing the truth in a Black woman's own living room—Cornelia reciprocates with "Damn you, then. . . . I hate you, too" (Douglas, *Can't Quit* 254)—encourages the women to openly confront and acknowledge the racial divide that separates them. They quickly move from racial accommodation to open confrontation. Tweet's voiced accusations—"talking all that shit about me being with you in New York. You ain't never *seen* me, *heard* me in your entire life and you talking that shit. I wasn't in no New York" (254–55)—resonate with William Alexander Percy's words quoted at the beginning of this chapter. Julia expresses her rage about her employer's prior unwillingness to acknowledge her Black help as a sovereign individual. Here Tweet clearly refers to Cornelia's deafness—both literal and metaphorical (her emotional inability to see or hear others for who they are). The breach of the code of silence, which leads to confrontation of oneself and the Other within the context of racial relations, is a prerequisite to racial reconciliation. Both of the women concerned have to realize their mutual distrust and simultaneous mutual dependence. Both have to overcome the physical expressions of their disabilities (deafness and speech impairment caused by aneurysm) that echo their

---

60. David Goldfield, *Black, White, and Southern* 2, qtd. in Sharpless 145.

emotional state. Cornelia's grief and anger at her own life allow her to search for and make real contact—"Cornelia, lost in her grief and tormented by less friendly voices, opens up to Tweet's story and allows herself to hear Tweet's counsel" (James 83). If this charged relationship is to survive the test of time, honesty seems to be the best policy: "The women come to their senses with the realization that they will be together again tomorrow and continue to need each other, probably forever" (James 88).

They can build their future on the remnants of the past—in Julia's living room Mrs. O'Kelly finally realizes she can and should reciprocate the kindness that came with the stories: "Cornelia's delayed maturation depends on working to save Tweet's life—and repaying Tweet['s] debts, which are long overdue" (Kissel 205). Yet, James's claim that "as both start to recover after catastrophic events, it is the bond of having cooked and cleaned and talked together for years that proves to be the sturdiest support on which to build a future" (88) has a partially faulty premise. In Cornelia's kitchen, only one woman talked: the other barely pretended to care to listen. Theirs was clearly not a relationship of social equals. Now, Julia's inability to speak[61] and unwillingness to listen to Cornelia marks a complete reversal. Before Julia's outburst, communication was again one sided. Only after embracing honesty, after dealing with the race issue and finally being able to say what is on their minds, can they truly engage in a meaningful exchange. Empathizing in retrospect with Julia's stories, Cornelia reaches out to her Black domestic servant: "You can't help it, no. Not what you've done for me or what I've done for you. . . . You can't take back what you've told me. It's here. It's mine. Mine, mine, mine. Not just yours" (Douglas, *Can't Quit* 255).

With her hearing aid turned on, coupled with a willingness to reach out to Julia and see in her another sovereign human being,[62] Cornelia is finally able to respond to her housekeeper's continuous failed attempts to communicate in her own kitchen. Tweet "reaches out, touches Cornelia's hand" and then sings the words of a Willie Dixon song, "Oh, I love you, baby, but I sure do hate your ways. . . . I say, I

---

61. Tweet's brain aneurysm, which blocks her speech, is a fitting metaphor for her rage about her stories not being acknowledged before.
62. Cornelia recognizes that people are complicated individuals, that they "are not made in ovens and iceboxes" (Douglas, *Can't Quit* 41), but she initially refuses to see Tweet's sovereignty, complexity, and implicit humanity.

love you, darling, but I hate your treacherous low down ways" (255, 256).[63] Minrose Gwin opines that this spatial movement represents the transformation of the women's relationship "from one of power and dominance to one of painful honesty and mutual love" ("Sweeping the Kitchen" 59). By moving toward honesty, understanding, empathy, and affection, their relationship is no longer a simple extension of the servant–served paradigm.

■　■　■

Rights, obligations, and duties that define sociocultural positioning (Harré 193) take the form of asymmetrical race relations in the South. None of the texts analyzed in this chapter offer easy solutions to the problem of complicated race relations in the domestic contact zones of the South either before or after the civil rights era.[64] Literary critic David Davis posits that "the transgressive friendships based on asymmetrical intimacy within the southern social hierarchy are too fraught to lead to happy endings because release from hegemony does not mean freedom. It means recognizing one's complicity with the systemic exploitation of domestic workers, which undercuts the sincerity of the relationship and causes feelings of guilt in the segregated South" ("Invisible in the Kitchen" 153).

It is true that subversive power is not self-liberating if it is wielded at the expense of others. However, mutual dependence, honesty, and affection offer a chance to rewrite relationships that have come to life in contact zones "involving conditions of coercion, radical inequality and intractable conflict" (Pratt 8). Indeed, while the interstitial spaces of pantry, kitchen, and dining room were still subject to either de jure or de facto segregation, they offered ground for negotiations of race relations in the American South. The potential in the relationships between White homemakers and Black help is a reminder of what Minrose Gwin envisioned for Southern literature: "anything can happen, anything is possible: new recipes are being formulated . . . a kind of

---

63. That struggle between love and hate has been long present in Tweet's life. She frankly confesses to Cornelia and herself: "I steal that gold barrette to remind me of it [hatred], in case I forget. . . . Sometimes I forget" (Douglas, *Can't Quit* 254).

64. I share Donaldson's opinion that Douglas's protagonists do not "appear to stride confidently into the future with a new sense of authority and confidence in the stories they are about to tell" (49–50).

fermentation is taking place which is transformative, radical and pro-foundly woman-centered" ("Sweeping the Kitchen" 54–55). Therefore, affectionate coexistence and meaningful communication across the color line in such contact zones is more likely to take place when racial asymmetry is removed from the equation. The texts analyzed demon-strate that personalities and changes in circumstances (be it a different space or life situation) are equally important for redressing the balance in inherently uneven relationships.

CHAPTER 2

Consuming Public Spaces

Performance of the Color Lines in Jim Crow Dining Cars, Stores, and Cafes

> Dwelling, moving about, speaking, reading, shopping, and cooking are activities that seem to correspond to the characteristics of tactical reuses and surprises: clever tricks of the "weak" within the order established by the "strong," an art of putting one over on the adversary on his own turf, hunter's tricks, maneuverable, polymorph mobilities, jubilant, poetic, and warlike discoveries.
>
> —Michael de Certeau, *The Practice of Everyday Life*

> Jim Crow always means less for the Jim Crowed and an unequal value for his money.
>
> —Langston Hughes, "What Shall We Do about the South?"

> This assumption that of all the hues of God whiteness alone is inherently and obviously better than brownness or tan leads to curious acts.
>
> —W. E. B. Du Bois, "The Souls of White Folk"

In *Purity and Danger*, anthropologist Mary Douglas explains that "bodily orifices seem to represent points of entry or exit to social units" (4). If we accept her claim that bodily boundaries are symbolical markers of boundaries around and between cultures, then we can "treat ritual protection of bodily orifices as a symbol of social preoccupations about exits and entrances" (127). Therefore, quite logically, "the orifices of the body . . . symbolize its specially vulnerable points" (122). These points need ritual protection that affords literal protection from the unknown. The threat of undesired food may analogously serve to maintain cultural traditions—thus becoming a metaphorical means of promoting and protecting the cultural unity of a social group. Consequently, not only what we put into our mouths, but also with whom and where we consume food, defines our social affinities and serves as a signifier of our socioeconomic class and status. Stephen Mennell and others suggest that "sharing food is held to signify 'togetherness,' and equivalence among a group that defines and reaffirms insiders as socially similar" (115). Hence, as a manifestation of racial discrimination, racial etiquette in the South prohibited physical or visual contact between two races during food consumption. Such taboos concerned both eating the same food and sharing the spaces of consumption.

Because eating out became progressively more common in the South from the beginning of the twentieth century, Southerners felt the need to regulate public eating spaces. The division into a "White" living room and "Black" kitchen, so emblematic of domestic racial relations, was transposed onto the public spaces of "For White" and "For Colored" sections of restaurants, cafes, and dining cars in the Jim Crow South. This chapter traces how Whiteness and White supremacy were articulated, performed, and sometimes contested in the Jim Crow South, spanning the period from the 1880s to the 1960s.[1] The texts selected for this analysis—Flannery O'Connor's "The Artificial Nigger," Ernest Gaines's "The Sky Is Gray," and Fannie Flagg's *Fried Green Tomatoes at the Whistle Stop Cafe*—will demonstrate communal complacency with and individual transgression of public segregated spaces of consumption. The analysis of these literary representations is framed by the *Plessy v. Ferguson* Supreme Court case (1896), which established the legal foundation for racial segregation, and the Civil Rights Act of 1964, which outlawed discrimination in public places, such as schools, workplaces, restaurants, hotels, and stores.[2]

---

1. Natalie Ring explains that "the term 'Jim Crow' refers to the system of racial segregation and oppression that existed primarily in the South from 1877 to the mid-1960s" (416).
2. In her historiographic study of Southern racist and interracial eating practices, *To Live and Dine in Dixie: Foodways and Culture in the Twentieth-Century South,*

The post-Reconstruction era, known as "Jim Crow," was regarded as "the 'final settlement,' the 'return to sanity,' the 'permanent system'" by White Southerners (Woodward 7), but for many African Americans it was a time of "symbolic slavery."[3] In the Jim Crow era "a dominant group was able to create a culture of segregation that extended well beyond the boundaries of its legal apparatus" (Hoelscher 661). Through the use of social pressure, legislation, and imposed black poverty, White Southerners segregated White and Black residential areas (Hoelscher 671) and public spaces. "The Jim Crow era marked the ascendancy of white supremacy and not only consisted of the social separation of the races, but more broadly included lynching and mob violence, the manipulation of the justice system, inequality in education, economic subjugation, and the elimination of black suffrage" (Ring 417). Jim Crow laws, Woodward claims, "in bulk and detail as well as in effectiveness of enforcement . . . were comparable with the black codes of the old regime . . . That code lent the sanction of law to a racial ostracism that extended to churches and schools, to housing and jobs, to eating and drinking" (7). Jim Crow laws existed in the South from the end of the Civil War; however "during the late nineteenth and early twentieth centuries, the southern states enacted a rash of laws that mandated racial segregation in every aspect of public life" (Brown and Webb 192). Even though laws mandating public segregation would have had the same objective, the laws themselves "differed from state to state and from city to city. The general pattern was nonetheless the almost complete circumscription of black public behaviour. . . . African Americans

---

Angela Jill Cooley chooses similar dividing dates. In her introduction Cooley states that she wanted to explore "the evolution of southern food culture from 1900 to 1964. During this period, southern food practices became progressively more public in nature and increasingly more in line with national norms. As national standards permeated southern foodways, by way of consumer products, national advertising, scientific cookery, public eating places, and chain restaurants, southerners responded with a mixture of eager acceptance, wary application, and determined intransigence, depending upon the circumstances" (2).
3. Williams-Forson explains that "scholars of black memorabilia refer to the period from the late 1880s to the 1930s as a time of 'symbolic slavery' because of the persistence of the Old South imagery" (*Building Houses* 58). Du Bois even perceives the Reconstruction and post-Reconstruction eras, with flagship Jim Crow laws, as a period of re-enslavement of African Americans. Du Bois claims that "no open-minded student can read them [the codes] without being convinced they meant nothing more nor less than slavery in daily toil" ("Reconstruction and Its Benefits" 784).

had to sit at the rear of streetcar trolleys and in the balconies of movie theatres. Some communities continued to prohibit blacks completely from public facilities, including libraries, parks and playgrounds" (Brown and Webb 192). The pervasiveness of laws, both locally and state sanctioned, that instituted policies of segregation turned this separation into a way of life. Through this system of racial abuses and insults, the Jim Crow South became an American apartheid.

Racial segregation in the South took two forms: de jure and de facto. The former "referred to the separation of the races as mandated specifically by law and de facto segregation occurred by custom or tradition" (Ring 417). During Reconstruction formerly enslaved people rarely confronted White Southerners openly about the customs of racial separation, which was the painful legacy of slavery. Thus, without statutory compulsion, both races reenacted the pre-*Plessy* status quo. However, "between 1890 and 1915, Southern states enacted an array of statutes that led to a more rigid and universal framework for the social separation of the races. This explosion of de jure segregation reflected Southern whites' growing unease about a younger, more assertive generation of African Americans who demanded respect and recognition of their rights" (Ring 417).

Southern states passed laws validating segregation, which enabled racial zoning strictures and denied African Americans equal access to public facilities such as restaurants, theaters, schools, and swimming pools. Local legislation, in the form of segregation ordinances, ruled biracial eating spaces in restaurants illegal: "Atlanta drafted its 1910 law that required racial segregation as a licensing ordinance. The law required eating places to obtain a license that would allow service to either whites or blacks" (Cooley, *To Live* 101).

Similarly, Birmingham, Alabama, the most segregated city in America,[4] voted in favor of discriminatory legislation. Cooley states that "in 1914, for example, after little debate, Birmingham's city council authorized an ordinance that required separate dining rooms for black and white café patrons" ("Eating with Negroes" 71–72).[5] Such a drastic

---

4. This evaluation of Birmingham is based on Charles Connerly's analysis of Birmingham's race-based planning legacy in *"The Most Segregated City in America": City Planning and Civil Rights in Birmingham, 1920–1980.*

5. The Birmingham ordinance, as Cooley observes in another article, "prohibited proprietors from 'conduct[ing] a restaurant or lunch counter at which white and

increase of laws mandating public segregation of eating establishments at the beginning of the twentieth century was a result of

> the most significant trend in public dining . . . the rise of lower-end or quick-order eateries. These spaces could not be easily regulated by relying on individual proprietors or communal censure. It was primarily the fear that lower-class whites and blacks would mingle, thereby threatening racial and gender hierarchies and the power of the white business class to maintain social control, that provided the incentive for white city authorities to attempt to create racially segregated eating space in the cities. (Cooley, *To Live* 15)

De jure segregation of public eating facilities received significant public support from White Southerners who believed that transgression of segregated spaces of consumption would not only violate their personal space but also, more importantly, would facilitate incorporation of the unwanted element into their social and moral order.

De jure and de facto segregation were not mutually exclusive. "Although Southern states passed an elaborate network of laws, de facto practices of segregation endured" (Ring 417). White Southerners instituted segregation as standard procedure in social interactions; the laws mandating public segregation (de jure) simply reflected a time-honored social practice of discriminating against African Americans in the social sphere (de facto). Thus, de jure segregation was a codified form of de facto segregation that made life under Jim Crow arduous for African Americans: "Segregation grew . . . in a compost of the old racial order, the paradoxically personalized but state-backed racial power that grounded the slave regime. Surviving the near-fatal wounds of emancipation and Reconstruction, this racial culture became the foundation of rural southern life throughout the early twentieth century" (Hale 124). Even if segregation was not enforced by law in all spheres of public interaction—there was no statutory mandate for every instance of interracial contact (Klarman 50)—de facto segregation generated inferior service, indifference, and humiliation, if not outright intimidation:

> Patterns of de facto segregation varied depending on the location, the traditions of a community, or even the whim of a white

---

colored persons are served in the same room.' The Birmingham Board of Commissioners passed the law unanimously with very little explanation or public commentary" ("The Customer" 262–63).

person. In most places, whites and blacks were expected to abide by an unspoken racial etiquette. For example, blacks could not enter a white home through the front door, address a white person by their first name, or refuse to give way to a white person on a sidewalk . . . and in many stores, blacks could not be served until white customers were finished. (Ring 417)

African American customers had to endure inferior service in public spaces (shops, restaurants, hotels, theatres, libraries, etc.). They encountered hostility and indifference from restaurant employees and could only purchase food at the "colored" window of segregated restaurants. Brown and Stentiford remark that "restaurants would not allow black customers to eat in the dining room, but required them to use the take-out counter only" ("Introduction" xix). Whether institutionalized by law or by custom, these instances of disfranchisement were "concerned with symbolism . . . Some Jim Crow statutes may have served similar functions, by expressing white political supremacy, regardless of whether the laws were necessary to effect segregation" (Klarman 50).

Although White supremacy and the resulting Jim Crow segregation were not solely Southern phenomena,[6] they found their most intense expression below the Mason-Dixon line:

Whites in all regions continued to think of themselves as a superior race and that belief fueled the rationale for racial prejudice, although in many places outside the South, the discrimination was more rooted in custom than in law. As punitive and degrading as Jim Crow was in the North and the West, however, it was never as bad as it was in the South. Jim Crow laws and customs were never so oppressive or as sadistically and savagely enforced as they were in the former Confederate States. (Block 119)

As Cooley points out, Southern racist culture, which gave rise to disfranchisement and segregation, had an enormous impact on Southern communities, which "implemented a particularly pernicious form of racial exclusion because they respected little of the fluidity that could be found in interracial interactions outside of the region" ("Eating with Negroes" 71). Unable to officially wield control over formerly enslaved people with a whip, Southerners had to devise symbolic ways to express their superiority in various social contexts. The

---

6. "Segregation existed in some parts of the North, yet by the turn of the century it had become a distinctly Southern phenomenon" (Ring 417).

more visible and disconcerting presence of African Americans in public and commercial spaces of consumption—shops, cafes, restaurants, and trains—precipitated and engendered the introduction of discriminatory legislation: "Racialized spaces could counter the confusion of appearances created by the increased visibility of a well-dressed, well-spoken black middle class" (Hale 130).[7] By traversing these spaces of consumption, however, African Americans breached the physical and psychological barriers imposed on them to prevent their upward class mobility to a formal middle-class status.

Any attempt by African American patrons to consume a meal in White eating establishments under Jim Crow was invested with a disruptive potential. Sharing a meal with the social "Other" indicated an affiliation between the races involved. Thus, such a creation of community across the color line would be, from the perspective of White Southerners, a potentially dangerous and morally dubious activity. With the awareness that sharing a meal engenders a sense of belonging and forges bonds, White Southerners regulated acts of consumption by segregating their domestic space into White dining rooms and Black kitchens. The same racial etiquette regulated commercial spaces of consumption. Angela Cooley persuasively advances the thesis that "in twentieth-century Southern food culture, the greatest 'sin' that whites could commit was the act of 'eating with Negroes'—a phrase that encompassed a variety of activities that included a white and black person breaking bread together" ("Eating with Negroes" 71) or eating in the same place. Committing the deadly sin of commensality—the practice of eating at the same table—or mingling socially with the Black "Other" would result in exclusion or shunning of the White transgressor. My reading of social interactions with food as the source of cultural anxiety and disjuncture is congruent with Angela Cooley's remarks that "because it [biracial dining] implicated significant racial constructs, white Southerners considered race taboos at the dining table to be

---

7. The increased mobility of African Americans created problems with their visible presence in Southern public spaces. A road guide called *The Negro Motorist Green Book*, later known as *The Negro Travelers' Green Book*, was published from 1936 to 1964 by Victor H. Green in order to provide instructions for safe and "embarrassment-free" travel. It was intended to provide Black motorists and tourists with information about establishments they could safely patronize in the Jim Crow South. The objective of the series was to "give the Negro traveler information that will keep him from running into difficulties, embarrassments and to make his trips more enjoyable" (1949 edition).

extremely important, and individual whites risked personal shame as well as family and community ostracism if they contravened this well-known proscription" ("Eating with Negroes" 87).

"Separate but Equal" Dining Cars[8]

The very prospect of sharing a meal with the racial Other was appalling to the majority of White Southerners. The fear of dining with those of inferior status, because of health concerns and the implications of social descent implied in interracial social mingling, was one that reverberated throughout the nineteenth and early twentieth centuries. In her autobiography, Virginia Foster Durr writes that "You couldn't eat with them in the drugstore or restaurant, because they were offensive, smelled bad, and were diseased" (253). The space of the dining car on a segregated train is another curious site of interracial consumption. At the beginning of the twentieth century, "a new law authorized railroad operators to refuse admittance of any colored person to the dining, Pullman, parlor, chair, or compartment cars" (Wynes 418).[9] The experience of Homer Plessy, Ida Wells,[10] Frederick

---

8. The analysis in this section is a significantly expanded version of my article "Consuming Racial Expectations in Flannery O'Connor's 'The Artificial Nigger,'" originally published in *Southern Exposure: Essays Presented to Jan Nordby Gretlund*, edited by Thomas Ærvold Bjerre, Clara Juncker, and David E. Nye, Department for the Study of Culture, University of Southern Denmark, 2017, pp. 153–66.

9. In her novel *Sula* Toni Morrison captures the impact of verbal abuse African American passengers had to suffer. The train conductor's contempt for and humiliation of Helene creates a rift between Helene and Nel, her daughter (19–20). Nel's determination to never let anyone humiliate her is an indirect response to her mother's apologetic attitude and accomodationist reaction to being shamed by a White conductor (21–22).

10. As a frequent rail passenger, Ida Wells experienced many instances of humiliation from train conductors. Because she aimed to uncover the mechanisms that exploit African Americans and demonstrate her civil rights as a Black person and a woman by occupying a seat in first-class carriages, commonly referred to as "ladies' cars," Wells became a victim of the color line in railroads. Sarah Silkey convincingly argues that "when Wells chose a seat in the first-class carriage, she was publicly asserting her right to be considered a lady" (47). Even though the first-class ticket legally entitled her to a seat in "ladies' cars," on many an occasion she was either forcefully removed to the smoky second-class car or evicted from the train altogether (McMurry 24–30). Wells's fierce refusal of such treatment, which created a lot of commotion among White passengers, deliberately assumed "unladylike"

Douglass[11] and countless other African Americans[12] and people then known as "mulattos," who were forcibly removed to the second-class cars, illustrates that

> the phrase "separate but equal" would long burn in the ears of African Americans, who knew intimately that while whites would uphold the "separate" part with zeal, the "equal" part was a complete fiction that no one, black or white, even pretended to believe. Rail cars for white passengers were almost always better than the single-class car reserved for blacks, the "Jim Crow car," or "smoke car."[13] Whites who could afford the higher price of a first-class ticket would have even greater comfort, while no amount of money could buy a black passenger out of the Jim Crow car. (Brown and Stentiford, "Introduction" xix)

The "separate but equal" doctrine rings hollow in the face of the fact that the condition of the Jim Crow cars bore virtually no resemblance to the first-class "White" cars. Langston Hughes perspicaciously observes that "to a South-bound Negro citizen told at Washington to change into a segregated coach, the Four Freedoms have a hollow sound, like distant lies not meant to be the truth in the land of the Jim Crow car" ("What Shall We Do about the South?" 3).

Unsurprisingly, the Mason-Dixon line is the demarcation line below which African Americans traveling south by train had to relocate to Jim Crow cars. Angela Cooley mentions the case of Essie Mae

---

behavior and posture in order to draw attention to the rules and mechanisms that "established a protected gendered and class-defined space that extended the 'domestic sphere' into public transportation" (Silkey 47).

11. In his autobiography, *My Bondage and My Freedom*, Frederick Douglass offers a vivid description of the incidents on the train, which included beatings, bruising, and forced removal along with the seat he clung to (399–400).

12. Among countless other instances of forced removals, there is the case of "Hugh Gloster, professor of English at Morehouse College, [who] riding as an interstate passenger, was illegally ejected from a train in his state, beaten, arrested, and fined because, being in an overcrowded Jim Crow coach, he asked for a seat in an adjacent car which contained only two white passengers. Legally, the Jim Crow laws do not apply to interstate travelers but the FBI has not yet got around to enforcing that Supreme Court ruling" (Hughes, "What Shall We Do about the South?" 4).

13. Langston Hughes similarly calls attention to the fact that "for his seat in the half-coach of the crowded Jim Crow car, a colored man must pay the same fare as those who ride in the air-cooled coaches further back and are privileged to use the diner when they wish" ("What Shall We Do about the South?" 3).

Washington-Williams, who "recalls her trip from Pennsylvania to South Carolina in the 1930s. She and her companions traveled in an integrated 'fancy parlor car' until they arrived in Washington, DC. At Union Station, they transferred to a segregated car with 'tattered seats' and an unspecified odor" ("Eating with Negroes" 81).[14] Historian Grace Elizabeth Hale's detailed observations about the spaces of Southern transportation are particularly revealing in this case. In her research Hale demonstrates that the Jim Crow car was typically adjacent to "the baggage car and the engine"; it was often "'a smoker cut in two,' and black passengers had to face the discomfort of having white smokers pass through the 'colored' section" (132).[15] With first-hand knowledge, Langston Hughes locates "the Jim Crow coach behind the engine, [it is] usually half a baggage car, next to trunks and dogs" ("What Shall We Do about the South?" 3).

The culture of segregation was even more vigorously upheld in the dining cars. Denied access to the diners and the railway station restaurants, most African Americans consumed their packed lunches in Jim Crow cars straight from shoeboxes. In his autobiography, James Weldon Johnson recollects preparing shoeboxes with tasty victuals: "In those days no one would think of boarding a train without a lunch, not even for a trip of two or three hours; and no lunch was a real lunch that did not consist of fried chicken, slices of buttered bread, hard-boiled eggs, a little paper of salt and pepper, an orange or two, and a piece of cake" (64–65).[16] Alternatively, they had to endure the humiliation of

---

14. Langston Hughes points to the symbolical importance of the capital city of the United States as the threshold of segregated means of public transportation: "After all, Washington is the place where the conductor comes through every Southbound train and says, 'Colored people, change to the Jim Crow car ahead.' That car, in these days and times, has no business being 'ahead.' War's freedom train can hardly trail along with glory behind a Jim Crow coach. No matter how streamlined the other cars may be, that coach endangers all humanity's hopes for a peaceful tomorrow" ("What Shall We Do about the South?" 6).

15. When Ray Stannard Baker, a White Midwestern journalist, reported on the spaces of Southern transportation in 1907, he had clearly never set foot in a Jim Crow car: "In almost no other relationship do the races come together, physically, on anything like a common footing. In their homes and in ordinary employment, they meet as master and servant; but in the street cars they touch as free citizens, each paying for the right to ride" (qtd. in Hale 133).

16. Shoebox lunches did not discriminate against African Americans' regional affiliation or social status. Even Black Northerners, such as for instance, Dorothy

being served food through a "dirty and ill-attended hole in the wall" (Hale 132),[17] which was not even a pale imitation of the proper dining cars patronized by White passengers.

The voices of dissent against racial segregation on the trains, as emblematic of systemic discrimination felt by African Americans,[18] were heard ever more frequently. The Niagara Movement, the precursor to the National Association for the Advancement of Colored People (NAACP), was the first organization for African Americans to officially protest against racial inequality in America. W. E. B. Du Bois and other members drafted a Declaration of Principles (1905) that opposed Booker T. Washington's accommodationist politics: "We refuse to allow the impression to remain that the Negro-American assents to inferiority, is submissive under oppression and apologetic before insults." They also addressed the issue of racial inequality: "Any discrimination based simply on race or color is barbarous, we care not how hallowed it be by custom, expediency, or prejudice." They particularly protested "against the 'Jim Crow' car, since its effect is and must be to make us pay first-class fare for third-class accommodations, render us open to insults and discomfort and to crucify wantonly our manhood, womanhood and self-respect" ("Declaration of Principles").

In response to a growing number of demands like those expressed in the Niagara Movement Declaration of Principles regarding access to the dining cars and first-class accommodations, to which a purchased

Height, the president of the National Council of Negro Women, could not expect to be admitted into the railway station restaurants. Jerzy Kamionowski recounts that "when Dr. Height had come to the South from New York for the first time in the early 60s, being hungry upon arrival, she had to eat a 'poor little meal out of a shoe box' . . . , since the rules of segregation did not allow blacks to eat in the railway station restaurant" (75).

17. Referring to the indignity African Americans passengers had to suffer, Langston Hughes connects equality of a citizen with the equality afforded by a consumer: "For his hamburger in a sack served without courtesy the southern Negro must pay taxes but refrain from going to the polls" ("What Shall We Do about the South?" 3).

18. Langston Hughes offers capitalist measures to resolve the systemic discrimination of his people: "Because transportation is so symbolic of the whole racial problem in the South, the Number Two thing [after pro-democratic education] for us to do is evolve a way out of the Jim Crow car dilemma at once. . . . Why not abolish Jim Crow entirely and let the whites who wish to do so ride in coaches where few Negroes have the funds to be?" ("What Shall We do about the South?" 5).

ticket entitled African Americans to their use,[19] in 1937 the railroads made concessions. Elizabeth Abel explains that "a 1937 Supreme Court case . . . required railroads to provide accommodations for African American passengers, [however] the railroads negotiated a compromise between providing a separate dining car and serving black and white passengers together in a common dining car by curtaining off two tables near the kitchen and making the call for African American diners before or, more often, near the end of the regular meal hour" (181).[20]

The curtain dividing the White clientele from the unwanted element was the symbolic and material price for integrating a common dining car. As an ironic visible marker of "separate but equal," the curtain relegated "unworthy" customers to a less-than-perfect location or serving time. The curtain is emblematic of racist practices in the South that, according to Angela Cooley, "identified whites as appropriate consumers of food and African Americans as secondary citizens in consumption culture." Cooley goes on to explain that in public eating facilities, "white supremacy prevailed, and over the next several decades, racial segregation laws united southern whites around a common ideology committed to the subjugation of black consumers" ("The Customer" 263). Such a curtain was a defensive mechanism against what White Southerners feared most: African Americans' demand to be perceived as human. The demand for respect could be enacted in eating facilities, voting booths, transportation, and school systems all across the South.[21]

---

19. Interestingly enough, opposition to Jim Crow cars also hides intraracial politics and classism as well. Willard Gatewood refers to elite African Americans who "were convinced that separate car laws were a white scheme to force 'respectable' African Americans to consort with 'uncouth' African Americans" (309). Clearly a feeling of class ascendancy/superiority took priority over their racial affiliation.

20. This legally impelled concession of Southern railroad companies to integrate dining cars seems also to be the result of pitting "market incentives [against] the desire to encode white racial supremacy within the changing features of the region" (Hale 133).

21. In *Intruder in the Dust* Stevens voices his objection against "the postulate that Sambo is a human being living in a free country and hence must be free" (100). Stevens goes on to instruct his young nephew that "someday Lucas Beauchamp can shoot a white man in the back with the same impunity to lynch-rope or gasoline as a white man; in time he will vote anywhen and anywhere a white man can and send his children to the same school anywhere a white man's children go and travel anywhere the white man travels as the white man does it" (100).

As a marker of legally sanctioned inferiority, the curtain of a dining car plays an important part in the cultural performance of racial segregation in Flannery O'Connor's "The Artificial Nigger."[22] Published in the *Kenyon Review* in 1955, the short story narrates a day trip two backwoods Georgians make to Atlanta. Mr. Head, a sixty-year-old White man, takes Nelson, his ten-year-old grandson, for his first visit to the city: "It was to be a lesson that the boy would never forget. . . . Mr. Head meant him to see everything there is to see in a city so that he would be content to stay at home for the rest of his life" (O'Connor, "Artificial" 251). Because they come from a rural, all-White Georgia county, the trip will also serve the purpose of initiating the grandson into a segregated society. However, the all-too-easy compartmentalization of people based on skin color is complicated by the rising African American middle class. Following a similar line of analysis, Rachel Hale points out that "whiteness itself was being defined in late nineteenth-century first-class train cars. When middle-class blacks entered the semi-public spaces of railroads, they placed their better attire and manners in direct juxtaposition with whites' own class signifiers" (128–29). White Southerners were wondering "what to do in public about eating and the 'problem' of a rising middle class of black southerners who could suddenly participate in the region's consumer culture as paying *citizen*-shoppers and diners? Whites were increasingly threatened by blacks' changing economic position in society, and also by their demeanor" (Ferris, *The Edible South* 247). The presence of such individuals would serve to undermine the racial superiority of poorer Whites; thus, when Mr. Head notices a wealthy African American parading down the aisle, his "serene expression changed. His mouth almost closed and a light, fierce and cautious both, came into his eyes" (O'Connor, "Artificial" 254). In the 1930s a wish to curtail democratic equality between races was a common sentiment among White Americans, especially among those from below the Mason-Dixon line. In 1939 Du Bois reported a prevalent White attitude that "the Negro is a problem in the American social order because his

---

22. O'Connor refused to delete the titular racial epithet. Ralph Wood relates that O'Connor explained to John Crowe Ransom, the editor of *Kenyon Review*, in which it was published, that changing it would "have sanitized the title [which] would have robbed the story of its real power, the power to invert racist intention into anti-racist redemption" (111).

aspiration and behavior are oriented toward a goal that dominant majority does not want realized" ("The Position of the Negro" 551). The African American passenger who provokes Mr. Head's quiet rage vividly exemplifies how social equality and acceptance do not necessarily follow legal freedom.

However, Mr. Head uses this encounter as a lesson to prove his grandson's racial ignorance. The first lesson for Nelson is to identify an African American when he encounters one. The grandson fails to pass the test, as he does not recognize the identity of the aforementioned wealthy passenger accompanied by two women:

> A huge coffee-colored man was coming slowly forward. He had on a light suit and a yellow satin tie with a ruby pin in it. One of his hands rested on his stomach which rode majestically under his buttoned coat, and in the other he held the head of a black walking stick that he picked up and set down with a deliberate outward motion each time he took a step. He was proceeding very slowly, his large brown eyes gazing over the heads of the passengers. (O'Connor, "Artificial" 254–55)

Misled by the passenger's attire and deportment, which do not conform to his prior racial presuppositions, Nelson naïvely misinterprets the man's identity. His misinterpretation reveals his innocent "color-blindness." He confronts his grandfather: "'You said they were black,' he said in an angry voice. 'You never said they were tan'" (255). Even though it is his grandfather who has exposed his racial naïveté, Nelson feels "that the Negro had deliberately walked down the aisle in order to make a fool of him and he hated him with a fierce raw fresh hate; and also, he understood now why his grandfather disliked them" (255–56). Rather than blame his grandfather for exposing his ignorance, or better still frankly admitting his own inexperience, Nelson projects his hatred onto the African American man, who has so ostentatiously expressed his wealth.[23] However, it will be in the dining car that the conflict

---

23. Nelson's hatred of the coffee-colored man only adds another layer to the already class-motivated antagonism between poor Whites and Blacks. William Julius Wilson explains why severing the potential allegiance between poor Whites and Blacks was convenient for the White elites: "The planter class of the South effectively prevented any economic or political cooperation or class allegiance between poor blacks and poor whites. As long as poor whites directed their hatred and

between wealth and racial otherness receives the most visible qualities of cultural performance.

The theoretical touchstone in my analysis of "consuming racial expectations" in O'Connor's short story will be anthropologist Milton Singer's discussion of cultural performance. His definition of cultural performance as one that possesses a "limited time span, a beginning and an end, an organized program of activity, a set of performers, an audience, and a place and occasion" (xii, qtd. in Madison 153–54) can be very useful here as a methodological guidepost. Reflecting on Singer's understanding of cultural performances, Soyini Madison sees them as "self-conscious and symbolic acts [that] are presented and communicated within a circumscribed space. Meaning and affect are generated by embodied action that produces a heightened moment of communication" (154).

In O'Connor's story, the symbolic acts of racial segregation take place in the dining car. On his tour to show his grandson the luxuries of the train, Mr. Head takes Nelson to the diner, which is "the most elegant car in the train. It was painted a rich egg-yellow and had a wine-colored carpet on the floor. There were wide windows over the tables and great spaces of the rolling view were caught in miniature in the sides of the coffee pots and in the glasses" (O'Connor, "Artificial" 256). There, during a limited span marked by the meal's duration, the grandfather and Nelson can witness the cultural performance of "racial otherness" in the making. The Black waiters and the White clientele perform their scripted roles reminiscent of the domestic relations between Black servants and White families or employers: "Three very black Negroes in white suits and aprons were running up and down the aisle, swinging trays and bowing and bending over the travelers eating breakfast" (256). The image of racial order in the diner replaces Nelson's earlier racial confusion and misidentification of the coffee-colored man. Grace Hale rightly observes that "visiting the dining car . . . [Nelson] draws assurance from the busy waiters, their 'very black' skins accentuated by their white suits, their work serving whites overriding

---

frustration against the black competitor, the planters were relieved of class hostility directed against them" (*The Declining Significance of Race* 54). The presence in public places of a middle-class Black consumer like the fictional coffee-colored man accentuates interracial alliances and antagonisms.

their somewhat saucy manner" (130–31). Such reassuring markers of White supremacy reappear frequently in Southern fiction. For instance, in *Fried Green Tomatoes at the Whistle Stop Cafe*, Ninny Threadgoode observes the Silver Crescent passing the fictional town of Whistle Stop. On the train supper is being served "with the colored waiters dressed up in their starched white jackets and black leather bow ties, with the finest flatware and silver coffeepots" (Flagg 102).

The negotiation of the racial order within a dining car, as a cultural performance, is effected through "an organized program of activity" (Madison 154). The culture of segregation relies "on performance, ritualized choreographies of race and place, and gender and class, in which participants knew their roles and acted them out for each other and for visitors" (Hoelscher 657). Indeed, the choreography of socially sanctioned racial relationships defines the place and roles of both Black waiters and White customers within the established racial order. A Black waiter approaching Mr. Head and Nelson naturally assumes servility, offering them "Space for two"; however, when the potential customers reply, "We eaten before we left," he assumes an air of superiority and responds, "Stan' aside then please" (O'Connor, "Artificial" 256). In expressing himself ungrammatically, a clear sign of his lower social status, Mr. Head betrays his own inability to participate fully in the privileges of the White race. Having realized that, the waiter expresses disdain, making "an airy wave of the arm as if he were brushing aside flies." In a tug-of-war of racial pretenses, Mr. Head and Nelson can only respond by not moving "a fraction of an inch" (256).

To prove his White privilege, Mr. Head wants to tour the kitchen in the dining car with Nelson, and thus invade another space where Black men can only enter in their capacity as servants or employees. Being denied access to it—"Passengers are NOT allowed in the kitchen!"—the chagrined grandfather feels compelled to regain his racially privileged position and reestablish his dominance. Unable to secure "natural" deference from the waiter, Mr. Head deflates the implications of the ban: "And there's good reason for that . . . because the cockroaches would run the passengers out!" (O'Connor, "Artificial" 256–57). Mr. Head may want to ridicule African Americans' supposed propensity for filth and disorder, but the joke is on him, and even more on the audience of the spectacle. The grin on Mr. Head's face and the laughter of the White clients in the diner underscore their hypocrisy and emphasize a lack of awareness regarding their ironic position. African American cooks and waiters are unable to maintain a hygienic environment in which to prepare food, and yet that very same food—supposedly "pure" fare, superior to Black culinary preferences—will be served to and consumed by White patrons in the diner.[24]

Apart from Mr. Head and his grandson, and the waiters, the coffee-colored man is another actor in this cultural performance of White supremacy. His presence in the diner car, made possible by his middle-class status, clearly disturbs the conventions of racial segregation, which are predicated on the supposed inferiority of the racial "Other." According to Hale, "racialized spaces could counter the confusion of appearances created by the increased visibility of a well-dressed, well-spoken black middle class" (130). Those African Americans who can afford to order from the diner menu,[25] whose "visible dress and deportment . . . belied any notion of southern blacks' racial inferiority" (Hale 128), have to be reminded of "their place" within the racial order. The coffee-colored man may be able to order a meal, which is a humiliating experience for those Whites who cannot; however, his potentially disruptive presence is defused by the curtain that serves to hide this breach while simultaneously confining him to his socially sanctioned place.

The curtain enforces the process of subordination through the imposition of "separate but equal" eating space: "The near corner of the diner, containing two tables, was set off from the rest by a saffron-colored curtain" (O'Connor, "Artificial" 256). It may be of different colors—saffron-colored or "green-as-poison" as in Toni Morrison's

---

24. Ironically, African Americans are deemed "too diseased and dirty to share a meal but . . . suitable for serving it" (Cooley, "Eating with Negroes" 70).

25. In Toni Morrison's *Jazz*, none of the passengers in the colored section of the fictitious train—the Southern Sky—eat in the dining car. Their economic situation prevents them from partaking of a meal in the diner: "If only they would tuck those little boxes and baskets underneath the seat; close those paper bags, for once, put the bacon-stuffed biscuits back into the cloth they were wrapped in, and troop single file through the five cars ahead on into the dining car, where the table linen was at least as white as the sheets they dried on juniper bushes; where the napkins were folded with a crease as stiff as the ones they ironed for Sunday dinner; where the gravy was as smooth as their own, and the biscuits did not take second place to the bacon-stuffed ones they wrapped in cloth. Once in a while it happened" (31).

Jazz[26]—but the curtain always points to the social inferiority of those it veils. Elizabeth Abel similarly calls attention to the fact that "the Jim Crow curtain reinstantiates white supremacy over wealthier and better dressed African American passengers by screening out of view all kinds of unsettling differences, those of social superiority no less than those of social inferiority" (331). Culinary preferences[27] and inferior spaces of consumption[28] "contributed to the process of marking African Americans—regardless of any personal characteristic—as inferior" (Cooley, "Eating with Negroes" 71).[29] However, separation of the

---

26. In Toni Morrison's *Jazz*, Violet and Joe take a train from Vesper County, Virginia, in 1906. An attendant comes through the colored section of the Southern Sky, which Violet and Joe have "naturally" boarded. He is "pleasant but unsmiling now that he didn't have to smile in this car full of colored people" (30). Advertising "breakfast in the dining car," the attendant wants "the whole coach to file into the dining car, now that they could" (31). The train crosses the Mason-Dixon line: "now that they were out of Delaware and a long way from Maryland there would be no green-as-poison curtain separating the colored people eating from the rest of the diners" (31). Now, the cooks and the waiters do not have to make up for the "separate but equal" situation, they do "not feel obliged to pile extra helpings on the plates headed for the curtain; three lemon slices in the iced tea, two pieces of coconut cake arranged to look like one—to take the sting out of the curtain; homey it up with a little extra on the plate. Now, skirting the City, there were no green curtains; the whole car could be full of colored people and everybody on a first-come first-serve basis. . . . Presided over and waited upon by a black man who did not have to lace his dignity with a smile" (31).

27. Angela Cooley observes that "many foods, such as chitterlings, pig's feet, and other inexpensive fare had long been associated with the African American community" (*To Live* 40). Moreover, as Cooley reports, "the middle-class blacks and lower-class whites . . . associated certain inexpensive meats, such as fatback and chicken giblets, as 'black people's food.' This represented a positive association for middle-class blacks, and consuming such foods connected them with their ethnic community. Lower-class whites looked upon such foods negatively because of the association with African Americans, and avoiding these foods reinforced their sense of white supremacy. . . . In this manner, Southerners associated food and eating behavior with their racial identity" ("Eating with Negroes" 73).

28. "African Americans dined at blocked-off, racially marked, and inferior tables" (Hale 284).

29. In her discussion of the function of the curtain to exclude and subordinate middle-class African Americans, Cooley quotes from Lillian Smith's memoir in which the Southerner recalled "the story of a young white girl who saw the president of a historically black university in Atlanta enter the dining car on a train. He sat behind a curtain to separate him from the dining space designated for whites. The girl had a difficult time believing that such an esteemed scholar, whom she had

inferior space of consumption by means of a curtain may be viewed as a ploy to veil the fact that there might not be many differences in dietary preferences between White and Black patrons, because certainly in many cases wealth was not the distinguishing feature. The taboo about commensality that White Southerners reinforced can be seen as a defensive mechanism against what sociologist Dollard calls "the shock of sameness" (92–93) rather than "alimentary racism" (Probyn 2)—a contempt or disdain for the food choices of other racial or ethnic groups. Hence, "the sight not of others eating but of collective eating 'on a basis of equality,' a reaction not to a difference in manners but to sameness in status" (Abel 181) is what may be disconcerting to White clients. The visceral disgust at primitive Blackness,[30] which affirms White racial superiority, assumes the form of disgust at the food choices of the racial Other. Thus, "to those invested in maintaining the racial caste system of that time, the illusion that blacks and whites ate differently reinforced their [White] sense of racial superiority" (Miller, *Soul Food* 29). Avoidance of physical contamination (an abject Black body, food, and appetites) masks a feeling of disgust at the possible moral contamination resulting from physical invasion of the body.[31]

The curtain always functions as "a visual shield" (Abel 181), be it a way of preventing either nausea[32] or disgust or indigestion induced by

---

heard speak at a church meeting, would be curtained away from the other diners. Her father, on the other hand, could not believe that an African American man would hold such a distinguished position as the president of a university . . . The mere fact of marking eating space as 'colored' served to mark the gentleman dining in this space as inferior in the father's mind" ("Eating with Negroes" 74).

30. According to William Miller, feelings such as disgust, repulsion, and revolt "convey a strong sense of aversion to something perceived as dangerous because of its powers to contaminate, infect, or pollute by proximity, contact, or ingestion" (*The Anatomy of Disgust* 2).

31. More about social anxieties about pollution and contamination of the body can also be found in Mary Douglas's works and Julia Kristeva's *Powers of Horror*, which adds the abject body to the equation of its dirtiness and a state of being out of its proper place.

32. "Nausea is produced by something entering the eye: a breach of psychosocial boundaries, a puncturing of a social membrane through one orifice that produces a reflex to expel through another" (Abel 181).

transgressive eating,[33] of imposing quarantine on the undesired element to prevent it from contaminating the environment, or as a reaction to "the shock of sameness." In O'Connor's short story, Mr. Head explains, with his air of superiority, "They rope them off" ("Artificial" 256). The "tremendous Negro" is curtained off for the benefit of both the rich White clientele—to maintain the illusion that they possess superior taste—and of the lower-class Whites—as a visual marker of their putative racial superiority. "Though Mr. Head and his grandson cannot even afford to eat on the train," explains Grace Hale, "the thin yellow fabric upholds their superiority, their belonging, their whiteness against the black man's roped-off wealth. The boy arrives in the city knowing 'niggers' as people who serve whites or inhabit spaces whose separateness and difference are clearly, visibly marked" (131). It never dawns on Nelson—nor is it verbalized by his grandfather—that the supposedly inferior Black man can afford to eat in the dining car, while they have to appease the pangs of hunger with a modest, home-made lunch. Mr. Head, an elderly White man of reduced financial means, cannot participate in the performance of Whiteness in the diner. Thus, beforehand he packs "a paper sack with some biscuits and a can of sardines in it for their lunch" (O'Connor, "Artificial" 252). One may charitably see the lunch bag as "suggesting the spiritual sustenance of the Gospel loaves and fishes" (Smith-Marzec 56); however, both preparing for lunch before the actual trip and lying to the waiter about it clearly suggest Mr. Head's fragile self-image regarding his own White superiority.

Cultural performances, according to Madison, "are consciously heightened, reflexive, framed, and contained" (154). A feature characterizing cultural performances is that they *show ourselves to ourselves in ways that help us recognize our behavior, for better or worse, as well as our unconscious needs and desires. When we perform and witness cultural performances, we often come to realize truths about ourselves and our world that we cannot realize in our day-to-day existence*"

---

33. In her essay "The Walls of Segregation Are Crumbling," published in the *New York Times Magazine* not long after the Supreme Court banned the use of curtains in interstate travel *(Henderson v. United States* 1950), Lillian Smith remarks: "Because of the old taboo about eating, Southerners know that the abolition of restrictions in dining cars is a profound cultural change. Today, it is a pleasant thing to report that Southerners are now watching each other eat as they travel through Dixie and no one has felt violent about it, no one has fainted, no one has had acute indigestion" (qtd. in Abel 181).

(Madison 154). In Mr. Head's case the self-reflection as a result of the cultural performance of White supremacy on the train is delayed. He is so entrenched in his racial superiority that he is unable to see his own hypocrisy, or, for that matter, that of the White race generally. However, the experience in the diner car illustrates that his very racism can paradoxically become "a vehicle for his salvation" (Smith-Marzec 52). In his *From Ritual to Theatre: The Human Seriousness of Play*, Victor Turner observes that "when we act in everyday life we do not merely re-act to indicative stimuli, we act in frames we have wrested from the genres of cultural performance" (122). Even though Mr. Head's reactions to the coffee-colored man and to the diner car waiters are inscribed in the scripts of racial superiority, and his actions on the train reveal a lack of any self-examination and self-reflexivity, they initiate what O'Connor calls "the working of grace for the characters" (*Mystery and Manners* 116).

The confrontation with the racial Other on the train, and in the dining car in particular, heightens Mr. Head's revelation about his questionable racial superiority at the sight of an ornament decorating one of the lawns in a White Atlanta neighborhood. It is a shabby, inappropriate plaster statue of an "artificial nigger" eating a watermelon, who is "meant to look happy because his mouth was stretched up at the corners but the chipped eye and the angle he was cocked at gave him a wild look of misery instead" (O'Connor, "Artificial" 268). Both the coffee-colored man and the statue have caricature-like qualities inherited from minstrel shows[34] and each is caught in the act of consumption. Both overlapping images of African Americans prompt Mr. Head to see himself and his world with new eyes: "He stood appalled, judging himself with the thoroughness of God, while the action of mercy covered his pride like a flame and consumed it. He had never thought himself a great sinner before but he saw now that his true depravity had been hidden from him lest it cause him despair" (269–70). It is the awed contemplation of the "artificial nigger" that reconciles Mr. Head and Nelson (Oates, "Mercy" 46) and "dissolved their differences like an action of mercy" (O'Connor, "Artificial" 269). However, it is the diner,

---

34. The narrator describes the coffee-colored client as "the tremendous Negro" who "had a heavy sad face and his neck bulged over his white collar on either side," while the waiter's eyes allude to Jim Crow minstrel shows: "The waiter wore large brown spectacles that increased the size of his eye whites" (O'Connor, "Artificial" 256).

which afforded the initial, troubled cultural performance of racial superiority, that serves as a catalyst. Since "cultural performances are not
only a reflection of what we are, they also shape and direct who we are
and what we can become" (Madison 154–55), the diner scene precipi-
tates Mr. Head's epiphany and his new understanding of mercy, even if
he is still unable to articulate this understanding with words.

The Dignity of Shopping

Apart from curtains in the dining cars acting as visible demarcation
lines of racial separation, other, invisible, walls divide the spaces of consumption. Ernest Gaines commented in an interview that "when you
say slavery ended one hundred thirty years ago, that wall is still there,
that law is still there. There are many of those walls that are still there,
invisible walls to most people, but they're still there" (Sartisky 258). The
color line, be it in the form of a curtain in the diner, a restaurant window sign saying "For Whites," or a set of unwritten but internalized
rules governing economic and social behavior in grocery and general
stores, "provided a way to order the more impersonal social relations
and potentially more subversive consuming practices of the new southern town life. White southerners nurtured their new racist culture to
contain the centrifugal forces of a much less isolated, less rural world"
(Hale 125). Encountering segregated spaces of consumption plays a dra-
matic role in the racialized socialization of James, the eight-year-old
Black narrator in Ernest Gaines's short story "The Sky Is Gray."[35] James
and his mother, Octavia, make a day trip from a poverty-stricken farm-
ing community in Louisiana to the more urban setting of Bayonne to
see a dentist.[36] The experience of the small-town spaces of consumption
in the 1940s functions as an eye-opener for the young boy on his journey to self-discovery.[37]

---

35. "The Sky Is Gray" is Gaines's first internationally published short story, which
originally appeared in *The Negro Digest* (August 1963) and was later included in
Bloodline, a collection of five short stories (1968).
36. Like William Faulkner's Yoknapatawpha or Gloria Naylor's Willow Springs,
Bayonne is an imagined territory invented out of whole cloth and settled by Ernest
Gaines's characters.
37. According to Valerie Babb, "The Sky Is Gray" functions as a story "in the bil-
dungsroman tradition" (24).

Through the process of socialization, "we internalize the norms and values of society, and learn [how] to perform the social roles in which we find ourselves" (Beardsworth and Keil 54). To survive in a segregated environment, African American children have to accommodate their personal and racial aspirations; they have to mold their personalities into conformity with the established systems of beliefs of Southern society. Hence, "their outlook and aspirations, their opportunities for development and self-expression, their attitudes and sentiments, are conditioned in one way or another by the traditionally sanctioned patterns of race relations in the area" (Johnson, *Growing Up* 274). Learning about "the taboos, prohibitions, and coercive symbols. . . . [that] constitute a vital element in the social environment of southern rural Negro youth" is part of the process of their socialization (280). In most so-called traditional families, the mother is responsible for edifying and nurturing her children, preparing them for a life in particular social circumstances,[38] and, in the Black household, according to Grier and Cobbs,

> the care and rearing of children falls even more heavily on the wife; she is the culture bearer. She interprets the society to the children and takes as her task the shaping of their character to meet the world as she knows it. This is every mother's task. But the black mother has a more ominous message for her child and feels more urgently the need to get the message across. The child must know that the white world is dangerous and that if he does not understand its rules it may kill him. (61)

James's socialization begins in his poverty-stricken home, where he is malnourished[39] and has to kill redbirds for dinner as a lesson both in

---

38. Having been drafted into the army, James's father cannot lift the responsibility of raising children from his wife's shoulders. Thus, Octavia has to adjust her parenting to include tough lessons in survival in the oppressive racist society.

39. James's family is in a dire economic situation, so the culinary repertoire does not include meat daily. Auntie Rose Mary says with resignation, "White beans and no salt meat ain't white beans" (Gaines 495). When Ty, James's brother, moans, "I'm getting tired of this old syrup. Syrup, syrup, syrup. I'm go'n take with the sugar diabetes. I want me some bacon sometime," Auntie reprimands him: "Go out in the field and work and you can have your bacon" (Gaines 495).

survival and manhood.[40] The culmination of the process takes place in the "little bitty town" of Bayonne (Gaines 499), in an unfamiliar world[41] where the Confederate flag still waves above the courthouse (Gaines 499). Specifically, the spaces of the hardware shop, cafe, and grocery store become the sites of agency where Octavia exhibits resilience[42] and shrewd survival tactics and where she negotiates her pride and dignity, virtues she wants to instill in her son.

The oppressed and disempowered employ what Robin Kelley calls "infrapolitics."[43] Kelley uses "the concept of infrapolitics to describe the daily confrontations, evasive actions, and stifled thoughts that . . . have a cumulative effect on power relations. While the meaning and effectiveness of various acts differ according to the particular circumstances, they do make a difference, whether intended or not" (8). In the

---

40. Two tiny redbirds cannot provide much sustenance for the whole family; however, they are a source of pride and self-confidence for James: "They was so little. I 'member how I picked the feathers off them and cleaned them and helt [sic] them over the fire. Then we all ate them. Ain't had but a little bitty piece each, but we all had a little bitty piece, and everybody just looked at me 'cause they was so proud" (Gaines 497). Even though James is mature beyond his age, Octavia has to teach him how to be a man who is able to provide for his family. Octavia has to adjust her mothering to the circumstances (poverty and racism). Consequently, William Burke's assessment of Octavia as being "cruel in eroding her son's gentleness and innocence, however necessary their tempering may be" (550), seems quite inadequate, if not myopic.

41. Karen Kossie-Chernyshev observes that even though "segregation, economic exploitation, and oppression were more pronounced in rural areas than in cities. . . . boundaries were less rigid in other rural spaces. Country stores, rural roads, and cotton gins were usually not segregated. Certain recreational activities were also not segregated. . . . Different from cities, most rural towns had few buses, hotels, or restaurants, all of which provided distinct stages for blacks and whites to play their prescribed roles" (646).

42. In her analysis of African American women migrants, Lisa Krissoff Boehm pays special attention to resilience, which is "the capability of a human being to continue on in the face of great adversity, . . . [it] is an often undervalued attribute; resilience is a form of courage, but it requires a continuity of spirit that is not necessarily a component of all types of bravery. . . . Resilience entails not only a momentary conviction of spirit, but a continued devotion to persisting in the face of adversity, a commitment to 'making a way out of no way'" (19).

43. Robin Kelley relates his concept of "infrapolitics" to James Scott's idea of "hidden transcripts," both referring to the struggles of subordinate groups, African Americans and peasants respectively, as invisible forms of political action. For more information, see James Scott, *Weapons of the Weak: Everyday Forms of Peasant Resistance*.

deeply segregated South, these "daily confrontations, evasive actions, and stifled thoughts" (Kelley 8) define the nature of African Americans' contacts with White Southerners.[44] Using subtle forms of infrapolitics, Octavia teaches her son how to work the racist system not to their advantage—because that is impossible due to their skin color—but rather to "their minimum disadvantage." The informal infrapolitics of the oppressed that Octavia uses are heuristic teaching methods rather than measures of disrupting power relations.[45] Robin Kelley claims that one "finds the hidden transcript emerging 'onstage' in spaces controlled by the powerful, though almost always in disguised forms" (8).

One such disguised form is the concealment of one's true self. Octavia instructs James not to look through the window at White people eating in a restaurant. James says, "Mama tells me keep my eyes in front where they belong" and she jolts her son when he accidentally runs into a White lady on the street (Gaines 499).[46] Octavia knows that appearance of "uppitiness" ascribed to such acts and gestures could

---

44. Locating infrapolitics on the Southern foodscape, Frederick Douglass Opie observes that "despite the outward appearance of deference, African Americans regularly resisted Jim Crow. Interviews with southerners indicate that African American customers and restaurant employees did not simply capitulate to conditions in the South but employed what one scholar calls 'infrapolitics.' In the case of segregated restaurants, infrapolitics included such everyday forms of resistance as theft, passing, and employing what one historian calls the 'cult of Sambohood': using grins, shuffles, and 'yas-sums' to get what one needed without violence" (*Hog and Hominy*).

45. While James Scott's arguments about everyday forms of peasant resistance are in a geographical sense far removed the plight of African Americans below the Mason-Dixon line discussed here, his idea of "hidden transcripts" is methodologically suggestive for work on disempowered Black Southerners. Thus, his observations about the forms and goals of peasants' everyday resistance are also relevant in the Southern context: "Most subordinate classes are, after all, far less interested in changing the larger structures of the state and the law than in what Hobsbawm has appropriately called 'working the system . . . to their minimum disadvantage.' Formal, organized political activity, even if clandestine and revolutionary, is typically the preserve of the middle class and the intelligentsia; to look for peasant politics in this realm is to look largely in vain" (*Weapons of the Weak* xv).

46. Frederick Douglass Opie explains that "before 1954, African American parents raised their children to cope with Jim Crow restrictions. Eugene Watts, from Waynesboro, Virginia, remembers: 'You didn't just walk into a white establishment,' you stood in front until somebody came out and typically said, 'Boy, are you lost?' It was then appropriate to stand, looking down at the ground, and politely reply, 'No sir, I would like to get something to eat.' African American elders made sure

prove ruinous. Thus Octavia belongs to a legion of Blacks who "learned to appear before whites as though they were zombies, cultivating the habit of casting the gaze downward so as not to appear uppity. To look directly was an assertion of subjectivity, equality. Safety resided in the pretense of invisibility" (hooks, *Black Looks* 254–55).[47] Perceived as provocative if not subversive, these behaviors might lead to lynching or another means of murder.[48] In her historical research Ritterhouse clearly states that the South was "a world where any black person who got 'uppity,' much less openly challenged the power structure, could get killed" (57). While avoiding eye contact may be construed as a sign of deference, in reality Octavia's role-playing and the hiding of her intentions is reminiscent of what Erving Goffman theorized about in his *Presentation of Self in Everyday Life*. Although Octavia does not embody the "ignorant, shiftless, happy-go-lucky manner" Erving Goffman ascribed to African American performance, her behavior certainly "underplay[s] any expressions of . . . spiritual strength, or self-respect" (25). The humble, tractable, and submissive manner that Octavia and other African American Southerners "felt obliged to affect during interaction with whites illustrates how a performance can play up ideal values which accord to the performer a lower position than he covertly accepts for himself" (Goffman 25).

that before black youths went downtown, they clearly understood the particularities, dictates, and customs of buying food at a white-owned restaurant" (*Hog and Hominy*).

47. bell hooks explains the importance of making African Americans cast their gaze downward as "an effective strategy of white supremacist terror and dehumanization during slavery centered around white control of the black gaze. Black slaves, and later manumitted servants, could be brutally punished for looking, for appearing to observe the whites they were serving, as only a subject can observe, or see" (*Black Looks* 254).

48. In *Negroes in American Society* Maurice Davie reproduces the table of offenses African Americans were charged with between the period 1882 to 1946 from the *Negro Year Book*, 1947, published by the Tuskegee Institute. The categories of "insult to white persons" and "all other causes" were among offenses punishable by lynching. Davie explains that "the other causes" category encompassed "minor offenses and trivial reasons, of which the following are examples: peeping in a window, not calling a white man 'Mr.,' writing to a white woman, sassing a white woman, trying to act like a white man, not knowing his place, attempting to vote, . . . being too prosperous, disputing over the price of blackberries, and enticing servant away" (346).

Hence, from the White perspective Octavia's actions might look like compliance and acceptance of her and her son's socially prescribed subservient position; in reality, however, she might be reenacting what could be perceived as a hidden transcript—registering a silent protest against segregation. To take shelter from the harsh weather while maintaining her inner dignity, Octavia enters the hardware store, where she pretends to be buying an axe handle in order to buy time for James to warm up next to a heater (Callahan 97). She seems to be well aware of the treatment African Americans receive in stores patronized by Whites: shopping in a White establishment means "submitting to the indignity of ill treatment by white sales people" (Sharpless 105). Black customers are subjected to "daily humiliations of being served last in stores" (Brown and Stentiford, "Introduction" xix), and the "seats around the stove . . . seemed at certain times reserved for white men" (Hale 173). Although "legal codes do not deny Negroes access to such establishments except where eating is involved, nor guarantee him the privileges usually accorded the white public," Johnson observes, in "the interracial situation in trade relations there is constant uncertainty" (qtd. in Hale 185).

This "constant uncertainty" reminds African Americans of their "double-consciousness," which Du Bois identified as

> a peculiar sensation, . . . this sense of always looking at one's self through the eyes of others, of measuring one's soul by the tape of a world that looks on in amused contempt and pity. One ever feels his two-ness,—an American, a Negro; two souls, two thoughts, two unreconciled strivings; two warring ideals in one dark body, whose dogged strength alone keeps it from being torn asunder. (*The Souls of Black Folk* 5)

Propelled by "double-consciousness," Octavia demonstrates to her son how to covertly challenge power relations, in order to avert the potentially humiliating consequences of asking for warmth in a White man's shop. James learns that the White owner seems to be colorblind when it comes to the purchasing power of a dollar.[49] The mother knows

---

49. Although the color line in segregated restaurants was clearly drawn, the one in shopping areas proved more elusive. Hale observes: "Inside shops racial identity could not be secured with segregation signs, which allowed for customers of both races while grounding black inferiority in inferior spaces. Certainly whites' desire

she literally cannot afford the luxury of an open rebellion but does she not want to accept pity. Therefore, Octavia silently works within and against racial etiquette in order to pursue her objective (to warm up her son in a store) while retaining her dignity in otherwise potentially debilitating circumstances. Exercising the art of masking her true intentions, or the act of dissimulation,[50] is reminiscent of the plight of African Americans so evocatively captured in Paul Laurence Dunbar's poem "We Wear the Mask."[51] Although this particular experience in the hardware store does not revolve around procurement or consumption of food, it establishes a set of useful guidelines for James to build on in his future confrontations with the White Other. When later on Octavia and James enter a cafe and a grocery store, James is already trained in the hidden transcript and the rituals of deference.

Two separate, but definitely not equal, worlds exist in Bayonne. White patrons enjoy the comfort and warmth of the restaurants, while James says, "we pass by another café, but this'n for white people, too, and we can't go in there, either. So we just walk" (Gaines 506). Blacks have to walk the streets in sleet and wind in order to eat in a black cafe about a mile out of town.[52] In an interview Gaines explains that Octavia and James

---

for absolute racial difference could have been met by excluding African Americans from 'white' stores—a solution practiced by most restaurants and often required by law—and by limiting black purchases of consumer items considered too fine for 'colored' consumers. To some degree these policies were pursued, but very few white southern businesses could afford to exclude a paying customer no matter their color, especially when the next store down the street would probably make the sale anyway. Within this most intimate geography of southern white consumption, then, the collective white need for superiority clashes headlong with white individuals' desire for greater income, and money often won" (188).

50. The act of dissimulation that Johnson ascribes to the Black youth equally well refers to all African Americans: "Among some of the youth outward conformity concealed inner discontent. . . . Outward submissiveness and respect may thus be, as often as not, a mask behind which these youth conceal their true attitudes" (*Growing Up* 296).

51. Paul Laurence Dunbar included his poem "We Wear the Mask" in the volume *Lyrics of Lowly Life*, published in 1896.

52. The black cafe in which Octavia has to wait until their visit at the dentist's, similarly to real-life eating establishments, operates outside the purview of "the urban consumer landscape" (Cooley, "The Customer" 258). Even though it seems to be a bit more respectable an establishment than the black dive Angela Cooley describes,

can't have any food or drink or anything "uptown." They must go "back-of-town" in order to eat and drink. Now, if I had wanted to hit the nail on the head, I could have put them in a white restaurant and had them thrown out, but by the fact that they have to go back-of-town, you know that they would not have been accepted uptown. . . . It's not hitting the nail on the head, but playing around it. I think this is much more effective. (Gaudet and Wooton 20)

Instead of expressing open and direct defiance or wallowing in self-pity in the face of a humiliating social situation, Octavia teaches her son the virtues and value of endurance, spiritual strength, and pride.[53] The distance to the cafe, the hostile weather, and the hunger they feel render James's lesson more painful and, consequently, even more salutary. Biding their time in freezing sleet is not an option. Neither is asking the cafe owners for "pity" warmth; indeed, as Octavia instructs her son, "Got to pay them something for they heat" (Gaines 510). James understands that Octavia, as the breadwinner, has to provide for and make sacrifices for her whole family, and this includes spending their grocery money on something for James to eat, which in turn means the hardship of walking back home in the damp and cold.

James has always been protective of his mother. In the cafe he poignantly expresses his love and care by making extra room for her next to the heater and by pretending he is not hungry: "ain't got but just three little old cakes there." James says, "I'm so hungry right now, the Lord knows I can eat a hundred times three, but I wan my mama to have one" (Gaines 511). They read each other's intentions like an open book; thus, "Mama don't even look my way. She knows I'm hungry, she knows I want it. I let it stay there a little while, then I get it and eat it" (511). Their exchange, expressed both through gestures and words, suggests that James is ready to assume the role of a responsible, caring, and mature provider for their family.

---

it apparently performs a similar function: it "provided public space for poor African Americans to congregate without the oversight of a white employer or white authorities" ("The Customer" 258).

53. Octavia does not want any open confrontation—either with White folks or with her own. In the cafe she politely accepts a rude invitation to a dance from an African American patron. However, she slams him against the wall and threatens him with her knife when the dance becomes inappropriate (Gaines 511).

The lesson of survival includes negotiation of one's respectability, dignity, and pride.[54] James will have the most vivid illustration of that when they are confronted by Helena, a little elderly White lady who owns a small grocery store. James realizes that her leaving the comfort of the store in order to approach two Black strangers passing by her store with an offer of food and warmth implies that the White lady has an unconventional character. Octavia interprets the dinner offer as patronizing and condescending, and thus, in order to preserve her own self-respect against behavior interpreted as an attempt to humiliate her, she turns around to leave the store. She is not in the habit of accepting pity food or warmth, and there is no reason she should change now. The White woman understands Octavia's pride and so she quickly adds: "Just a minute . . . The boy'll have to work for it. It isn't free" (Gaines 513). A game of wills is enacted/played, in which both women work to establish and then negotiate their pride:

> "We don't take no handout," Mama says.
> "I'm not handing out anything," the old lady says. "I need my garbage moved to the front. Ernest has a bad cold and can't go out there."
> "James'll move it for you," Mama says.
> "Not unless you eat," the old lady says. "I'm old, but I have my pride, too, you know."
> Mama can see she ain't go'n beat this old lady down, so she just shakes her head.
> "All right," the old lady says. "Come into the kitchen." (513)

This exchange teaches James that survival should depend neither on compromising your self-respect nor on charity, however nobly intended. James learns that African Americans are supposed to respond to offers of food and shelter "with [the] dignity and equality his mother teaches him. She'll eat the food only if she can keep her sense of herself as an equal, and this means that she and the kind old White woman set the terms of the situation together" (Callahan 98). Octavia's personal situation synecdochally refers to the general plight of disempowered

---

54. "Embracing respectability did help many African Americans maintain an inward sense of integrity and self-respect as they lived their lives in the shadow of Jim Crow, and this included many blacks who were poor and uneducated, not just the black middle class" (Ritterhouse 57).

African Americans. Survival should not be based on relying on others because the oppressed may then become susceptible to systemic abuse: "Dependency on the philanthropy and good will of others leads to vulnerability when that support is no longer forthcoming" (Roberts 113). Building one's future on expecting good will and charitable acts from others deepens the preexisting vulnerability and subjection of the disempowered. Octavia knows the cost of losing contact with reality, however harsh it is. Dependency on charity creates vulnerability, and so do dreams. The confrontation of dreams with reality can be physically painful. James says, "I smell bread cooking. I look, then I see a baker shop. When we get closer, I can smell it more better. I shut my eyes and make 'tend I'm eating. But I keep them shut too long and I butt up 'gainst a telephone post" (Gaines 512). James learns the hard way that a lengthy stay in the world of make-believe can hurt.

Empathizing with the plight of the African American mother and son, Helena comes up with a plan to feed Octavia and her son without robbing them of their dignity by offering handout food. She has to mask her sympathy as a business transaction: the boy helps with the rubbish, and in exchange he and his mother can eat in Helena's kitchen.[55] Otherwise, inviting Black strangers into one's kitchen would be an open subversion of socially sanctioned racial relations for which Octavia may not be ready. Although Helena may be masking the true intentions behind her offer, Octavia is certainly masking the extent of her hunger and poverty. The nutritional value of the offered meal, which consists of "rice, gravy, meat . . . some lettuce and tomato in a saucer . . . a glass of milk and a piece of cake there, too" clearly exceeds their daily menu. James says, "It looks so good, I almost start eating 'fore I say my blessing" (Gaines 514). Octavia's restraint in eating such a feast—"she's eating slow like she's thinking" (514)—is not only a stratagem to teach James not to devour the food but also a way to maintain his dignity. By her manner of consumption Octavia also may wish to conceal her true self (her actual poverty and hunger), both as a means of preserving her own estimate of herself and, more

---

55. James does not fully understand power negotiations; hence, he attempts to look inside the rubbish cans, which seem too light for him: "I tell myself I ain't go'n be nobody's fool, and I'm go'n look inside this can to see just what I been hauling" (Gaines 514).

importantly, as a precautionary measure against any future patronizing gestures.

Even if Helena's kitchen seems to be a friendly space for the oppressed Other, the store is a potentially oppressive space where, unlike self-service grocery stores, the shopkeeper assists and often interferes with the customer's selection of merchandise.[56] Octavia does not have to experience the tension[57] and uncertainty typically connected with the particularities and customs of buying food, which were often part of African American customers' experience in White stores. Certainly one reason for that is the lack of any White clients in the store in whose presence the rituals of deference would have to be enacted. Commenting on these rituals, Hale observes that "African Americans often had to wait until all whites were served to take whatever grade

---

56. Using the example of Piggly Wiggly, Sharpless comments on the meaning and impact of the introduction of self-service groceries for African American customers:

> The self-service grocery store, pioneered by Piggly Wiggly in Memphis in 1916, often proved more comfortable for domestic workers. One entered through a turnstile, picked up a basket, selected one's own merchandise without assistance or interference from a grocery store employee, and queued to pay. A 1925 ad touted the egalitarian nature of Piggly Wiggly: "Just one kind of store for every kind of people, where the high and the low, the rich and the poor, all meet and are accorded the same kind, courteous treatment. Here you see with your own eyes and select with your own hands the food you buy without interruption from anyone" . . . By the 1940s, self-service grocery stores treated their customers with courtesy and equality, for the most part, but at the meat counter, sociologist Charles Johnson observed, "personal contacts are unavoidable" and caused African Americans "most embarrassment." And the chance always existed that the employer might disapprove of the employee's selection of food. (37)

57. "In the segregated South, trips to the store could be fraught with tension. First, the store itself could be the site of much conflict. Maya Angelou recalled going to the butcher shop in Stamps, Arkansas, in the 1930s. White people were served first, even if the butcher were in the middle of an order for African American customer. Next came the domestic workers buying for their employers: 'In fact, a black maid or cook would be served before us, because her order was intended for white people.' And last came the African Americans buying for themselves. While some domestic employees might have enjoyed the privilege of stepping to the head of the line, for others it must have felt awkward to be rude to one's peers on behalf of one's employer" (Sharpless 37).

of cornmeal, molasses, or sidemeat clerks would give them" (173).[58] The other reason is that rather than exercising the prerogative of her social status to control what Black Southerners buy (shopkeepers could easily disapprove of and deny the purchase; Hale 172), Helena once more wants to show her kindness of heart and cuts more salt meat than warranted for the purchase price. Hence, another elaborate dance of expressing and accepting generosity in connection with food ensues between the two proud women, this time over two bits' worth of salt meat. Octavia's lessons on the importance of saving face while confronting a dire economic situation culminate in flat refusal of the excess meat.

After a stalemate—Octavia's comment "That looks like awful lot of meat for a quarter" meets with Helena's response "Are you telling me how to run my business?" (Gaines 516)—Octavia, with perfect composure, expresses her gratitude about the earlier dinner and intends to leave the shop. With a realization that her act of kindness might be construed as patronizing, Helena stops her customers and cuts off half of the meat. Octavia meets her opponent in the game of wills with a confrontational look in which she displays strength of character and self-respect. Deferential avoidance of eye contact was one of the basic prescriptions of racial etiquette that defined and reaffirmed African Americans' supposed inferiority and subservience. In fact, Octavia has previously admonished her son to keep his eyes "in front where they belong" in order to avoid open confrontation with White patrons of the cafe they are passing (499). To retain their mutual dignity and establish temporary equality, these two women "elaborately split the difference, the facts of the situation never explicit, always implicit. Finally, James's mother upholds both the woman's generosity and her own dignity with a simple, direct ritual statement: 'Your kindness will never be forgotten'" (Callahan 98).

Offering and accepting kindness should never be at the expense of one's self-respect and sense of self-worth. The lessons in the hardware store, the Black cafe, and Helena's kitchen and shop teach James

---

58. In *Etiquette of Race Relations*, Doyle explains that in "places of business, the Negro should stand back and wait until the white has been served before receiving any attention and in entering or leaving he should not precede a white but should stand back and hold the door for him. On the streets and sidewalks the Negro should 'give way' to the white person" (qtd. in Hale 189).

that one should use everyday acts of resistance to uphold one's dignity even in the most oppressive circumstances, gracefully accept individual acts of kindness, and never allow others to steal one's sense of self-worth with handouts. As such, the dignity a Black mother instills in her son becomes, as bell hooks explains, "a radically subversive political gesture" (*Yearning* 43).[59] Even though Octavia cannot overcome White privilege, she can bear dependency with dignity and teach her son never to devalue or efface his true self. Octavia's final comment—"You not a bum . . . You a man" (Gaines 516)—made to James on a street when the boy is trying to turn up his coat collar to protect himself from the heavy sleet, is part of Octavia's program to instill personal responsibility, dignity, and pride in James and prepare him well with "hidden transcripts" to face the challenges posed by White supremacy.

The Transgressive Cafe[60]

The South's social order, based on White supremacy and gender subordination, is reflected in the space of the cafe in Fannie Flagg's *Fried Green Tomatoes at the Whistle Stop Cafe*. The titular cafe, run by two White women, Idgie Threadgoode and Ruth Jamison, becomes a site of contestation of that social order. During the first decades of the twentieth century Idgie and Ruth, the main heroines, move out of their respective homes into the back of the cafe. Their decision to run a cafe

---

59. bell hooks further explains: "I want us to respect and understand that this effort [of black women] has been and continues to be a radically subversive political gesture. For those who dominate and oppress us benefit most when we have nothing to give our own, when they have so taken from us our dignity, our humanness that we have nothing left, no 'homeplace' where we can recover ourselves" (*Yearning* 43).

60. This section appeared in print as "The Whistle Stop Cafe as a Challenge to the Jim Crow Bipartition of Society in Fannie Flagg's *Fried Green Tomatoes at the Whistle Stop Cafe*" in *Roczniki Humanistyczne*, vol. 64, no. 11, 2016, pp. 169–84. Parts that concern the restaurant business also received a less in-depth evaluation in my 2013 article "Zapisy na stole, wywrotowe jedzenie: heteronormatywność i pomidory, *Smażone zielone pomidory*" ("Table Inscriptions, Subversive Foodways: Heteronormativity and Tomatoes, *Fried Green Tomatoes*"), in *Inne Bębny. Różnica i Niezgoda w Literaturze i Kulturze Amerykańskiej* (*Different Drums: Difference and Dissent in American Literature and Culture*), edited by Izabella Kimak, Ewa Antoszek, and Katarzyna Czerwiec-Dykiel. Wydawnictwo UMCS, 2013, pp. 28–46.

together has twofold significance: they reject domesticity, a socially pre-scribed space for women; and they act on their increased sensitivity to help the disempowered and oppressed—the Black and the poor. As such the Whistle Stop Cafe is a space where their identities are nego-tiated and redefined in the context of racial oppression and gender subordination.

In the patriarchal American South, homes "immediately connote the private sphere of patriarchal hierarchy, gendered self-identity, shelter, comfort, nurture and protection" (George 1). As a contact zone between different genders, homes are ideologically charged. The importance of home "lies in the fact that it is not equally available to all. Home is the desired place that is fought for and established as the exclusive domain of a few. It is not a neutral place" (George 9). This lack of ideological neutrality is reflected in the fact that White patriarchy domesticated Southern women through "the Cult of True Womanhood."[61] Its separate-spheres ideology placed women on domestic pedestals: various cookbooks advocated the kitchen as "women's sacred domain" (qtd. in Levenstein 31 f.49), and claimed that "the view of woman's place is very traditional, and her happiness is seen in preparing food and enjoying domesticity" (qtd. in Grubb 166–67). Some women envisioned more for themselves beyond their patriarchally prescribed enclosure in domesticity and decided to con-test patriarchal control of the feminine—like Idgie and Ruth, who use "their access to food to challenge political and economic hierarchies" (Lindenfeld 227).

When women emerge from their domestic seclusion and still per-form quintessentially feminine tasks, they violate the established order and enjoy a degree of agency in doing so. Volition seems to be a key factor determining one's satisfaction and fulfillment in any endeavor or enterprise. Idgie and Ruth, like their historical counterparts "in the restaurant business, . . . remaining true to home values . . . often decried the profit motive. Although they [women in the restaurant business] sought financial success, many said they found their gratifica-tion in terms of self-expression" (Whitaker 99). With no need to make a profit, running a restaurant or cafe becomes a way of expressing one's

---

61. More about the attributes of true womanhood in Barbara Welter's article "The Cult of True Womanhood: 1820–1860."

values. Idgie and Ruth's cafe becomes a symbol of the human capacity for empathy and affection that make possible the creation of an environment where people seek a modus vivendi between races and classes, even if pragmatically based on concessions and compromises.

Charity to all regardless of skin color runs in the Threadgoode family: Poppa Threadgoode "owned the only store in town. . . . Poppa couldn't say no to anybody, white or colored. Whatever people wanted or needed, he just put in a sack and let them have it on credit. Cleo said Poppa's fortune had walked right out the door on him in paper bags. But then, none of the Threadgoodes could ever say no to anybody" (Flagg 26). Idgie herself has been a Robin Hood of sorts from Alabama. Under cover of night, Idgie, with the help of Grady Kilgore, the local sheriff and part-time railroad detective, redistributes government supplies to the disempowered: "During the Depression . . . this person called Railroad Bill would sneak on the government supply trains and throw stuff off for the colored people. Then he'd jump off before they could catch him. This went on for years, and pretty soon the colored started telling stories about him. . . . Sipsey said, every Sunday in church, they'd pray for Railroad Bill, to keep him safe" (331–32).

However, only the ownership of the cafe affords Idgie and Ruth a possibility to feed the hungry, make a social statement, and earn a decent living at the same time. The women find a way to turn their cafe into a social mission. *The Last Supper*, the picture Ruth hangs in the cafe (50), best captures their perception of their business as self-expression and a genuine calling. Their business model seems to resemble the business models of restaurants operated by middle-class women in America of the 1930s, who, by "providing valuable social services," claimed "to make the whole world homelike. . . . Some women spoke of the restaurant business as a way of recovering an ancient female vocation [of feeding humanity] that had been wrongfully usurped by men" (Whitaker 91). For Idgie and Ruth, running a cafe is not based on a single individual act of kindness; rather, the entire enterprise revolves around altruism and empathy. Hence, in just two years from its opening, "the name of the cafe was written on the walls of hundreds of boxcars, from Seattle to Florida" (Flagg 30) and as such it becomes a signpost for all those in need.

Ownership of a restaurant, cafe, or other eatery does not necessarily mean rejection of domesticity; it does, however, perpetuate the domination of women while promoting the creative use of their culinary talents and moral values. The seventeenfold increase in women's ownership of restaurants between 1890 and 1930 (Whitaker 90) testifies to the strong demand for women who could apply their familiarity with culinary activities and social sensitivities in inspired ways. At the same time, one cannot deny the importance of "social and economic changes in the early twentieth century" that "enlarged women's opportunities to carry home-based skills and values into the sphere of business" (89). Because "there persists within the middle-class American psyche a longing for an idealized home," restaurants and cafes offering home-style fare, or "home cooking," "have lured middle-class Americans by promising to restore the very traditions" of domesticity (Barbas 52). Thus the image of traditional domesticity, which centers on the private space of the family table, is brought to public eating establishments. Angela Cooley similarly remarks that "restaurants that were established outside of the home used wholesome advertising to tie themselves to familial settings. . . . Many public eating places tried to create similarities between dining in and eating out" (*To Live* 81). By alluding to the ideal of the American home, cafe proprietors and restaurateurs bring the values of patriarchal homes into the public sphere; indeed: "eating establishments were supposed to uphold the same moral standards expected of the southern home" (133).

However, in the early twentieth century a widening spectrum of public eating facilities, from restaurants catering primarily to White elite patrons, to lunch rooms, to lower-class establishments such as cafes,

> represented a potential threat to cherished white middle-class ideals related to the home and family. They [White Southerners] worried about a variety of alleged public immorality that might threaten the white family, and public restaurants represented particular points of entry for vice. . . . Public eating places represented public venues where a primarily domestic activity took place. Home continued to be the primary site of dining for southerners which meant that any potential new food culture developing in public places represented an active threat to the private concerns. (Cooley, *To Live* 62)

The very existence of a large variety of public eating establishments, which allow for "socializing, eating, drinking, and intermingling of all sorts" (106), poses a threat to White supremacy. The diversity of customers could also challenge the homogeneity of White domestication: "urban lunchrooms and cafés saw a more diverse dining population with a motley assortment of various ethnicities, classes, occupations, genders, and races, meeting and intermingling in one form or another" (114). Hence, the relationship between public eating places and private dining rooms, much like their correlative activities of eating out and dining in, is not simply based on exteriority.

The White patriarchal values connected with domesticity and veneration of White womanhood are metaphorically inscribed on the table; indeed, the private space of the table at the heart of the house becomes the very embodiment of White supremacy. Thus, the simple act of dining out carries significant ideological implications: the private space of the table is transposed onto the public space of any dining area—from restaurants through cafes to lunch counters. Hence, such public eating establishments

> are sites at which social boundaries are negotiated . . . sites of incorporation and exclusion, serve the more immediate aim of negotiating the imaginary and permeable contours of the nation. When those boundaries are felt to be in jeopardy, the rules of commensality are carefully patrolled. At commercial eating places, which open up the matrix of the family home, the walls that defend and stand for the sanctity of the private house and of the female body at the heart and hearth will be reproduced in the meanings ascribed to restaurant walls. (Abel 161)

Allowing two races to eat together in the same dining space would violate White patrons' sense of proper racial mores. Thus, as Hale explains, "because they made public the decidedly home-centered rituals of eating, cafes, restaurants and diners usually served only one race" (187).

In *Consuming Geographies*, Bell and Valentine claim "these loci of food consumption" can facilitate "community building and cohesion"; public eating facilities become cornerstones of the community, where "food retains its 'communicative' role" (106). In doing so, a neighborhood restaurant or a cafe becomes a signifier for the local community. Public patronage of such an eating establishment may therefore provide the means and opportunity to redefine and negotiate one's identity, both individual and collective. In *The Great Good Place*, Ray Oldenburg claims that these venues, in terms of their importance in people's lives, are third only to home and workplace. Such "third places" are "people's own remedy for stress, loneliness, and alienation" (Oldenburg 20); they offer not only "escape or time out from life's duties and drudgeries" (21)[62] but also "experiences and relationships afforded there and nowhere else" (21), mainly because the "*raison d'etre* of the third place rests upon its differences from the other settings of daily life and can best be understood by comparison with them" (22). If third places are "places where community is most alive and people are most themselves" (20), then clearly Idgie and Ruth's cafe is the third place in the fictitious town of Whistle Stop. In her bulletin, *The Weems Weekly*, Dot Weems confesses "it seems to me that after the cafe closed, the heart of the town just stopped beating. Funny how a little knockabout place like that brought so many people together" (Flagg 385–86). The reference to the aesthetics of the Whistle Stop Cafe ("a little knockabout place") also endows it with another characteristic feature of third places: that they are "taken for granted and most have a low profile" (Oldenburg 42).

As the product of the love between Idgie and Ruth, the flourishing cafe becomes the heart of the community, catering in several ways to the sundry needs of various people across color and class lines. The Whistle Stop Cafe on several accounts seems to be dissimilar to the "new" public eating places Angela Cooley studies. In contradistinction to real-life establishments, such as "stands, lunchrooms, cafés, and cookshops" that "often represented ephemeral establishments that did not stay open for longer than a year or two" ("The Customer" 250), the Whistle Stop Cafe stays in business for forty years (June 1929–June 1969). Cooley's research reveals that typical restaurant "menus specialized in 'quick order' foods, such as sandwiches, that could be prepared quickly and cheaply," while Ruth and Idgie's cafe offers a wide repertoire of Southern specialties, all prepared by their Black cook, Sipsey: buttermilk biscuits, skillet cornbread, coconut cream pie, pecan pie, Sipsey's Southern-fried chicken, grits, candied yams, and fried green tomatoes. However, both the "new" public eating places and their

---

62. Mencken called another third space—the tavern—"a quiet refuge" and a "hospital asylum from life and its cares" (qtd. in Oldenburg 21).

fictitious representative do "not cater to an elite clientele"; neither do they "bother with expensive décor," nor "provide separate facilities for the accommodation of women" ("The Customer" 250).

Third places seem to be perfect spaces for social performance in which "action, reflection, and intent are not marked as they are in cultural performances. Social performances are the ordinary, day-by-day interactions of individuals and the consequences of these interactions as we move through social life" (Madison 155). Oldenburg's explanation inscribes social performance in the functions of third places, which "are an ordinary part of a daily routine. The best attitude toward the third place is that it merely be an expected part of life. The contributions that third places make in the lives of people depend upon their incorporation into the everyday stream of existence" (37). Social performances, which constitute such everyday interactions among individuals, are reenacted in places like the Whistle Stop Cafe. What draws regular visitors to a third place is the fellow customers: "the right people are there to make it come alive, and they are the regulars" (Oldenburg 33). Like a home, a third place offers "the psychological comfort and support that it [a home] extends" (Oldenburg 42). Individuals "feel at home and comfortable" (Oldenburg 22) in a third place, mainly because its "character . . . is determined most of all by its regular clientele and is marked by a playful mood, which contrasts with people's more serious involvement in other spheres" (Oldenburg 42).

The regulars who frequent the Whistle Stop Cafe comprise its inner circle, negotiating and enacting cultural scripts while there, on which, according to Madison, all social performances are built (155). However, Jim Crow's bipartition of society precludes the possibility of the cafe becoming a neutral ground that theoretically is supposed "to level their guests to a condition of social equality" (Oldenburg 42). Oldenburg explains the function of a leveler, which "by its nature, [is] an inclusive place. It is accessible to the general public and does not set formal criteria of membership and exclusion. . . . Third places counter the tendency to be restrictive in the enjoyment of others by being open to all and by laying emphasis on qualities not confined to status distinctions current in the society" (24). Because segregation received significant public support under Jim Crow, the inclusiveness of a third place, or rather its lack, in such a "separate but equal" social context confirms that "social performances become examples of a culture's or sub-culture's particular symbolic practices" (Madison 155). One such symbolic practice is designating "colored" and "White" ordering and sitting sections in public eating facilities, or simply the refusal to serve African American customers, as a reaction to "the increasing tendency for white women to dine and work in public eating places, a constantly changing and growing New South population, and an atmosphere already concerned with the notion of racial purity" (Cooley, *To Live* 100). While not infected by racist ideology, Idgie and Ruth are aware of the consequences of breaching segregation barriers. They run a cafe, in which "all the railroad people ate . . . colored and white alike. . . . [Idgie]'d serve the colored out the back door. Of course, a lot of people didn't like the idea of her selling food to the coloreds, and she got into some trouble doing it, but she said that nobody was gonna tell her what she could and could not do" (Flagg 51). The voiced and staged objections by Ku Klux Klan sympathizers and members to the serving of Black patrons are based either on the taboo of commensality or revulsion regarding White women serving food to Black men. Notably, the source of both objections indirectly implied violation of Southern cultural norms via oblique but well understood references to the sexual nature of White female service.[63]

Idgie is aware that commensality would violate the racially pure personal space demanded by White regulars of her cafe, which in turn might not only boil their blood[64] but trigger violent performances of authority under the cover of white sheets. Idgie straightforwardly explains this concern to Ocie Smith, an African American railyard worker: "You know that if it was up to me, I'd have you come on in the front door and sit at a table, but you know I can't do that. . . . There's a bunch in town that would burn me down in a minute, and I've got to make a living" (Flagg 53). "The bunch in town" that Idgie mentions

---

63. After conducing sociological research in a group of Southern counties, Johnson drew a list of rigid taboos, which are not to be breached under any circumstances, the first three include: "Negroes may never marry whites . . . never dance with whites . . . never eat with whites" (*Growing Up* 277–78).

64. John Dollard quoted a "professional southerner" whose blood boiled when he "went North, to see Negroes riding streetcars side by side with whites, to see them eating in the same restaurants, to see Negro men and white women together" (44).

is an allusion to a thriving KKK chapter, whose vigilante-like activities attempt to "restore morality in both the private and public sectors" (Piacentino 411). The Ku Klux Klan, "also popularly known as the Invisible Empire," was originally founded in 1866 in Tennessee. One historian of the Klan, David A. Horowitz, has explained that "reacting harshly to post–Civil War threats to white supremacy and Democratic rule, Klansmen defied the law with acts of terrorism and intimidation against newly freed African-American slaves, Union army occupiers of the southern states, and white Republicans" (2) until laws passed in 1870 and 1871 forced them to disband. The Invisible Empire rose from the ashes in 1915, shortly after the release of *The Birth of a Nation*, which fueled Klan recruitment (Piacentino 410). Its hooded members "advocated white supremacy, intending through their influence and their secret and subversive activities to resurrect a social order in which blacks would be restored to their former permanent subservient status to a white, male-dominated society" (410). With membership soaring to several million in the 1920s, the Klan "flourished at the grassroots level, reflecting a sense of American identity and civic engagement that was shared by many white Protestant Americans in the aftermath of World War I" (Pegram x).

Aware of the KKK's racism and religious bigotry but armed with strong moral views on segregation and business acumen, Idgie refrains from openly transgressing racial etiquette, in which "the separation of blacks and whites at mealtime, however minimal or artificial, was among the most strictly enforced rules" (Ritterhouse 24). If she wants to stay in business, Idgie cannot openly defy the racist status quo; she has to make concessions. She chooses one of the most common accommodations in such a social context. Continuing to justify her actions to Ocie Smith, Idgie instructs him: "I want you to go back over to the yard and tell your friends, anytime they want anything, just to come on around to the kitchen door" (Flagg 53). Such a decision bespeaks the cafe's social mission to feed humanity but at the same time prevents cross-racial fraternizing. It is illustrative of

> a more common compromise[, which] was a rear door or side window carry-out option that preserved the front door/back door structure of plantation culture and avoided the symbolic implications of sitting down together; the hierarchy was further maintained by requiring African Americans to bring their own

paper bags for sandwiches and buckets for ice cream and Coke. (Abel 179)

The act of selling food to the disempowered, both African Americans and poor Whites, through the kitchen door can be construed as one of the social performances that are "formed, understood, and reiterated through cultural scripting" (Madison 155).

Proper racial conduct is displayed in everyday interactions between White and Black customers of the Whistle Stop Cafe through cultural scripts, which are expressed and negotiated by, for example, denying African Americans access to the dining section of the cafe through the front door. However, even that concession is viewed as a transgression of racial segregation. Idgie is confronted by the town sheriff, Grady—who is both her admirer and a KKK member—about the Klan's objections to her business policy: "Idgie, you ought not to be selling those niggers food, you know better than that. And there's some boys in this town that's not happy about it. Nobody wants to eat in the same place that niggers come, it's not right and you just ought not be doin' it" (Flagg 53). Acknowledging how "Klan membership in many communities was . . . an open secret and included public officials, Protestant ministers, and ordinary and prominent citizens alike" (Pegram 6), Idgie downplays, if not downright emasculates, Grady and his fellow Klansmen: "Well, Grady, tell you what. The next time those 'some people' come in here, like Jack Butts and Wilbur Weems and Pete Tidwell, I'll ask 'em if they don't want anybody to know who they are when they go marching around in one of those stupid parades you boys have, why don't they have enough sense to change their shoes?" (Flagg 54).

This "bunch of grown men getting liquored up and putting sheets on their heads" (Flagg 54), as Idgie succinctly describes them, violently denies any kinship or equality with African Americans. The Klansmen "fused purity reform and community activism with a controversial heritage of racism and nativism" (Horowitz 1). With "a reformist zeal" its hooded members objected to anything they "deemed morally scandalous or dangerous to the preservation of a socially conservative American value system" (Piacentino 411). They saw themselves as "the guarantor of traditional social morality" (Horowitz 3). They reviled biracial dining because "food sharing, or commensality . . . is a great signifier of community, and anthropologists have emphasized its role in kinship and reciprocity ties in countless cultural settings" (Bell and Valentine 106).[65] The Klan enforced social boundaries and disrupted the ability of diners from both races to cement bonds while sharing a meal, because "not only . . . [are] the proprieties of food seen as being incorporated into the eater, but, by a symmetrical process, the very absorption of given foods is seen as incorporating the eater into a culinary system and into the group which practices it" (Beardsworth and Keil 54).

Because Idgie dismisses the warnings, Grady turns to Ruth in order to appeal to her better sense of propriety. Ruth counters Grady by referencing the visual politics of Jim Crow: "Oh Grady, what harm can it be to sell a few sandwiches out the back door? It's not like they're coming in and sitting down. . . . They are not hurting anybody, Grady" (Flagg 54). Ruth's retort reflects the fact that "sharing a meal, or even an eating space, performs a . . . charged symbolic function" (Abel 164). Ruth manages to defuse the crisis by removing African Americans from the dining section of the cafe to the rear entrance, where they are less visible to the White clientele. Unable to deny the logic of Ruth's arguments, Grady has to concede "Well . . . okay for now, I guess," only to remind her that he represents the voice of authority:

---

65. The vehement opposition to any kinship, equality, or reciprocity ties that lies at the core of the taboo against interracial commensality is wonderfully illustrated in Virginia Foster Durr's *Outside the Magic Circle: The Autobiography of Virginia Foster Durr*. Durr writes that she saw a Black girl sitting at her table in the dining room during her sophomore year at Wellesley College. Her visceral reaction reveals the depth of her Southern upbringing: "My God, I nearly fell over dead. I couldn't believe it. I just absolutely couldn't believe it . . . I promptly got up, marched out of the room, went upstairs, and waited for the head of the house to come . . . I told her that I couldn't possibly eat at the table with a Negro girl. I was from Alabama and my father would have a fit. He came from Union Springs, Bullock County, and the idea of eating with a Negro girl—well, he would die. I couldn't do it" (56). However, after nightlong considerations, motivated by an ultimatum from the head of the house, Virginia changes her mind. A challenge from Emmie, Virginia's friend, is also not without significance: "Why would you kiss and hug them [an old Black cook] and not eat with them?" (57). Virginia's decision to go along with breaking the taboo is made easier by a realization that her father does not have to know about the breach of his daughter's Southern conduct. Durr confesses: "I did eat with that Negro girl for about a month, and I came to realize that in that time that it wasn't the Negro girl I was afraid of. It was my father's reaction I feared. She was a perfectly nice girl, well-mannered and intelligent. She used the right fork and all. She was a Southerner, too" (58).

"But you make sure you keep them at the back door, you hear me?" (Flagg 55). However, Ruth's solution also exposes the hypocrisy of the visual politics of Jim Crow: African Americans cannot consume food in the company of White people, not even the very food they themselves have been preparing. After averting the threat of open conflict looming over the cafe, Ruth and Idgie, even if they seemingly accept Jim Crow's bipartition of society and feed Blacks and the homeless through the kitchen back door, act in accord with their strong sense of justice: "the only thing that changed was on the menu that hung on the back door; everything was a nickel or a dime cheaper. They figured fair was fair" (Flagg 55). Such a strategy shows a combination of Idgie and Ruth's strong moral views on segregation and their basic sense of decency and Christian morality.

Quite interestingly, the cafe becomes the site of bonding across both color and gender lines against White chauvinist domination and abuse. The twofold oppression converges in the person of Frank Bennett, a Klansman who repeatedly beats his wife Ruth and brutally abuses Blacks, among them Sipsey. As a result of unified efforts on the part of his victims, Frank ends up on the cafe's menu. This justice is administered to prevent the kidnapping of Ruth's baby and is meted out with a deadly frying pan by Sipsey and Jim Smokey 'Lonesome' Philips, a former vagrant who had found both work and home at the Whistle Stop Cafe. To get rid of the incriminating evidence (Bennett's corpse), Idgie uses a Southern festivity as a cover-up. Idgie has Big George, Sipsey's son, start the hog-boiling season earlier than usual: "It was another ice-cold Alabama afternoon, and the hogs were boiling in the big iron pot out in back of the cafe. The pot was bubbling over the top, full of long-gone hogs that would soon be smothered with Big George's special barbecue sauce" (Flagg 207). What is left of Frank is then served to the unwitting patrons of the cafe, including detectives investigating his disappearance. Big George's new secret flavor in the sauce becomes a signifier of culinary resistance to the oppression of the weak: both women and African Americans. The sexist pig Bennett becomes a "barbecued pig," a "secret" that gets "hidden in the sauce" (Lindenfeld 239).

Barbecue is not simply quintessential, iconic Southern food.[66] The

---

66. As a Southern specialty, barbecue is pervasive and omnipresent; South Carolina is even divided into four discrete "barbecue regions" with varying

celebration of pork during BBQ fests is a public spectacle of community, "the communal eating festivals . . . [seek] to reinforce the bonds of family and community by preserving their rich culinary traditions" (Levenstein 41). John Shelton Reed, Tennessean sociologist, claims that barbecue transgresses all social boundaries in the South: a "good barbecue joint may be the one place you'll find Southerners of all descriptions—yuppies, hippies, and cowboys, Christians and sinners, black and white together" (47). Zora Neale Huston similarly claims in her autobiography that barbecue will be significant in the utopian, postracist future: "Maybe all of us who do not have the good fortune to meet or meet again, in his world, will meet at a barbeque" (286).

The cafe is certainly no "raceless" pit barbecue joint;[67] the hog-boiling season and resulting barbecue are cultural performances informed by and expressing racial relations and status quo under Jim Crow. Steven Hoelscher's definition of a cultural performance as "the sorts of nonordinary, framed public events that require participation by a sizable group and that, as planned-for public occasions, invest their participants with meaning" (661) captures the meaning of barbecue in the town of Whistle Stop. The inclusiveness of the festivity seems to subvert, even if temporarily, the Jim Crow bipartition of society—openly sharing the same kind of meat not only prepared but, more importantly, also consumed by Blacks constitutes a transgression of the savage–civilized polarity[68] imposed by White supremacy. Cultural

---

distinctive sauces (Kovacik and Winberry 208–9). The importance and diversity of barbecue in the South cannot be underestimated; a long list of scholarly works devoted to this social event testifies to such a claim: Andrew Warnes's *Savage Barbecue: Race, Culture, and the Invention of America's First Food* (University of Georgia Press, 2008), Elizabeth S. D. Engelhardt's *Republic of Barbecue* (University of Texas Press, 2009), Robert F. Moss's *Barbecue: The History of an American Institution* (University of Alabama Press, 2010), and James R. Veteto and Edward M. Maclin's *The Slaw and the Slow Cooked: Culture and Barbecue in the Mid-South* (Vanderbilt University Press 2011), to mention only the newest additions to this field of research.

67. Andrew Warnes contends that "pit barbecue culture is often said to be raceless . . . during the Jim Crow period many such joints were among the few places where black and white southerners could eat together. . . . The owners and customers alike saw these joints as free and de facto non-white spaces in which certain uncivilized appetites could find release" (*Savage Barbecue* 102–3).

68. There is "the strong assonance between the words *barbecue* and *barbaric*" (Warnes, *Savage Barbecue* 6), due to a semantic context: "all *barbarians* must

performances, such as the production and consumption of barbecue, "are reflexive instruments of cultural expression and power in which a group creates its identity by telling a story about itself" (Hoelscher 661). Big George's barbecue is held in high esteem by the White residents of Whistle Stop. Indeed, Grady even brags to the Georgia detectives investigating Frank Bennett's disappearance: "That nigger makes the best goddamned barbecue in the state. You've gotta get yourselves some of that, then you'll know what good barbecue is" (Flagg 208). The fame of Big George's barbecue transcends municipal limits: years later Ninny Threadgoode recalls that "people drove all the way from Birmingham to get it" (Flagg 302). However, praise for the cook is leveled by a rhetoric of cleanliness and purity, which inscribes inferiority onto the other race. Angela Cooley perceptively captures how, during hog-killing season, inferiority is imprinted on Blackness: "Requiring African Americans to perform the most distasteful chores in food production—such as cleaning out a pig's intestines—reinforced the connection that whites tried to create between blackness and filth" ("Eating with Negroes" 79).[69]

Anthropologist Mary Douglas observes that "if food is treated as a code, the message it encodes will be found in the pattern of social relations being expressed. The message is about different degrees of hierarchy, inclusion and exclusion, boundaries and transactions across boundaries. . . . Food categories therefore encode social events" ("Deciphering a Meal" 61). Hence, the BBQ event, in catering to both White and Black patrons of the cafe alike, indicates the possibility of biracial cooperation and consumption: everyone is included in the celebrations of barbecue. Boiling and serving human flesh is not simply a vehicle for concealing incriminating evidence of Frank Bennett's murder, even though "white masculine dominance literally becomes an object of consumption" (Lindenfeld 239). With Idgie making the decision to barbecue the corpse, the backyard barbecue becomes her statement of power through which she expresses her objection to and

---

barbecue and all who barbecue must be barbaric" (Warnes 7). Barbecue is an event when "supposedly civilized members" of society are growing "tired of their civilized life, seeking respite from its dry protocols in the form of this somehow savage, somehow necessary food" (Warnes 104).

69. In many ways, this relegation of distasteful tasks to those deemed socially inferior is reminiscent of India's caste system.

resistance against racial and gender oppression.[70] Thus, as Shari Zeck rightly phrased it, "White women and African Americans are not opposed in this film, but rather they cooperate in ridiculing the world of evil white men. To confront racism, one must also confront violence against women, and vice versa" (227).

■ ■ ■

Where we eat defines not only who we are, but also who we are not. Thus, public spaces of consumption act as demarcation lines that either include us in or exclude us from social groups. Cultural hierarchy is formed through the invitation or denial of participation in social activities. Thus, the "projection of community ideals and their embodiment in material form . . . creates an artificial though nonetheless real symbolic order that operates to provide not information but confirmation, not to alter attitudes or change minds but to represent an underlying órder of things, not to perform functions but to manifest an ongoing and fragile social process" (Carey 15).

The ritual and processual view of communication James Carey proposes could also be applied to the analysis of eating rituals as a performance. Food consumption in public eating facilities such as the diners, cafes, and restaurants is a symbolic process where collective consciousness is communicated, individual identities shaped, and alliances negotiated or contested. In the Jim Crow South, patrons, depending on their skin color, find themselves either excluded or included. The public spaces of food consumption mark the boundaries of intimacy and define acceptable social distance in cross-racial contact. Thus, it would be hard to disprove Angela Cooley's claim that public eating spaces, if viewed through the prism of interracial dining, are "spaces of conflict, social control, and resistance" ("The Customer" 244).

It is no coincidence, then, that African Americans used food

---

70. Yet it should be stated that the cafe's potential as a statement against racial and gender subordination is not fully explored in the novel. After all, it is a Black woman, Sipsey, who is the cook in a cafe run by two White women, not the other way round. Lorna Piatti-Farnell lucidly demonstrates that Ruth and Idgie fail to implement their radical racial sentiments: "Behind the closed doors, the division of labor in the café's kitchen still shows signs of racial stratification" (58).

consumption, especially commensality, to register racial dissent during the civil rights movement. As Susan Kalcik observes, "eating together or eating similar foods in similar ways is an expression of equality, which is why integrating restaurants was so important in the Civil Rights movement in the United States" (49).

CHAPTER 3

A Sweet Taste of Victory

Food and Social Drama at the Lunch Counter

I've made up my mind not to order a sandwich on
light bread if the waitress approaches me
with a pencil. My hat is the one I wear
the Sundays my choir doesn't sing. . . .

. . . .

Because I'm nonviolent I don't act or
react. When knocked from the stool
my body takes its shape from what
it falls into. The white man cradles
his tar baby. Each magus in turn.

—Thylias Moss, "Lunchcounter Freedom"

At the rate things are going here, all of Africa will be free
before we can get a lousy cup of coffee.

—James Baldwin, *Nobody Knows My Name*[1]

For protest to succeed, it must produce a feeling of moving
ahead; it must force people to take notice of injustice; and it
must win new allies.

—Bayard Rustin, *Strategies for Freedom*

---

1. James Baldwin's quote comes from an article titled "A Negro Assays on the
Negro Mood," originally published in the *New York Times*, March 12, 1961, later
published as a chapter, "East River, Downtown: Postscript to a Letter from Harlem,"
in Baldwin's *Nobody Knows My Name: More Notes of a Native Son* (1961).

By creating "separate but equal" spaces of consumption during the Jim Crow South, White Southerners pretended that the gaping racial wound did not exist. They orchestrated a reality where everyone "knew" their place in society. However, as Victor Turner states, "social life . . . even its apparently quietest moments is characteristically 'pregnant' with social dramas. It is as though each of us has a 'peace' face and a 'war' face, that we are programmed for cooperation, but prepared for conflict. The primordial and perennial agonistic mode is the social drama" (*From Ritual* 11). When African Americans openly acknowledged segregation as systemic abuse, stared into it, and saw it for what it was, the social drama of the civil rights movement ensued. Nonviolent confrontation, be it in the form of school desegregation (in Little Rock), a bus ride (Rosa Parks in Montgomery), or an order of coffee (the Greensboro Four at Woolworth's), follows the pattern of social drama, whose structure, according to Victor Turner, is based on four phases: breach, crisis, redressive action, and resolution. Anthony Grooms's "Food that Pleases, Food to Take Home," the short story chosen for analysis in this chapter, depicts the social drama of individual characters in the broader sociohistorical context of the civil rights movement. A close reading of the short story will reveal the complexities of the racial situation in the American South. Application of Turner's social drama theory will expose various factors that informed the actions of Grooms's main heroines ranging from hesitant (troubled conscience), mild (the nonviolent resistance), to very confrontational (the explosion of anger seething beneath the surface). An order of a hamburger with some fries and orangeade becomes a symbolic means of acknowledging the racial wound, an act that offers the characters a chance not only to confront or upset the racial status quo but also to reevaluate their own beliefs.

Even though I illustrated and analyzed in the previous chapter the mechanisms of and ideology behind "separate but equal" spaces of consumption during the Jim Crow South, it is pertinent to mention the decades leading to the desegregation of public eating places. For the White ruling class, public eating facilities were regarded as an extension of the private act of dining in:

> Public eating places in southern urban areas reflected the broader cultural conflicts among middle-class white authorities and various lower-class elements, each attempting to mold public urban

space to meet their own desires, needs, and anxieties. Public eating establishments, because they simultaneously represented home and quintessential urban space, played a key role in new urban identities. (Cooley, "The Customer" 242)

However, as various public spaces of consumption proliferated, the food-scape of the urban South had to undergo changes:

Public establishments lost the regulating influence of family and community mores, which engendered cultural conformity through a combination of communal values, experiences, and censure. Instead, the assortment of races, socioeconomic classes, ethnicities, and genders that gathered in southern urban areas projected their own identities into public eating places. (Cooley, "The Customer" 242)

Thus, faced with such imagined threats to White supremacy, White Southerners, who "were generally uninhibited in pursuing their segregationist impulses" (Klarman 93), adopted and enacted "obviously impermissible segregation ordinances" in order to preserve social peace and protect racial purity (93).

Yet, as White supremacist ideology attempted to control and restrict access to public eating facilities, socioeconomic reality pulled in the opposite direction by allowing for and embracing a diversity of paying clientele. First of all, "new lifestyles necessitated different eating habits with people eating different foods, moderating the amounts of food they ate at different times of the day, and finding new consumer outlets for their dining convenience and pleasure" (Cooley, *To Live* 148). The patrons of public eating facilities (be they African Americans or lower-class Whites), as the correlative of mass consumption, "both depended upon and created a new geography of shopping. In this complex layering of places, whites interacted with African Americans as consumers, as both indirect and direct violators of both localized and regional rituals of racial deference" (Hale 125).

Second, in a tug-of-war between ideological and economic imperatives, some White owners of eating establishments chose bread/income over principles/White supremacy: "The same economic pressures that led to the tacit desegregation of department and grocery stores in the thirties operated for restaurants as well. Although the taboos on interracial eating were far more stringent and tenacious than those on commercial transactions, eating places (unlike drinking fountains or restrooms) were subject to the same financial exigencies, and a range of compromises were struck between ideological priority and economic gain" (Abel 177–78). If cross-racial contact was unavoidable (for whatever reason), then at least the extent of that contact could be limited to minimize the presumed damage. Racial purity (uncontaminated Whiteness) and domination (supremacy) were at stake in interracial eating facilities. As a preemptive strategy to avert potential contamination, owners erected partitions[2] and posted signs in restaurants and at lunch counters to designate "colored" and "White" ordering and seating sections.

As such, the signs "White Only" and "Black Only" were a visual "anti-pollution" barrier. These signs responded to anxieties that "extended beyond the body . . . and permeated very basic concerns about the soul. Some southerners worried that eating places might serve as potential sites for activities considered immoral and that bodily pollution might result. This possibility was particularly disturbing in public locations where people consumed as if in their private homes" (Cooley, "The Customer" 251). Angela Cooley perceptively captures the connection between interracial eating and morality: "For the southern white middle class, public eating establishments implicated concerns about bodily pollution and threats to racial purity in many other ways as well. An obvious concern involved the possible association of white women and black men in public eating spaces" (*To Live* 96). Apparently, for some White Southerners there was only a tiny step from interracial eating to interracial sex: "interracial eating threatened social structure more profoundly than by offering opportunities for social intermingling: a limited focus on the slippage from the social to the sexual would simply elide eating with sex rather than pursue the more intriguing question of their structural parallels" (Abel 160).[3] Thus, any

---

2. As an example, Marcie Cohen Ferris remarks that in "Birmingham, segregation ordinances in 1950s outlawed whites and blacks from being served in the same room in a restaurant, unless they were separated by a '7-foot or higher' partition. The law also stipulated separate street entrances for whites and blacks into segregated dining facilities" (*The Edible South* 248–49).

3. Langston Hughes points to the North to prove how inherently illogical it is of Southerners to directly connect interracial dining and marriages: "It might be pointed out to the South, for instance, that the old bugaboo of sex and social equality doesn't mean a thing. Nobody as a rule sleeps with or eats with or dances with

suggestion of desegregating eating places under Jim Crow would meet with virulent opposition from most White Southerners, who employed eugenics to explain their stance: African Americans were supposedly "too diseased and dirty to share a meal" with (Cooley, "Eating with Negroes" 70) and posed a threat to Whiteness (fear of miscegenation)[4] in public eating facilities.

The injunction against "eating with Negroes" and taboos prohibiting interracial sex were connected by the intimate nature of these activities: "eating and sex both involved intensely personal activities that entailed consumption in its most intimate form. In both cases, the human body consumes a substance which thereby becomes a part of the body" (Cooley, *To Live* 63). With this conflation of the implications of interracial eating and interracial sex in mind, it should not come as a surprise that many a Southern mother warned her daughter to "be careful about what enters your body . . . what enters and leaves the doors of your body is the essence of morality" (Smith, *Killers of the Dream* 87–88). The parental advice offered to Lillian Smith resonates well with Mary Douglas's claim that "nothing is more essentially transmitted by a social process of learning than sexual behavior, and this of course is closely related to morality" (*Natural Symbols* 69). Such a parental warning thrives on the parallel anxieties connected with the contamination of pure White female bodies by a purportedly abject element:[5] be it in the form of inferior food consumed with the supposedly

---

or marries anybody else except by mutual consent. Millions of people in New York, Chicago, and Seattle go to the same polls and vote without ever cohabiting together. Why does the South think it would be otherwise with Negroes were they permitted to vote there? Or have a decent education? Or sit on a stool in public place and eat a hamburger? Why they think simple civil rights would force a Southerner's daughter to marry a Negro in spite of herself, I have never been able to understand" ("What Shall We Do about the South?" 6).

4. In her research, Angela Cooley observes that the "presence of women in unregulated establishments created the potential for sexual interactions and race mixing;" hence "miscegenation was no doubt at the heart of many food consumption issues with which urban authorities wrestled" (*To Live* 15; "The Customer" 258, respectively).

5. Cooley explains that "like the consumption of food, sexual activity also involved the invasion of the human body by a foreign substance which could thereby become a part of the body. For white southerners, sexuality represented the absolute foundation for racial purity and the means by which whiteness or blackness was transmitted from parent to child" (*To Live* 10).

inferior race or the threat of miscegenation polluting the racial purity of Whiteness,[6] the very foundation of Southern supremacy:

> White southerners respected a deeply ingrained commitment to protect their bodies—and thereby their race—from potential sites of pollution. . . . In the public sphere, protection from bodily pollution necessitated regulation in the form of health codes and racial segregation laws. Such laws protected racial purity by ensuring that pure food entered the white body in the public sphere and by protecting white women—the source of racial purity—from perceived dangers, particularly those related to white female sexuality. (Cooley, *To Live* 63)

Thus, the protection of female bodies synecdochally refers to the protection of Southern supremacy. Elizabeth Abel aptly observes that "Jim Crow signs at local eating places attempt to protect a white social body whose boundaries seemed at risk of penetration . . . the body of collective eaters, joined by the incorporative dynamics of a different orifice, constitute a permeable and consequently privatized site of social replication. Interracial eating . . . threaten[s] to breach the fabric of white national reproduction" (168). The social implications of interracial eating bring to mind Julia Kristeva's concept of the abject: the other that "disturbs identity, system, order. What does not respect borders, positions, rules" (4), and as such invests the space of interracial public consumption with a subversive potential.

The parental instruction Lillian Smith summons in her memoir *Killers of the Dream* captures the social intentions of White supremacy, inscribed—as it were—on a White female body; hence prescriptions of female conduct in public carry symbolic expression: "eating with Negroes" is one step away from "sleeping with Negroes." The body—in this particular case the body of a White woman—is "simultaneously a physical and symbolic artifact, . . . both naturally and culturally produced, and . . . securely anchored in a particular historical moment" (Scheper-Hughes and Lock 6). Thus, a Southern woman is both the physical body and the social body, the interrelationship of which is perfectly reflected in Mary Douglas's general observations about the body:

---

6. For an exhaustive discussion of a relationship between food and racial purity, see Kyla Wazana Tompkins, *Racial Indigestion: Eating Bodies in the 19th Century*; and Sharon Holland, *Erotic Life of Racism*.

The social body constrains the way the physical body is perceived. The physical experience of the body, always modified by the social categories through which it is known, sustains a particular view of society. There is a continual exchange of meanings between the two kinds of bodily experience so that each reinforces the categories of the other. As a result of this interaction the body itself is a highly restricted medium of expression. The forms it adopts in movement and repose express social pressures in manifold ways. . . . all the cultural categories in which it [the body] is perceived . . . must correlate closely with the categories in which society is seen in so far as these also draw upon the same culturally processed idea of the body. (*Natural Symbols* 69)

Such a multifaceted perception of the body was systematized by Nancy Scheper-Hughes and Margaret M. Lock into three perspectives, which are methodologically suggestive for the present analysis: the individual body as "understood in the phenomenological sense of the lived experience of the body-self"; the social body, referring to "the representational uses of the body as a natural symbol with which [we ought] to think about nature, society, and culture" (7); and "as a *body politic*, an artifact of social and political control" (6). The collective "White" body (a.k.a. Southern patriarchy), when threatened with miscegenation, may devise mechanisms of regulating the conduct of individual "White" bodies in order to prevent contamination (edible or sexual): "When the sense of social order is threatened . . . the symbols of self-control become intensified along with those of social control. Boundaries between the individual and political bodies become blurred, and there is a strong concern with matter of ritual and sexual purity, often expressed in vigilance over social and bodily boundaries" (24).

Scheper-Hughes and Lock posit that a body politic concerns "the regulation, surveillance, and control of bodies (individual and collective) in reproduction and sexuality, in work and in leisure, in sickness and other forms of deviance and human difference" (7–8). Thus, through a set of social norms a body politic differentiates "us" from the social "Other," and regulates social relations through scripts of desired behaviors. To uphold segregation in the South, White supremacy developed its own body politic (no eating or sleeping with the "inferior" race). Because "the stability of the body politic rests on its ability to regulate populations (the social body) *and* to discipline individual bodies" (8), the Southern body politic promulgated carefully detailed proscriptions in the form of its infamous Jim Crow laws. The need to regulate the collective public eating seems to derive from the fact that "points where outside threats may infiltrate and pollute the inside become the focus of particular regulation and surveillance" (23–24). Elizabeth Abel's perception of the social body in the context of the visual politics of Jim Crow seems to confirm that "both integrated and differentiated, bounded yet partially permeable, the physical body is a central image of the social body; bodily orifices stage and represent defining, vulnerable, hence carefully regulated points of entrance to or exit from social wholes. Ingestion figures absorption into the social body; hence, sharing a meal, or even an eating space, performs a more charged symbolic function than common labor or travel on a common carrier" (163–64).

The symbolic function of sharing food or sharing an eating space is a ritual of absorption/initiation into the social group. Elizabeth Abel perceptively posits that "collective eating ritualizes the constitution of the social body though the shared consumption of common substances. What is incorporated in these acts is not only the consumed substance but also the individuals who collectively consume it" (164). Rituals of eating thus clearly function as mechanisms of social control (*body politic*).

Lunch Counter Sit-Ins

Taking advantage of the multivalence of the concept of the body, the analysis of foodways can be conceptualized in a similar way. Food can be viewed from three perspectives: the "individual" food (a food product, or the physical act of eating), symbolic food (socially symbolic consumption, such as commensality), and the *food politic* (regulation of eating practices and spaces). During the civil rights movement a cup of coffee—the individual beverage ordered at the Woolworth's counter—assumed a symbolic dimension in a cultural performance that exposed the fact that the *food politic* both reflected and promoted racial segregation that consigned African Americans to inferior spaces of consumption, and by extension to an inferior social position, through a forced display of deference to White Southerners. The virulent opposition of Southern White supremacists to African Americans' nonviolent demands to be served at the same lunch counters as Whites demonstrates that the fight over desegregation of public eating places accentuated "the intimate associations . . . among food, consumption, race, body, and identity" (Cooley, "The Customer" 241). Much as the "White" side of the social spectrum feared, integrating public eating facilities would have consequences affecting other aspects of social life.

White Southerners did not believe that Black youth possessed "either motivation or ability to organize an insurgency against segregation" (Webb 59),[7] yet four Greensboro university freshmen staged a lunch counter sit-in that galvanized African Americans into openly demanding equal rights. It is safe to say that, as Cuthbert-Kerr remarks, "the sit-in movement was sparked by a sit-in in Greensboro" (732). On February 1, 1960, four young male students from North Carolina Agricultural and Technical College—David Richmond, Ezell Blair Jr., Joseph McNeil, and Franklin McCain—sat down to request service and ignited a nationwide struggle. These four protestors, called "the Greensboro Four," after having purchased some items in the local F. W. Woolworth's department store, "sat down at the lunch counter and ordered coffee. The White waitresses refused to serve the students and directed them to a stand-up counter.[8] The students remained seated. Feeling an '[i]ntense sense of pride, [and] a bit of trepidation,' the students remained seated until closing and returned the next day" (Cooley, *To Live* 228).

Their nonviolent protest was far from spontaneous, as Wolff points out. Indeed, they did "not come to Woolworth's on the spur of the moment; they were fully aware of what they were doing and fully expecting to be arrested. In fact, bond was waiting for them" (Wolff 15–16). The Greensboro Four belonged to the National Association for the Advancement of Colored People, and "through their participation in the NAACP Youth Wing, they became well informed about the effects of Jim Crow laws on their lives, their family, and the black

---

7. In this context, it is not amiss to say that "the sit-ins took the older black political leadership by surprise, [but] most supported the campaign" (Brown and Webb 296). As Klarman remarks, the cynics within NAACP "who had expected the demonstrations quickly to 'fizzle out, panty-raid style' were disappointed" (373).
8. Suzanne Bilyeu provides the details: "A black woman working at the lunch counter scolded the students for trying to stir up trouble, and the store manager asked them to leave" (24). When they refused to leave, the store manager instructed his staff to ignore the four, as he "didn't want any disruptions that would scare away customers" (26).

community" (Essien 348). At NAACP meetings, during which the sit-in demonstrators "spent many hours discussing ways in which they could participate in the integration movement" (Cuthbert-Kerr 732), they learned not only how to recognize but also how to nonviolently agitate against racial disfranchisement, discrimination, and segregation.

Richmond, Blair, McNeil, and McCain were the snowflakes that started the avalanche of nonviolent protests. A discussion of sit-ins as a new tactic developed by the civil rights movement would be "a false periodisation of history that ignores the continuity of black protest that occurred over the course of many decades. The sit-in tactic had been pioneered by the Congress of Racial Equality (CORE)[9] during the 1940s" (Brown and Webb 295). Angela Cooley rightly posits that "although the Greensboro sit-in spawned an excitement among university students toward equal rights, the sit-in movement had earlier antecedents. Starting in the 1940s, CORE triggered a similar, albeit less publicized, direct action campaign targeted in segregated restaurants primarily located outside of the South" (*To Live* 232).[10] The earliest instances of northern protests took place in 1943 as sit-ins at Jack Spratt's Coffee House and Stoner's Restaurant, both staged in Chicago. Later cases would include sit-ins in St. Louis in 1949, and in Baltimore in 1952 (Stentiford 604). The NAACP Youth Council and CORE were behind such peaceful sit-ins as the "Royal Seven," when a group of African Americans from Durham, North Carolina, staged a sit-in at the Royal Ice Cream Parlor in June 1957 (the protestors were arrested for trespassing);[11] the integration of Dockum Drugs in Wichita, Kansas, after a month-long lunch-counter sit-in in August 1958; and the desegregation of the Katz Drug Store lunch counter in Oklahoma City, also in August 1958. During the 1950s many similar sit-in demonstrations failed to attract the attention of the national media. It was the February

---

9. August Meier and Elliott M. Rudwick's *CORE: A Study in the Civil Rights Movement, 1942–1968*, offers a comprehensive, lucidly written assessment of the organization.

10. Suzanne Bilyeu is of the same opinion that "earlier sit-ins in the Midwest and the South had, in some cases, led to the integration of local lunch counters. But they were mostly isolated incidents that hadn't gained momentum. The Greensboro sit-ins happened at just the right time and place" (25).

11. The ingenuity of the legal system to arrest sit-in demonstrators (charging the customers with trespassing) was motivated by the fact that racial segregation laws were "generally categorized as business licensing ordinances or health codes, not criminal violations" (Cooley, *To Live* 240).

1960 sit-in campaign in Greensboro, followed by demonstrations in Nashville a fortnight later, whose desegregation of lunch counters was best organized and the largest in scope, that finally achieved national media visibility. The sit-ins staged in those two locations "caught the imagination of the entire nation and received extensive and generally favorable coverage in national newspapers and on television" (Klarman 373). These instances in both Greensboro and Nashville created tension and social unrest by disturbing the racial status quo for the first time so far south of the Mason-Dixon line. According to David Brown and Clive Webb, the 1960 sit-in campaign "represent[ed] an important shift in black political action. None of the earlier protests had taken place in the heartland of the Jim Crow South, nor had they attracted national publicity" (296).

Apart from challenging Jim Crow segregation, the sit-ins also gal-vanized many students into action. As an instrument of grassroots antisegregation resistance, the sit-in campaign united students in forc-ing Woolworth's and other establishments to change their segregation-ist policies. To systematize the efforts and capitalize on the enthusiasm of the many student protestors who embraced the movement, in April 1960 a conference, sponsored by the Southern Christian Leadership Conference (SCLC),[12] was held at Shaw University in Raleigh, North Carolina (Wallach, "Civil Rights Movement" 159). Ella Baker, then executive director of the SCLC, met with 126 student delegates from Southern states "to discuss how to build on the political momentum created by the protests" (Brown and Webb 297). A new organization—the Student Nonviolent Coordinating Committee (SNCC)[13]—was founded, encouraged by Ella Baker, who believed that a more demo-cratic "group-centered leadership" should replace an organization built on the cult of personality surrounding the Reverend Martin Luther King Jr. (Brown and Webb 297). Baker reminded the students about the

---

12. Jessica Harris explains that "the Southern Christian Leadership Conference . . . , a loose confederation of churches, community organizations and civil rights groups, was formed, and it started to gain prominence and the support of liberal whites north and south. Soon it began to challenge the power of the National Association for the Advancement of Colored People . . . , the traditional black lead-ership organization, which had been instrumental in the passing of the historic *Brown* decisions in 1954" (*High on the Hog*, Chapter 9).

13. For an extensive and insightful study of the SNCC, see Iwan Morgan and Philip Davies, eds., *From Sit-Ins to SNCC: The Student Civil Rights Movement in the 1960s.*

desired impact of their nonviolent protests: "Whatever may be the difference in approach to their goal, the Negro and white students, North and South, are seeking to rid America of the scourge of racial segregation and discrimination—not only at lunch counters, but in every aspect of life" (375).[14] A similar sentiment was expressed in a "Wanted: Picketers" leaflet that was distributed in March 1960 at the University of North Carolina: "WHY WE PICKET—WE DO NOT PICKET . . . just because we want to eat. We can eat at home or walking down the street. . . . WE DO PICKET . . . to enlist the support of all (whatever the color) in getting services in business places that will grant us dignity and respect" (qtd. in Ferris, *The Edible South* 260–61).

The SNCC used the nonviolent sit-in tactic to intrude on the complacency of the White majority by refusing to behave in accordance with the subservience expected of them and, by extension, challenged the social disfranchisement that such subservience represented. The sit-in demonstrations made it "absolutely clear that the Negro is not satisfied with segregation" (Klarman 379).[15] Kwame Essien's assessment of the Greensboro Four's success—they "were successful in the sit-in movements partly because they employed nonviolent strategies" (349)—synecdochally refers to the whole sit-in campaign in which "nonviolence remained the underlying philosophy" (Cuthbert-Kerr 737).[16]

---

14. However, Gavin Wright claims, "the Greensboro students were not seeking a specific economic objective, and they were not planning a test case on constitutional grounds. But they were angry at the symbolic injustice of lunch counter exclusion and frustrated at the lack of progress since the *Brown* decision six years before" (80). Similarly, Julian Bond, an American social activist, recalls the impact of Ella Baker's "Bigger Than a Hamburger" speech: "I can remember it being an eye-opener to me, because I really had not thought about much more than a hamburger. We were doing lunch counter sit-ins, we wanted to integrate the lunch counters, and that was the deal. I knew that racial problems extended far beyond lunch counters. But I didn't see us doing anything like that, 'till she mentioned it there. So it was a real eye-opener, a real big step, a big leap for me. And I think it was for a lot of the other people too" (qtd. Hampton and Fayer 63).

15. Half a century after the events, Franklin McCain, one of the original Greensboro Four, confessed: "I felt that this could be the last day of my life. But I thought that it was well worth it. Because to continue to live the way we had been living—I questioned that. It's an incomplete life. I'd made up my mind that we absolutely had no choice" (Bilyeu 25).

16. For more information about nonviolent campaigns, consult James Peck, *Cracking the Color Line: Nonviolent Direct Action Methods of Eliminating Racial Discrimination*.

Student protestors were instructed and trained in Gandhian techniques of "nonviolent direct action" against the evil of inequality and segregation. Despite advances in the fight for racial equality (e.g., *Brown v. Board of Education*), de facto segregation was still the norm across the Southern United States in 1960.[17] Nonviolent confrontation leading to disruption of the entrenched racist status quo was deemed necessary.

In his "Letter from Birmingham Jail," Martin Luther King Jr. explained that nonviolent direct action was the only viable option as it "seeks to create such a crisis and foster such a tension that a community which has constantly refused to negotiate is forced to confront the issue. It seeks to dramatize the issue that it can no longer be ignored." However, as King explained in his Nobel Peace Prize lecture, this crisis should only be resolved peacefully; therefore,

> nonviolence in the civil rights struggle has meant not relying on arms and weapons of struggle. It has meant noncooperation with customs and laws which are institutional aspects of a regime of discrimination and enslavement. It has meant direct participation of masses in protest, rather than reliance on indirect methods which frequently do not involve masses in action at all. ("Peace and Justice")

King's Nobel lecture, delivered on December 11, 1964—almost five years after the Greensboro Four entered Woolworth's to challenge and erode Jim Crow segregation—captures the essence of the nonviolent approach to protest that he advocated:

> We will take direct action against injustice despite the failure of governmental and other official agencies to act first. We will not obey unjust laws or submit to unjust practices. We will do this peacefully, openly, cheerfully because our aim is to persuade. We adopt the means of nonviolence because our end is a community at peace with itself. We will try to persuade with our words, but if our words fail, we will try to persuade with our acts. We will always be willing to talk and seek fair compromise, but we are ready to suffer when necessary and even risk our lives to become witnesses to truth as we see it. ("Peace and Justice")

---

17. In his "Letter from Birmingham Jail," King summed up the protracted process of gaining racial equality in the American South: "The nations of Asia and Africa are moving with jetlike speed toward gaining political independence, but we still creep at horse-and-buggy pace toward gaining a cup of coffee at a lunch counter."

The sit-in demonstrators, and other nonviolent civil rights protestors, believed that the hurt and anger of the disfranchised had to be voiced so that social justice could finally prevail. As the leader of the civil rights movement, King expressed the view that in order to establish peaceful relations, grievances needed to be redressed: "I believe in this method because I think it is the only way to reestablish a broken community. It is the method which seeks to implement the just law by appealing to the conscience of the great decent majority who through blindness, fear, pride, and irrationality have allowed their consciences to sleep" ("Peace and Justice"). The aim of exposing and intruding upon the complacency of White Southern Christians,[18] according to King, was to seek understanding, reconciliation, and redemption. The desired result of his movement's nonviolence, therefore, was the vanquishing of social injustice, not individual people.[19]

The sit-in protests began in Greensboro, North Carolina, but mushroomed far beyond the state's borders. On February 2, the day after the Greensboro Four ignited the protest, they "were accompanied by twenty-three of their fellow classmates. By the end of the week, there were more than 300 student protesters" (Brown and Webb 295). The sit-ins swept across the South, generating a much greater level of social disruption than any other civil rights protest; the "Greensboro protest prompted an almost instant movement" (Cuthbert-Kerr 733). Students across the country, both Black and White, became active participants in the civil rights movement. As the sit-ins multiplied, by "April, seventy-eight communities had been affected by demonstrations involving 70,000 student activists, 3,000 of whom were arrested" (Brown and Webb 296). Not surprisingly, nonviolent protests set off a chain of counterreactions by defenders of the South's racial status quo. The forms of this nefarious backlash varied from putting signs in the windows saying "NO TRESPASSING," "We Reserve the Right to Service the Public As We See Fit," and "CLOSED—In the Interest

---

18. In "Letter from Birmingham Jail," King expressed his hope that "the white religious leadership of this [Birmingham] community would see the injustice of our cause and, with deep moral concern, would serve as the channel through which our just grievances could reach the power structure." However, he claims it was White ministers who put White consciousness to sleep: "In the midst of blatant injustices inflicted upon the Negro, I have watched white churchmen stand on the sideline and mouth pious irrelevancies and sanctimonious trivialities."

19. Based on "The King Philosophy."

of Public Safety" (Williams, *Eyes on the Prize* 127–29), to "abusive and violent resistance from the local white population as the Ku Klux Klan, Citizen's Council, and other white supremacists [who] staged counter protests and dumped condiments and water on them" (Cooley, *To Live* 228).

Staunch defenders of segregation gathered to harass the protestors, smearing the food they had ordered on the faces of the nonviolent protestors as an act of humiliation (Ferris, *The Edible South* 255). Store managers threatened the protestors with legal action (Cuthbert-Kerr 733), and "vigilantes and law enforcement officers . . . use[d] 'fascist-like tactics,' including tear gas, police dogs, and fire hoses" (Klarman 379). Such actions were part of Anne Moody's experience, which she recorded in her powerful memoir *Coming of Age in Mississippi* (1968). Moody recounts violent attacks ranging from chanting "anti-Negro" slogans, putting nooses around the protestors' necks, dousing them with ketchup and mustard, smearing them with pies, beating them with brass knuckles, kicking them, or rubbing salt into their bleeding wounds (Chapter 22). Despite those intentionally provocative reactions, "southern black youngsters, together with sympathetic whites, sat in at restaurants, lunch counters, and libraries; 'stood in' at movie theaters; 'kneeled in' at churches; and 'waded in' at beaches. All told, an estimated 70,000 people participated in such demonstrations, and roughly 4,000 were arrested. More than a hundred southern localities desegregated some public accommodations as a result" (Klarman 373). Instead of individual legal battles in courtrooms, students chose to take to the streets and segregated public places as a form of nonviolent direct action. For the first time, the struggle to end racial injustice combined legal action[20] and political endorsement[21] with direct public protest. This shift was perceptively captured by journalist Louis Lomax: "They were proof that the Negro leadership class, epitomized by the NAACP, was no longer the prime mover in the Negro's social revolt. The demonstrations have shifted the desegregation battles from the courtroom to the marketplace" (qtd. in Williams, *Eyes on the Prize* 136).

---

20. "The federal government also stepped in, and U.S. Attorney General William Rogers negotiated with the owners of chain stores in the South to end segregation" (Cuthbert-Kerr 735–36).

21. Sit-ins "were endorsed by many northern, and a few southern, politicians of both parties, including President Eisenhower, Vice President Nixon, and the leading Democratic presidential contenders" (Klarman 373).

The tremendous impact of the sit-ins on banning racial segregation by businesses offering food, accommodation, and entertainment to the public cannot be denied.[22] Yet the victories were unevenly distributed, because in "the Deep South, where resistance to racial reform remained most determined, the sit-ins failed to secure the desegregation of lunch counters, as white authorities launched a repressive crackdown on the demonstrators. However, in the more moderate Upper South the students successfully forced white businesses to integrate their facilities" (Brown and Webb 297). It took the Civil Rights Act of 1964 to outlaw racial segregation in public places. Essein concluded that "nationally, the most far-reaching results of the confrontational tactics inspired by the Greensboro Four during the sit-ins contributed to the 1963 March in Washington, the Civil Rights Act of 1964, and the passage of the Voting Rights Act in 1965" (349). The latter two, according to King, "came as a bright interlude in the long and sometimes turbulent struggle for civil rights: the beginning of a second emancipation proclamation providing a comprehensive legal basis for equality of opportunity" ("Peace and Justice").

"Bigger Than a Hamburger"

A Virginia-born poet, short story writer, and novelist, Anthony Grooms included "Food that Pleases, Food to Take Home" in his 1995 short story collection *Trouble No More*, which won the 1996 Lillian Smith Award for Fiction (Dickson-Carr 113). In 2006, *Trouble No More* was selected as the "Book All Georgians Should Read" by the Georgia Center for the Book. His only novel, *Bombingham* (2001), was praised for "its combination of lyricism, complex characters, and a delicate balance of history, politics, and a focus on simple humanity" (Dickson-Carr 113)—qualities that define *Trouble No More*. The narrators and protagonists in *Trouble No More* are "youths living during or after the Civil Rights movement, attempting to make sense of a world in which their ordinary wants and needs come into conflict with racism" (Dickson-Carr 113). Annie McPhee and Mary Taliferro, the two African American heroines of "Food that Pleases, Food to Take Home," are not

---

22. "The civil rights protests didn't end with a cup of coffee at Woolworth's. In 1963, another series of demonstrations in Greensboro . . . targeted movie theatres and cafaterias, as well as discriminatory hiring practices" (Bilyeu 27).

exceptions. Inspired by the sermon of their pastor, Reverend Bill Green, Annie and Mary decide to "demand their rights" at the lunch counter of a local store in Louisa, Virginia.[23] Their lunch counter demonstration is concerned with what Ella J. Baker, the executive director of the SCLC in 1960, famously described as "something much bigger than a hamburger or even a giant-sized Coke" (375). Their demand to be served reverberates with Ella Baker's aforementioned assumption that such direct protests "are seeking to rid America of the scourge of racial segregation and discrimination—not only at lunch counters, but in every aspect of life" (375).

Instead of "degenerate[ing] into pamphleteering,"[24] or "appropriate[ing] the movement as a satisfying morality tale in a larger American progress narrative" (Metress 148), or even presenting the civil rights sit-in demonstrations as ideologically homogeneous and unanimously nonviolent,[25] "Grooms's stories highlight the fact that African American communities are never monolithic, always comprising people allied to divergent factions but with their own personal and political problems that often parallel one another" (Dickson-Carr 113). A lack of social homogeneity, according to renowned British cultural anthropologist Victor Turner, fosters the potential for social dramas, which "reveal 'subcutaneous' levels of the social structure, for every 'social system' . . . is composed of many 'groups,' 'social categories,' statuses and roles, arranged in hierarchies and divided into segments" (*From Ritual* 10–11). Such is the case with the morally equivocal tone of Mary Taliferro and Annie McPhee's struggle for their rights in rural Louisa. The method of their resistance to racial segregation, be it Mary's head-on confrontation or Annie's strategy of nonviolent resistance, illustrates the four phases that Victor Turner ascribed to a social drama: breach, crisis, redressive action, and resolution. A breach in the status quo, if

---

23. The short story might be set in a not-altogether-fictitious rural area. Louisa is Anthony Grooms's hometown.

24. Reviewing *Trouble No More*, Diptiranjan Pattanaik remarks that Grooms "never allows the potentially combustible materials that define the black existence and quest for self-realization in America to degenerate into pamphleteering" (193).

25. Recent children's books, such as Andrea Davis Pinkney's *Sit-In: How Four Friends Stood Up by Sitting Down* and Carole Boston Weatherford's *Freedom on the Menu: The Greensboro Sit-Ins*, present the civil rights sit-ins as ideologically homogeneous and unanimously nonviolent. Both books use the 1960 Woolworth's sit-ins as historical source material for a literary interpretation of the struggle for integration narrated through the eyes of young Southern Black children.

not predicted and appeased, easily escalates into full-blown conflict. When conflict is stirred up, the parties involved have to negotiate and establish a new status quo. The cathartic and self-reflexive process of redressive actions may lead to a reconciliation—in other words, to "the reintegration of the disturbed social group" (Turner, *From Ritual* 71)—or, if negotiations fail, to a regression into crisis because of "the social recognition of irreparable breach between the contesting parties," owing to "permanent cleavage between the parties involved" (71). Whether the outcome of the social drama in Louisa can be interpreted as reintegrative or divisive depends not only on the aspirations of and methods used by the agents of change—Mary and Annie—but on their sensitivity and humanity.

A breach in the social status quo—the first phase of social drama—is not an accidental action. The act of overt nonconformity to the imposed social relations is always informed by social and historical circumstances. Recognizing that the "breach may be deliberately, even calculatedly, contrived by a person or party disposed to demonstrate or challenge entrenched authority" (Turner, *From Ritual* 70) entails accepting the fact that a challenge to segregated public eating places would not be possible if it were not for the changes in the Southern "eating out" landscape. Angela Cooley brilliantly captures the favorable conditions for such changes:

> The development of public eating spaces starting in the early twentieth century reveals an increasingly urban and mobile South attempting to accommodate more concentrated, diverse populations and an increasingly consumption-oriented culture. The leisure experience of dining out, which at one time had been limited primarily to a privileged elite feasting in carefully prescribed environments, gave way to a more motley assortment of lower-class establishments that hosted assorted crowds who ate out for necessity, convenience, or entertainment and often partook of a variety of less wholesome activities of urban indulgence. ("The Customer" 241)

Often family owned and operated, those new local eating establishments—stores with lunch counters or low-end eateries—catered to the appetites of the middle and lower classes. They transformed the Southern "dining landscape" so that it encompassed a wider demographic spectrum of clients.

The patronage of locally owned eating establishments more often than not reflected their proprietors' values and beliefs.[26] Their owners, often staunch defenders of segregation, made some concessions to African American customers—their dollars could buy them produce but that same money did not guarantee them service at the lunch counter:

> For the very accessibility and anonymity of the lunch counter made its symbolically invested boundaries dangerously permeable. Undefended by the economic mechanisms that regulate access to more expensive restaurants, lunch counters confer the mantle of social membership on anyone who eats, assimilating them indiscriminately to a kind of national space. At these uniquely affordable and American eating sites, the social distinctions traditionally drawn by norms of commensality, which differentiate those who are invited to sit at the social table from those who are excluded, were in special jeopardy. (Abel 165)

White supremacists believed that presence of both races at one lunch counter had to be avoided to protect racial purity[27]—hence the division into "White" and "Black" sections at the counter. Ironically, because of economic motivations and ideological imperatives in the 1930s, "lunch counters became the only social site at which sustained eye-to-eye encounters between the races were both imposed and proscribed" (Abel 161).

The emerging fast-food restaurants, such as White Castle, and the ubiquitous presence of national chains such as Woolworth's, an inexpensive five-and-dime store, manifested a similar social practice of

---

26. Cooley remarks that "the white supremacists that held out the longest for segregation tended to own and operate family restaurants that they treated like their own homes. For this reason, distinctions between the public and private were vague in their minds and ignored in their business practices. They interpreted civil rights victories as personal assaults on the white southern home and as a threat to the nature of whiteness. For civil rights activists, attacking segregation at lunch counters and other public eateries confronted the decades-long connection between food consumption and whiteness" (*To Live* 231).

27. Cooley observes that "lunch [counter] sit-ins implicated an important aspect of southern culture for white supremacists as well, specifically the maintenance of racial purity. Many of those who defended restaurant segregation most voraciously, such as Atlanta restaurateur Lester Maddox, actively connected it to notions of miscegenation and racial purity" (*To Live* 231).

racial apartheid, albeit on a larger scale. Because of its national character, Woolworth's, in principle, exhibited a democratizing tendency to invite and serve all customers. The emergence of chain stores in the South offered a promise of "sameness" with the Yankee scenes of consumption "bringing standardized food, service, and décor to very different geographic locales[;] one could purchase lunch anywhere and partake in identical scenes" (Abel 164). The fact that the lunch counters in department stores and drugstores were supposed to serve the purpose of "economic and social leveling (customers reduced to the same lowest common denominator and aligned along a counter rather than affiliated in groups around a table)" (165) troubled some White segregationists. "These spaces undoubtedly created a conundrum for the well-established segregation laws and racial customs that governed dining in public places in the South" (Cooley, *To Live* 224–25). Rather than embodying a promised space of consumption "anonymous, mechanical, and devoid of emotional content" (Abel 164), lunch counters in the South became a performative space, where Jim Crow segregation was obeyed and then later challenged.

Although the accessibility of merchandise at five-and-dime chain stores was supposedly determined only in dollars, in reality, and in common with family-owned establishments, it was measured in colors as well. The retailer did not discriminate against the "color" of the money spent on merchandise offered in the store; in other words, "Black money was good in these stores, but it only went so far" (Cooley, *To Live* 224). However, the purchasing power of a dollar was magically gone once African American customers wanted to sit down and be served at the lunch counter. In cases when "black customers wanted to eat, they had to purchase food to go or stand at designated 'colored' sections. In these chains, local control over service policies allowed segregation to prevail wherever it was provided for by law, custom, or the discretion of local management" (224–25). Hence, as Rebekah Kowal perceptively opines, "even as cash registers equalized shoppers, regardless of race, store lunch counters separated them solely on that basis. Woolworth's lunch counter, then, epitomized the illogic of segregation and symbolized the hypocrisy of white store owners who would take money from blacks when they shopped but not when they dined" (146–47). Somehow Woolworth's slogan—"Everybody's Store"—rings hollow in this context.

When protestors contrive to effect a breach, they have to carefully choose the place of coordinated protest. Thus, Greensboro's downtown Woolworth's lunch counter, now a civil rights landmark, was clearly targeted due to its significance—both local and national. On a local level, Woolworth's, located close to the "Crossroads of the Carolinas," was one of the few convenient and fairly inexpensive places to eat in Greensboro's deteriorating downtown area (Wolff 13). The store served a social function as well, as Rebekah Kowal explains: it was "one of the few places downtown where black and white residents came into social contact, since the white-owned shops in suburban shopping centers were mostly inaccessible to black people. In other words, routinely separated in their neighborhoods, schools, churches, and businesses by prohibitions and habit, the city's inhabitants mingled as they shopped in department stores like Woolworth's" (146). Miles Wolff also observes that Woolworth's position was secured on the town's foodscape: the food served there was "adequate, and the store's bakery, which [made] its own cakes and pastries, [was] one of the better bakeries in the city" (13). On a national level, Woolworth's status as a national chain store made it a likely candidate to stage a protest: "Woolworth's was chosen specifically because it was a national chain and was vulnerable to pressure from outside the South" (Cuthbert-Kerr 733).[28] Not only did sit-in activism in Woolworth's receive national media coverage; the "news of the Greensboro sit-in spread quickly through a network of young activists, often connected to black colleges, black churches, and local civil rights groups in the South" (Cuthbert-Kerr 733).

Christopher Metress claims that "the civil rights movement circulates in American memory" not only through historical but also verbal artifacts such as literary representations (141). His analysis of the reemplotment of Martin Luther King Jr.'s memoir (*Why We Can't Wait*) in Anthony Grooms's novel *Bombingham* provides eloquent arguments for "the cognitive value of literary discourse in the production of social memory" (141). Extending his arguments to other literary representations of the movement, I propose an analysis of Grooms's short story "Food that Pleases, Food to Take Home" as a creative and valuable

---

28. Stentiford concurs that "the Woolworth's lunch counter was one of the nation's largest restaurant chains, and often was responsible for a large percentage of each store's profits. As a national chain, it was more vulnerable to the negative publicity the incident [of sit-ins] brought" (604).

means of "enriching our understanding of the black freedom struggle of the mid-twentieth century" (Metress 141). In this short story, Grooms exhibits what Metress dubbed the ability of literature "to keep alive the movement's power to speak effectively to the unresolved challenges of our times" (148). By capturing the moment of social crisis and change enacted at real-life Southern lunch counters, Grooms's "social drama" offers exactly what Metress advocates: "a more expansive view of civil rights history" (Metress 141).

The historical background of Mary and Annie's protest against the discriminatory exclusion of African Americans in public eating places is firmly established at the beginning of the short story:

> Annie McPhee wasn't sure about what Mary Taliferro was telling her. Mary said that colored people in Louisa should stand up for their rights. They were doing it in the cities. Mary said that Channel Six from Richmond had shown pictures of Negroes sitting in at lunch counters. . . . Walter Cronkite had shown pictures from Albany and Birmingham. Negroes were on the move. (Grooms, "Food" 133)

To add righteousness to their planned protest, Mary refers to Reverend Green's sermon, from which she deduces that "the Lord helps them that helps themselves. . . . The Lord will part the Red Sea of injustice and send down the manna of equal rights" (134). If Black people underplay self-respect and do not demand equal treatment, the reverend's sermon implies, White people will not treat them with the respect due to all humans regardless of the color of their skin. Annie and Mary answer his call to action, albeit with different levels of enthusiasm and different fears. Instead of marching down Main Street to "tell them white folks that we want our rights" (133), as Mary suggests and that Annie is sure everyone would be scared to do, they decide instead to stage a protest at May's Drugstore, a local business with a lunch counter in Louisa.

As the protest's initiator, Mary has a more participatory voice than Annie, who seems timid, jittery, and defensive. Mary illustrates a more militant dimension of Black activism, and consequently she would most likely be perceived by Whites as what Charles Johnson called an "uppity nigger" who, as he describes, "does not 'know his place' and dangerously disturbs race relations by trying to be what he is not and never can be. . . . He demands rights instead of requesting favors. He stirs up other Negroes by 'inventing' wrongs. He is, if anything, more dangerous than the 'bad nigger,' because he is more subtle in linking his annoying pretenses with values otherwise approved by the culture" (*Growing Up* 281).

Even Mary's appearance and body language reflect her refusal to sell herself short and accept a socially subservient position. Her belligerent attitude is emphasized not only in her "determined stride" but more importantly in her attire (Grooms, "Food" 135). On the one hand, the women "put on Sunday suits, high heels, and pillboxes" (134), casting themselves as respectable members of the middle class.[29] Mary and Annie's elaborate attire adheres to the dress code recommended by the organizers of sit-ins in Greensboro: "Students will wear dress attire or other pertinent clothing. (Young ladies are urged to look their best and gentlemen wear ties.)" (Kowal 138).

On the other hand, both women are elaborately attired in order to provoke White people. Their description—"they dressed to kill" (Grooms, "Food" 134)—carries the same semantic context in the case of both women—they are dressed in fancy clothes to impress and provoke others. The fact that they are in their finery demonstrates that they are, to use Ralph Ellison's expression, "stewards of something uncomfortable, burdensome" (431). However, Mary's ostentatious fashion announces her contentious—even confrontational—attitude toward White people.[30] Rather than disguise her anger and hostility toward White society, she flaunts them. Indeed, she can hardly contain her fury: "White people make me sick. Every last one of them. Sick. What I'd really like to do is to take ole lady May by her scrawny little neck and

---

29. To coordinate a response to the Greensboro sit-ins, Mayor George Roach appointed an "Advisory Committee on Community Relations" (Martin, "Let's All Sit Together"). Woolworth's management yielded to public pressure and informed the Advisory Committee about the store's desegregation on July 21, 1960. The final decision of Woolworth's manager to "serve all properly dressed and well-behaved people" neatly reverberates with Annie and Marie's elaborate attire to underscore their middle-class respectability ("The Greensboro Chronology").

30. Actually, Mary may be less pugnacious than she leads Annie, and even herself, to believe. The choice of the time of their performance would testify to that: "They parked at the far end of the onestoplight street deserted in the cool midmorning. People were at work in the factory, or in the fields, or at the schools. The few people they passed stared at them, but no one knew them" (Grooms, "Food" 134–35). If she truly wanted their protest to be noticed and consequently to sit "up there on Walter Cronkite" (134), then she might have chosen a more suitable time.

choke her. . . . I'd like to kick a piece of her butt" (Grooms, "Food" 135). With the benefit of hindsight (the outcome of Mary's actions in May's store), one might risk the statement that Mary's aggressive words and actions acquire promissory character.

Their exaggerated costume—"Mary wore her good wig. They put on lipstick and rouge and fake eyelashes" (134)—may also be interpreted as an emblem of negotiating their identity. Mary and Annie seem to be acting on the principle that "once visible, it [the breach] can hardly be revoked" (Turner, *From Ritual* 70). They have been brought up in a world where Whiteness is synonymous with being American; they know, to use George Lipsitz's words, that "whiteness never has to speak its name, never has to acknowledge its role as an organizing principle in social and cultural relations" (*The Possessive Investment* 1).[31] Thus, in order to act against the absence of racial being, which takes the form of imposed invisibility in public spaces, these two African American women make a spectacle. The aura of theatricality surrounding them bears the markings of cultural performances that "provide an intricate counterpoint to the unconscious practices of everyday life, as they are stylistically marked expressions of 'otherness' and identity" (Hoelscher 661). Thus, Mary and Annie, by requesting service at the lunch counter, make a social stance against social exclusion. The act of challenging racial segregation laws, which acquires features of staged theatrical activity, becomes a cultural expression of "the dissensus with visuality"[32]—the invisible that refuses to be unseen.

Mary and Annie decide to articulate and perform their subjectivity in May's Drugstore, one of the typical family-operated lunch places in the South, which "often started as a sideline to some other business enterprise. Such places generally did not feature the fancy décor, architecture, or cuisine of finer dining establishments. The seating arrangements, décor, and menus of quick order establishments revolved

---

31. In a similar fashion, Hoelscher posits that "many people . . . merge their perceived absence of racial being with the nation, enabling whiteness to become their unspoken but most profound sense of what it means to be an American, and, by necessity, making all other racialized identities an Other" (662).

32. In his discussion of the emancipation of enslaved people, the right to subjectivity, and countervisuality, Nicholas Mirzoeff refers to Rancière's explanation of "the dissensus with visuality," which is "a dispute over what is visible as an element of a situation, over which visible elements belong to what is common, over the capacity of subjects to designate this common and argue for it" (478).

A SWEET TASTE OF VICTORY

around function" (Cooley, *To Live* 114). The lunch counter installed in May's Drugstore seems to be generic:

> Along the left wall was a linoleumtopped lunch counter with five backless stools anchored in front of it. It was junked with jars of pickles, loaves of sandwich bread, buns and cake plates bearing doughnuts and pies. The spigots of a broken soda fountain were partially hidden in the clutter. Behind the counter was a grand mirror with ornate framing. It was placarded with menus and handwritten signs announcing "specials." The mirror was grease-spattered on one side from a small electric grill that sat on a shelf. On the other side, two huge coolers stood bubbling lemonade and orangeade. A broken neon sign above the mirror announced, "FOOD THAT PLEASES, FOOD TO TAKE HOME." High above were shelves on which rested plastic wreaths of cemetery flowers. (Grooms, "Food" 136)

By installing a lunch counter, a store owner can offer customers a wider range of service, thus generating more profit. However, a lunch counter adds to the "racial messiness of consumer culture" (Hale 186) by creating the aforementioned conflict of accepting "Black" money for purchased goods but not for service at the lunch counter. The sign above the lunch counter attempts to clear up the "racial messi-ness" resulting from "the hypocrisy of allowing African Americans to shop in the store, but preventing them from using the lunch counter" (Cuthbert-Kerr 733). If we accept Abel's claim that "signs at eating places elsewhere attempt to regulate points of cultural entry through a relatively conscious process of selection" (170), then this particular sign serves as a reminder of de facto, if not de jure, Jim Crow segrega-tion. The sign positions a customer both outside and inside the patri-archal home—the food offered at this lunch counter is so pleasing that you can take it home and your family will love it.[33] The host of a White family home is implied by the sheer "White" ownership of the store. Thus, the wording of this sign serves as an invitation to a "White" house. Through these allusions to home and hearth, the sign maintains White supremacy—"White supremacists continued to connect places where food was consumed to racial purity and to the decorum of the

---

33. Much like signs, slogans performed a similar function in this context. For instance, in 1966 the McDonald's chain "increased the family feel of the company by introducing the new slogan 'The Closest Thing to Home'" (Cooley, *To Live* 226).

white southern home" (Cooley, "The Customer" 265). Capitalizing on the image of the White family home, this sign resonates with the connection between racial purity and the rigid structures of segregation upheld both in domestic and public spaces.[34]

If we alter our frame of reference for a moment and turn from the White owner and implied White customer to an African American consumer, then quite interestingly, the rhetoric of the sign "FOOD THAT PLEASES, FOOD TO TAKE HOME" regresses from inclusion to exclusion. As Abel observes, "signs regulate access to eating places" (170); thus, the wording of this particular sign finds resonance with Jim Crow restrictions, under which "only white patrons could use the seats, black patrons had to either get their food to go, or eat it while standing" (Stentiford 604). An invitation to sit down at the lunch counter, an act that would replicate the feeling of communion of individuals at the table in a family home, is removed from the sign—here Black customers are disinvited from the fellowship of the table. The sign "invites" Black customers to be satisfied with takeaway food; they are prevented from being incorporated into the social and moral order. Thus a "Black" expulsion from commensality replaces a "White" invitation. During the first half of the twentieth century, African Americans *seemingly* accepted "racial erasure" from public eating establishments and other social places through acts of forced subservience. However, once African Americans begin to challenge discrimination, once they refused to concede to the manners of subservience, then the segregation signs become "as much admissions of weakness as labels of power" (Hale 193). The condition of the sign in May's Drugstore—it is a broken neon sign, after all—suggests that tensions concerning racial relations have reached such unprecedented levels that the social situation is beyond repair. The social order imposed by Southern White supremacists no longer functions as intended. The wreaths of cemetery flowers placed on the shelves above the sign augur the demise of Jim Crow.

When Mary and Annie enter the store with the intention of contesting Jim Crow discrimination, they make their voice of dissent heard and their once latent rebellion visible. The physical clash between disciplinary measures of segregation (the agents and signs of White

---

34. Cooley remarks that "many white southerners continued to make [connection] between food consumption, racial purity, and—by implication—the home to which such matters ultimately alluded" ("The Customer" 265).

supremacy) and "antidiscipline" of those forced thus far to submissiveness (African American consumers) constitutes the second phase of the social drama in the South during the civil rights movement.[35] Victor Turner asserts that the crisis is "a momentous juncture or turning point in the relations between components of a social field—at which seeming peace becomes overt conflict and covert antagonisms become visible. Sides are taken, factions are formed" (*From Ritual* 70). Mary and Annie decide to expose the injustice in cross-racial relations through the direct action of civil disobedience. Hence, their creative performance is clearly part of a social drama, which, "in its full formal development, its full phase structure, . . . is a process of converting particular values and ends, distributed over a range of actors, into a system (which may be temporary or provisional) of shared or consensual meaning" (Turner, *On the Edge* 203).

By demanding to be served at a lunch counter in areas designated for "Whites only," African Americans created disharmony in the Southern status quo. Chaos, threats, and fear of the social consequences of interracial dining are evoked by the fact that "one main message of food, everywhere, is *solidarity*. Eating together means sharing and participating. The word 'companion' means 'bread sharer' (Latin *cum panis*). . . . we evolved as food sharers and feel a natural link between sharing food and being personally close and involved" (Anderson, *Everyone Eats* 125). Against the claims of the defenders of segregation that "the eating in public places by people who are perfect strangers can mean only one thing, and that is that they are both or severally hungry," an explanation offered two weeks after the advent of sit-ins at Woolworth's (Abel 163), African Americans knew—and White counterdemonstrators did not wish to acknowledge—the fact that the act of interracial public consumption is not ideologically neutral. As Abel

---

35. My understanding of discipline and antidiscipline stems from the work of Michel de Certeau, who postulates an interesting dynamic between everyday practices. In his book *The Practice of Everyday Life*, Certeau explains that his goal is "not to make clearer how the violence of order is transmuted into a disciplinary technology, but rather to bring to light the clandestine forms taken by the dispersed, tactical, and makeshift creativity of groups or individuals already caught in the nets of 'discipline.' Pushed to their ideal limits, these procedures and ruses of consumers compose the network of an antidiscipline" (xiv–xv). My reading of Grooms's short story applies Certeau's analysis more narrowly to explore the conflict in Southern public eating facilities.

explains, "Eating together in public means more than 'only one thing,' which is why the prospect of interracial eating provoked the anxiety that needed to be calmed" (163). Hence, the disharmony in the status quo stirred by the demand to be served at a "White" lunch counter was rightly identified as demanding full rights of citizenship,[36] and as such, was an "exercise for the spread of American democracy" (Cooley, *To Live* 231).

Social dramas, arising in conflicts, are units of disharmonious social processes (Turner, *Dramas* 37–41). The processual form of social drama, according to Turner, replicates the processual view of culture, which moves through the phases of structure and antistructure. Turner posits that humankind "grows through antistructure, and conserves through structure" (*From Ritual* 114). Thus structure creates status quo and order within systems; it preserves culture (Turner, *From Ritual* 36). Madison contends that "structure is all that which constitutes order, system, preservation, law hierarchy, and authority" (160). However, order comes at a cost. Its costs are social obligations and legal restraint.[37] In the American South the obvious cost of imposed social order/structure was the disfranchisement of African Americans. Acting against their social exclusion, if not erasure, African Americans begin to object publicly and pointedly during the civil rights movement to their systemic and individual abuse. They devised creative ways of challenging the Jim Crow social order[38]—by not giving a seat to a White

---

36. The assertion of the right to equal treatment is present in various accounts of the events in Greensboro. For instance, one of the students told United Press International, "We believe, since we buy books and papers in the other part of the store, we should get served in this part" (qtd. in Lewis 86). Analyzing similar voices led Cooley to believe that "the ability to participate in conspicuous consumption became an important element of American democracy. Civil rights activists considered sit-ins and other forms of direct action protest toward discrimination in public eating places to be important elements for accessing these and other rights of citizenship" ("The Customer" 264).

37. Victor Turner asserts that "in people's social structural relationships they are by various abstract processes generalized and segmentalized into roles, statuses, classes, cultural sexes, conventional age-divisions, ethnic affiliations, etc. In different types of social situations they have been conditioned to play specific social roles. It does not matter how well or how badly as long as they 'make like' they are obedient to the norm sets that control different compartments of the complex model known as the 'social structure'" (*From Ritual* 46).

38. Victor Turner connects creativity and innovativeness with antistructure:

person, or ordering coffee at a "White" lunch counter. The creativity of their nonviolent protest reveals the latent antistructure, which, according to Turner, is the "dissolution of normative social structure, with its role-sets, statuses, jural rights and duties" (*From Ritual* 28).

Mary and Annie seem to be agents of antistructure, which, according to Madison, "constitutes human action beyond systems, hierarchies, and constraints" (160). The women no longer want to concede to the manners of subservience imposed on them by the social order. However, they understand the social and legal consequences of their transgression of public eating places—instead of sitting with Walter Cronkite, Annie bitterly remarks, they might end up sitting in the Louisa jail (Grooms, "Food" 134).[39] For this very reason, initially their gestures and bodily reactions are marked with a mixture of anxiety and excitement:

> Mary pushed closer to the counter, took a deep breath, and pulled herself up onto the first stool. She sat for a moment, her eyes as excited as a child's on a fairground ride. "You ever sit on one of these?" She caught herself for being too loud. She put on a serious face, her lips folded under so as not to look too big, placed her feet on the shiny circular footrest, and adjusted her skirt.
>
> Mary beckoned to Annie to sit on the stool beside her, and gingerly as a child testing hot bathwater, Annie sat. She pulled herself up on the stool, forgetting to smooth her skirt as Mary had done. She sat ready to jump down at any moment. (Grooms, "Food" 136–37)

Sally, a heavy woman with a soft face who works both as a May's shop assistant and a counter waitress, immediately recognizes these customers as a threat to the status quo—"When she saw the girls, the woman looked confused for a moment, then she looked frightened and wrung her hands. 'May I help ya?' she asked" (Grooms, "Food" 137). The confusion and fear written on Sally's face, combined with the fact that she has no vested interest in helping out (she is the owner's sister-in-law

---

"liminal and liminoid situations . . . are the settings in which new models, symbols, paradigms, etc. arise—as the seedbeds of cultural creativity" (*From Ritual* 28).

39. The legal repercussions of Mary and Annie's daring endeavor are ominously represented by the location of May's Drugstore on the urban landscape. When both women enter the street where May's is located, "Annie looked straight ahead down the street of wooden and brick shops. The perspective was broken by the courthouse square and the little brick jailhouse beside it" (Grooms, "Food" 135).

from West Virginia),[40] are all grist for the protestors' mill when it comes to challenging Jim Crow segregation.

Emboldened by the favorable circumstances, Mary wants to place an order. From the very beginning of the story, she does not seem to advocate the philosophy and methods of nonviolence, which Sally clearly senses, standing back "as if ready to retreat into the storage room" (Grooms, "Food" 137). When Mary states her demand—"We don't want no takeout. . . . We want to eat at the counter like White folks. We want you to write it down on your little pad and bring us silverware wrapped in a napkin"—the shop assistant blanches (Grooms, "Food" 137). Her defensive statement, "I can't served colored," ignites Mary's open rebellion. At this stage of confrontation, Mary's manner is still civil, though not particularly friendly: "'Why can't choo?' Mary said. She tried to sound sophisticated. 'You have the food. You have the stove. All we want is a hamburger and some fries.' She pointed to the orangeade. 'And some of that orange drink'" (Grooms, "Food" 137). Behind Mary's cool logic lies a social demand, to use Ella Baker's phrase again, of "something much bigger than a hamburger" (375). If it were just about the dish, Mary would gladly accept takeout. But she seems to have her mind and heart set on an open confrontation. Mary may share the goals with sit-in protestors in Greensboro, but when the conflict escalates she progressively negates all the prescriptions of nonviolent demonstrations.

Annie is the one interested in nonviolent and peaceful desegregation; on their way to May's Drugstore, she reminds Mary: "We're

40. Angela Cooley remarks that "the earliest sit-ins tended to take place at national chains and local department stores, such as Woolworth's, S. H. Kress, Howard Johnson's, or Rich's, in which store managers had no proprietary interest. The managers generally refused to serve African Americans based on community custom and local law. Most managers responded to sit-ins by closing the counter, ordering all customers to leave the premises, and calling the police" (*To Live* 239). When Black protestors occupied the lunch counter seats on the principle "sit until served," the waitresses could not serve White customers either. Hence, sit-ins diminished sales. Thus, bending under economic pressure, "six months after the sit-ins began, Harris, the manager of the Greensboro Woolworth's, finally relented: The sit-ins had already cost him $150,000 in lost business. On July 25, 1960, the lunch counter served its first black customers—four Woolworth's employees who worked in the store's kitchen" (Bilyeu 27). Similarly, Miles Wolff posits that it is the reduced revenue in Woolworth's and other shops affected by sit-ins that led to the desegregation of lunch counters: "Economic pressure, not constitutional mandate, appears the best explanation for the success of the sit-ins" (174).

suppose to be peace demonstrators. . . . let's do this the right way. Let's just go in and ask to be served" (Grooms, "Food" 135). Her language and actions exemplify caution, self-discipline, and moderation, the very qualities that were supposed to define the actions of nonviolent demonstrators.[41] Her response to the shop assistant's plea for understanding of the position she is in embodies the essence of nonviolence: "'Yes, ma'am,' Annie said, then cleared her throat, took a deep breath, fought to control her jittery voice. 'We just want our rights'" (137). Her careful manner of articulation and succinct phrasing reflect what Martin Luther King Jr. envisioned for a nonviolent protest: "We do not want to instill fear in others or into the society of which we are a part. The movement does not seek to liberate Negroes at the expense of the humiliation and enslavement of whites. It seeks no victory over anyone. It seeks to liberate American society and to share in the self-liberation of all the people" ("Peace and Justice"). The second part of Annie's statement wonderfully illustrates the essence of African American nonviolent protest, which, according to John Franklin, "is clear, straightforward, unequivocal, and without threats or even guile. Quite often it appeals to the humanity of the perpetrators, and it relies on the paradox, the inner contradiction of the position against which it speaks" (97). Hence, Annie indirectly makes clear that her desire to be served at the lunch counter should not be construed as an attack on an

---

41. The Greensboro Four formed the Student Executive Committee for Justice in order to guide other students in organizing and staging sit-ins. During the Greensboro sit-ins, nonviolent protestors were offered scripts of possible conversations between a White female counter waitress and a Black customer at the lunch counter. Such typical exchanges exuded students' caution and self-discipline. In his article "Students Hit Woolworth's for Lunch Service," published in the *A&T Record* on February 5, 1960, Albert L. Rozier Jr. included the conversation between Blair, one of the Greensboro Four, and the counter waitress at Woolworth's:

Blair: I'd like a cup of coffee, please.

Waitress: I'm sorry. We don't serve colored here.

Blair: I beg to disagree with you. You just finished serving me at a counter only two feet from here.

Waitress: Negroes eat on the other end.

Blair: What do you mean? This is a public place, isn't it? If it isn't, then why don't you sell membership cards? If you do that, then I'll understand that this is a private concern.

Waitress: Well you won't get any service here.

(qtd. in Kowal 140–41)

individual person (an opponent in racial strife), but rather an attempt to defeat the evil system of segregation, oppressive policies, and unjust acts.[42]

In contradistinction to Annie, Mary does not show herself as cautious, friendly, or nonthreatening, even though nonviolence was supposed to win understanding and friendship—two necessary steps, according to Dr. King, to redemption and reconciliation in racial relations.[43] Mary is certainly not interested in peacefully bringing about desegregation; instead, she wants to make a spectacle of occupying a seat at the lunch counter on the principle that she has the right to "sit until served." She unabashedly admits that she wants to make a stand: "'I'm not taking a step until I get served,' Mary said. 'I don't care if Miss May—if the owner—ain't here. You in charge and I want my rights'" (Grooms, "Food" 138). Not only does she engage in the confrontational exchange of arguments, which sit-in protestors were prohibited from doing, but she also strikes back, both verbally and physically, when Mrs. May's sister-in-law declines to serve her.[44] The conflict escalates on both sides. As Mary becomes more aggressive, the waitress moves from defensive to offensive. Sally begins with a preemptive withdrawal ("I don't want any trouble"), then an offer of takeout ("I will give you some food if you'll just take it home"), through a veiled threat ("Mr. May will be back from the hospital soon and . . . please . . ."), to a threat of legal action ("I don't want to have to call the police. Don't make me call nobody") (137–38).

There is a breach in Sally's defensive strategy, however. Mary,

---

42. All those goals of nonviolence were mentioned by Martin Luther King Jr. in his "Letter from Birmingham Jail."

43. King envisioned a path toward redemption and reconciliation, via friendship and understanding, in his *Stride toward Freedom*. A commentary on these and the other tenets of King's philosophy of nonviolence is provided by the Martin Luther King, Jr. Center for Nonviolent Social Change, http://www.thekingcenter.org.

44. Mary's confrontational stance is reminiscent of the Black Panthers' direct action as a response to police brutality and economic oppression in Black communities. Apart from their combative attitude and disruptive actions, the Black Panthers were committed to their communities. In the late 1960s, for instance, in order to improve the lives of African Americans, they organized the Free Breakfast for Children and Free Food for the Public programs, which "sought to 'bend the bars of empire' by sustaining community through alternative food spaces" (Slocum 313).

showing her "war" face, immediately notices the inherent illogic of her opponent's response and turns it against the waitress:

> "If it were up to me . . ." the woman said. "If it were up to me, I would be glad to serve you. I don't mind colored. Honest. I'm from West Virginia."
>
> "It *is* up to you," Mary said, a crooked, dimpled smile on her face. "Who else is here? How come you don't want us Negroes to have our rights?" (138)

With her fighting spirit adjusted high to fit the external circumstances, Mary moves far from the nonviolent negotiations advocated by King and embraced by sit-in protestors. For Mary, a White person is either a segregationist or not; there is no gray in-between area and she does not account for the individual circumstances a person may find themselves in. Therefore, Mary's unequivocal condemnation of the gray area allows her to notice her opponent's faulty reasoning and use it against her. Not as blinded by anger at and hatred of White people as Mary is, Annie shows greater sensitivity to other people's plight. Having heard moans from the storage room since approaching the counter, Annie adjusts her actions accordingly: "Maybe Mrs. May was dead, she thought, and someone was crying. They shouldn't be causing this trouble if Mrs. May was dead. 'Well, maybe we should come back when Mrs. May is here,' Annie said vacantly" (138).

The resulting offer of a takeout sandwich that Sally makes to Annie represents the epitome of that very grayness, the condescending charity used as a precautionary measure to appease a conflict; Mary therefore interprets it as offensive:

> "Ain't that some mess?" Mary said, putting her hands on her hips. "You even give us food, but you don't want us to sit and eat it like people. You rather see us go out back and eat it like a dog. I know how you white people is. I done seen it. You have your damn dog eat at the table with you, but you won't let a colored person. Do I look like a dog to you?" (138)

Not only does Mary compare the predicament of African Americans to domesticated, servile, and submissive creatures, but also—and even more importantly—she raises the issue of visibility. The social body is what is at stake in the act of collective eating, the social body that is shaped and expressed not only by those who eat together but, crucially, by those who see them doing so. Elizabeth Abel offers an interesting observation about social barriers demarcated by the visibility of the social body:

> The sense of the nation that had been formed by collective eating was renegotiated in terms of collective seeing. The social body was constituted not by those who ate together, but by those who saw each other eating together. . . . [T]o not see others eating (even if one heard them) was equivalent to not eating with them. This reconstitution of the social body in terms of those seen eating together is simply a strong version of a commonplace of social dining: that one goes to restaurants not only for their oral gratification but also for the social incorporation gained by being seen, and by seeing oneself, eating in the company of others. (180)

Thus, Sally acts as a guard of social barriers that the social Other should not break. As an agent of social order, the waitress has to safeguard it from the intrusion of an alien, unwanted element. Her response of "I can't served colored" removes the responsibility for social exclusion from herself and onto the collective White hegemony, whose law she is obliged to obey.

When Sally looks "to see if somebody white [is] out there," she may be doing so for two reasons. For one, White people in the store might support her endeavors to contain the crisis by either intimidation or threatening legal action. However, she also might be looking to see if anyone can see female African American customers being served by a White woman. Thus, her offer of takeout food eliminates the element of the problematic visibility of African Americans sitting and eating at the lunch counter. Bearing in mind that, as Harry Golden mockingly observed, "it is only when the Negro 'sets' that the fur begins to fly," the semantic context of a takeout offer and "the Vertical Negro Plan" Golden proposed are the same. He conceived this plan to solve the problem of segregation in public spaces in a 1956 *Carolina Israelite* editorial of that title.[45] Golden satirically advocates the return of Vertical Segregation: "Since no one in the South pays the slightest attention to a VERTICAL NEGRO, this will completely solve our problem" (106). According to Golden's observations, White Southerners have accepted coexistence with Blacks in public spaces such as shops, because

---

45. "The Vertical Negro Plan" appears in Golden's *Only in America* (1958).

customers of all colors stand, walk, and mingle.[46] However, the equality of customers and the purchasing power of their money ends the moment they decide to sit down. Then all the problems begin. Clearly meant as a measure to ridicule White Southerners' hypocrisy, Golden's article argues that equality in the South can be achieved by simply making African Americans *stand* at lunch counters, in schools, or in offices.[47] Interestingly enough, Woolworth's stores in Greensboro attempted to achieve equality of their customers by enforcing their version of Vertical Negro segregation: the stores "allowed black customers to purchase merchandise, but they could not eat with white customers sitting by the counters. Also, blacks could eat while standing" (Essien 348–49).

Since the "out of sight, out of mind" solution can no longer be applied in May's Drugstore—Mary and Annie have ostentatiously settled themselves on the lunch counter stools—Sally has to contain the crisis. Her responses to Mary's increasingly confrontational stance are a logical consequence of the social exchange. At first these responses involve both defensive and protective practices, which, as Erving Goffman stated, "comprise the techniques employed to safeguard the impression fostered by an individual during his presence before others" (7). However, Mary's verbal escalation disrupts the projected definition of civil relations between two races: "'I'll tell you what *is* my business . . . This here piece of pie is. And I got a good mind to help myself to it right now.' She reached out for the lid of the pie plate" (Grooms, "Food" 139). If Mary were to use tact and respect in interacting with her opponent, she would be operating in accord with the precepts of nonviolent protest, which according to Dr. King, "seeks to secure moral ends through moral means. Nonviolence is a powerful and just weapon.

---

46. In his editorial, Golden demonstrates that "one of the factors involved in [North Carolina's] tremendous industrial growth and economic prosperity is the fact that the South, voluntarily, has all but eliminated VERTICAL SEGREGATION. The tremendous buying power of the twelve million Negroes in the South has been based wholly on the absence of racial segregation. The white and Negro *stand* at the same grocery and supermarket counters; deposit money at the same bank teller's window; pay phone and light bills to the same clerk; walk through the same dime and department stores, and *stand* at the same drugstore counters" (106; emphasis added).

47. Golden suggests removing all desks from schools (because then students would be made to stand all day) and introducing only standing-up jobs as ways to achieve racial equality in the South ("The Vertical Negro Plan").

Indeed, it is a weapon unique in history, which cuts without wounding and ennobles the man who wields it" ("Peace and Justice"). Unwilling to internalize the values of nonviolence, Mary's hostile behavior not only generates anomie but also affects Sally's reactions.

This correspondence between one's self-projection and the demand to be treated accordingly had been posited by Erving Goffman in his *Presentation of Self in Everyday Life*, published in 1959 before the advent of the Greensboro sit-ins:

> Society is organized on the principle that any individual who possesses certain social characteristics has a moral right to expect that others will value and treat him in a correspondingly appropriate way. Connected with this principle is a second, namely that an individual who implicitly or explicitly signifies that he has certain social characteristics out to have this claim honored by others and ought in fact to be what he claims he is. (6)

Because Mary does not attempt negotiation, instead simply making demands—"'I told you I wanted it here.' She jabbed her finger on the countertop. 'Why don't you admit it? You just like every white person I ever seen. Just as prejudice' as the day is long'" (Grooms, "Food" 139)—the confrontation does not unfold according to her plan. The threat of violence implicitly suggested in her body language cannot secure her desired social equality, because, as King said,

> Violence as a way of achieving racial justice is both impractical and immoral. . . . It solves no social problem: it merely creates new and more complicated ones. Violence is impractical because it is a descending spiral ending in destruction for all. It is immoral because it seeks to humiliate the opponent rather than win his understanding: it seeks to annihilate rather than convert. Violence is immoral because it thrives on hatred rather than love. It destroys community and makes brotherhood impossible. . . . It creates bitterness in the survivors and brutality in the destroyers. ("Peace and Justice")[48]

Sensing the impending downward spiral of verbal assault, if not outright physical violence, Sally wants to pacify the situation: "Don't be

---

48. Such an opinion is clearly alien to Mary and other more militant social and political activists. Mary rejects the gradualist principle of achieving goals (King's nonviolence). Rather, her behavior and actions show an affinity for drastic change and direct confrontation (Malcolm X's stance).

ugly. . . . Just take it and go" (Grooms, "Food" 138). Mary treats another preventive offer of a takeout made to compensate for the situation as a sign of weakness. This realization gives impetus to her rising hatred and violence. As a response to Sally's offer, "Mary stood stiffly, smiled. There was a small silence. 'Serve me,' she demanded" (139) without heed to Martin Luther King Jr.'s advice "not [to] seek to satisfy our thirst for freedom by drinking from the cup of bitterness and hatred" ("I Have a Dream"). The more Mary's responses fill with vitriol and violence, the more the weakness in her espoused values is exposed.[49]

Once the civility of such an interaction breaks down, both sides of the confrontation adjust their expectations and methods of conflict resolution to fit the situation at hand. Erving Goffman states that

> when an individual projects a definition of the situation and thereby makes an implicit or explicit claim to be a person of a particular kind, he automatically exerts a moral demand upon the others, obliging them to value and treat him in the manner that persons of his kind have a right to expect. He also implicitly forgoes all claims to be things he does not appear to be and hence forgoes the treatment that would be appropriate for such individuals. The others find, then, that the individual has informed them as to what is and as to what they ought to see as the "is." (6–7)

In a sense, Mary will get what she wanted. Using argumentative and violent verbal exchanges, accompanied by correspondingly aggressive body language, Mary creates a hostile enemy in Sally, who will retaliate using methods adequate to the standards Mary has set:

> "Serve your goddamn self," the older woman said, her voice rising to a screech. . . . "Serve yourself." The woman had turned toward Mary. Her entire body trembled, her hands, now unclasped, fanned the air. She pushed a loaf of sandwich bread across the counter toward Mary. She slapped a package of hamburger buns, causing it to sail and hit Mary on the shoulder. She threw Dixie

---

49. King opines that "the ultimate weakness of violence is that it is a descending spiral, begetting the very thing it seeks to destroy. Instead of diminishing evil, it multiplies it. Through violence you may murder the liar, but you cannot murder the lie, nor establish the truth. Through violence you may murder the hater, but you do not murder hate. In fact, violence merely increases hate. So it goes. Returning violence for violence multiplies violence, adding deeper darkness to a night already devoid of stars. Darkness cannot drive out darkness; only light can do that. Hate cannot drive out hate: only love can do that" (*Where Do We Go from Here* 64–65).

cups, plastic forks and paper napkins. Mary ducked below the countertop. "Serve yourself," the woman screamed. "Eat all the goddamn food you want." (Grooms, "Food" 139)

Because Sally sinks to Mary's level, the confrontation does not play out quite as predictably as Mary has wished or hoped for. Forcing equality at the expense of others and demanding compliance to aggressive demands not only violates the tenets of nonviolence advocated by Martin Luther King Jr., but more importantly for Mary, they are contrary to her own self-interest. She is mentally prepared for possible legal repercussions (she admits to not being afraid of going to jail) but she seems not to have taken into account the fact that once she cannot contain her personal enmity toward the waitress, her aggressiveness may foster hostility and strong-arm methods aimed at her and her cause.

Even though the conflict reaches the stage where antagonisms have brought latent racial conflict out into the open, there is still room for redressive action, as Turner notes:

> In order to limit the contagious spread of *breach* certain adjustive and redressive mechanisms . . . are brought into operation by leading members of the disturbed group. These mechanisms vary in character with such factors as the depth and significance of the breach, the social inclusiveness of the crisis, the nature of the social group within which the breach took place, and its degree of autonomy in regard to wider systems of social relations. The mechanisms may range from personal advice and informal arbitration, to formal juridical and legal machinery, and to resolve certain kinds of crisis, to the performance of public ritual. (*From Ritual* 70; emphasis in original)

Quotidian life eliminates the need for reflection about the social order; only the redressive phase of social drama "involves a scanning of and reflection upon the previous events leading up to the crisis that has now to be dealt with" (Turner, *On the Edge* 199).[50] Redressive action offers interpretation of the genesis of social crisis, which in turn can lead to reintegration of fractured social structures. Depending on the

---

50. According to Turner, "the redressive phase, in which feedback on crisis is provided by the scanning devices of law (secular ritual) and religious ritual, is a liminal time, set apart from the ongoing business of quotidian life, when an interpretation . . . is constructed to give the appearance of sense and order to the events leading up to and constituting the crisis" (*From Ritual* 75).

A SWEET TASTE OF VICTORY

effectiveness of negotiations and mechanisms of redressive actions, the conflict might be contained or it might escalate. As Dr. King posits, "every crisis has both its dangers and its opportunities. It can spell either salvation or doom" ("Peace and Justice").

These verbal negotiations between Sally and her two recalcitrant customers, which escalate into expressions of physical frustration, have been accompanied by increasingly agonized sounds in the storage room, "as if someone, or some animal, were grieving" (Grooms, "Food" 136), underscoring the gravity of the dispute over the lunch counter. Initially Annie cannot define the source of this "deep and pathetic" moan, emitted by "something monstrously sorrowful . . . almost a groan [vibrating] in her chest" (139). Her instinctive reaction to "[hold] onto the seat of the stool" at the sound of the moans, which she can feel "in the pit of her stomach" (138), replicate her jitteriness and anxiety about demanding equal rights.

Mary and Sally's confrontation takes an unexpected turn when the source of the sounds discloses itself in the "slow, awkward swaying" (138) of a man emerging from the storage room. At the sight of Willie, a big man with thick fingers, who looks "like an animal, a hurt animal" (139) moaning for his mother, Annie trespasses on the space inaccessible to customers; she goes behind the counter gate, where Sally and Willie had been safe from the outside world. Only here does Willie's peculiar condition reveal itself in its entirety:

> his barrel chest, bulging out in odd places under a pinnedtogether plaid flannel shirt; then his thick neck, stiffly twisted so that one ear nearly lay against his hulking shoulder. His lips were thick and flat. One side of his face was higher than the other, like a clay face misshapen by a child's hand. His eyebrows were thick ridges that ran together at the top of his wide flat nose. (140)

On further inspection, Annie notices "drool in the corners of his mouth. He had gray eyes that swam lazily in their sockets. Now she looked at the offered hand. It was the whitest hand she had ever seen, with thick, hairy knuckles and nubbed nails" (140). The process of othering, which stigmatizes African Americans as inferior, is reversed here. Annie's surprise at the whiteness of Willie's grotesque hand reveals how torn in opposite directions she is, between the endemic distance to White people as the "Other" and her compassionate understanding of the impact of Willie's "otherness" on Sally's situation: "She had never touched a white boy. She reached out for the hand hesitantly. . . . She saw her hand, so obviously brown, move into her focus, and then move closer and closer to the pale hand until her fingertips touched it" (140). Annie's reaction to Willie implies that she does not see him as a freak or a monster, later assessments of Willie offered respectively by Mr. May and Mary. Willie manifests Patricia Yaeger's concept of "throwaway bodies" in Southern fiction, bodies "whose bodily harm does not matter enough to be registered or repressed."[51] Endowed with emotional intelligence, Annie sees Willie as a deeply hurt man in need of understanding and empathy. By patting Willie on his grotesque, white hands, Annie resists inflicting violence upon his spirit (the result of the process of "social othering"), which can be equally damaging as violence to the body.

Annie's moment of epiphany at the sight of Willie and her touching his hands clearly demonstrate that, despite she and Mary not initially understanding the position Sally is in, Annie realizes that only by desisting from treating others as the collective evil "Other" and shedding prejudice, does one have the moral right, as Goffman posits, "to expect that others will value and treat [one] in a correspondingly appropriate way" (6). Hence, Annie cannot demand compassion and respect if she does not treat Willie and his mother with understanding and sensitivity. Sally's explanation of Willie's condition— "Just born thatta way, child. Just born like that" (140)—acquires new, deeper significance for Annie. A realization of their shared status as disadvantaged within Southern society—both as racial Other and a White, grotesque anomaly—allows Annie to see the need for restoring a broken community beyond racial divisions—but not at the expense of anyone. The encounter with the "freak"[52] reminds Annie not only of the

---

51. *In Dirt and Desire: Reconstructing Southern Women's Writing 1930–1990*, Yaeger explains, "We must pay attention to the difficult figure of the throwaway body—to women and men whose bodily harm does not matter enough to be registered or repressed—who are not symbolically central, who are looked over, looked through, who become a matter of public and private indifference—neither important enough to be disavowed nor part of white southern culture's dominant emotional economy" (68).

52. The word *freak* used in this context when referring to Willie is not meant as a judgmental assessment of his status in society, but rather is used in connection with his ability to inspire epiphany in Annie. Flannery O'Connor elucidated the relationship between the sanctity of human life and the presence of "freaks" in Southern literature: "Whenever I'm asked why Southern writers particularly have a penchant

sanctity of human life regardless of color or shape, but also of the fact that all life is interrelated. Only through nonviolent love and the understanding that makes it possible can one resist injustice.

This epiphany cannot be part of Mary's experience, as she does not try to understand Sally's predicament. Nor does she look for ways in which the waitress could possibly become their ally. Mary again misinterprets a repeated offer of food as a weakness of the "enemy" to be exploited. Weakness is provocative, whereas strength, both physical and of character, may deter from possible attacks. Hence, the reconciliatory potential of the food offer escapes Mary:

> "See," the woman said. She looked at Mary. "See. We are just people like you are. We don't want to hurt nobody. Not a soul." She took back the man's hand and smiled at Annie. "Tell you what. I'll cut us all a piece of pie."
>
> "Can we have it at the counter?" Mary glared at the woman, her lips poked out.
>
> The woman sighed loudly. "Won't you understand?"
>
> "Then eat it by yo'self." (140–41)

An offer to share food, as probably the profoundest enactment of human connection, has the potential to call forth the good in one's opponent. Whereas Sally's earlier offers of takeaway food were meant to silence the voice of racial dissent, or eliminate the sight of it,[53] sharing this pie implies Sally's attempt at commensal reconciliation with her African American customers. As a sign of good will, her commensality transcends racial ties, encouraging an experience of unity and understanding. However, Mary's virulent response suggests that for her, such an offer to share food exacerbates racial inequality, rather than representing symbolic reconciliation.

The redressive phase of social drama situates reconciliation between structure and antistructure, in a liminal state that, according to Victor Turner, is "essentially interstitial, betwixt-and-between" (*On*

---

for writing about freaks, I say it is because we are still able to recognize one. To be able to recognize a freak, you have to have some conception of the whole man, and in the South the general conception of man is still, in the main, theological" (*Mystery and Manners* 44).

53. Turner claims that in order to restore peace, "those with a strong interest in maintaining the *status quo ante*. . . . attempt to apply *redressive machinery*—to 'patch up' quarrels, 'mend' broken social ties, 'seal up punctures' in the 'social fabric'" (*From Ritual* 10).

the Edge 263). This phase of Turner's social drama is thus situated on the threshold between alternate systems, regulations, or styles of organization.[54] Turner claims that during the transition period, "there has to be an interfacial region or . . . an interval, however brief, of *margin* or *limen*, when the past is momentarily negated, suspended, or abrogated, and the future has not yet begun, an instant of pure potentiality when everything, as it were, trembles in the balance" (*From Ritual* 44). Turner notes that such a period of transition may "generate and store a plurality of alternative modes of living"; thus liminality is also a form of ambiguity (33).[55] It invites "speculation and criticism" (47). Hence, Turner suggests that liminality is creative and reflexive but, by its very nature, can also be destructive (47). The commensality implied by the social antagonists at May's Drugstore sharing a pie can be understood as a *liminoid* phenomenon, which, according to Turner, is experimental in character, exists on the margins of social and political structures (54), and inverts properties of already consolidated order.[56]

During a liminoid moment like cross-racial consumption in public eating spaces, all the participants in the social performance—in this case, the waitress and her customers—would merge into a transient unity in *communitas*, to which Turner ascribes dynamism, immediacy, and spontaneity.[57] The *communitas* has "a relational quality of full unmediated communication, even communion, between definite and determinate identities. Such *communitas* would essentially be a

---

54. Turner explains that the term *limen* is the Latin word for *threshold*, which implies transition between systems or structures (*From Ritual* 41).

55. Turner posits that "liminality is, of course, an ambiguous state, for social structure, while it inhibits full social satisfaction, gives a measure of finiteness and security; liminality may be for many the acme of insecurity, the breakthrough of chaos into cosmos, of disorder into order, rather than the milieu of creative interhuman or transhuman satisfaction and achievements. Liminality may be the scene of disease, despair, death, suicide, the breakdown without compensatory replacement of normative, well-defined social ties and bonds" (*From Ritual* 46).

56. "'Meaning' in culture tends to be generated at the interfaces between established cultural subsystems, though meanings are then institutionalized and consolidated at the centers of such systems. Liminality is a temporal interface whose properties partially invert those of the already consolidated order which constitutes any specific cultural 'cosmos'" (Turner, *From Ritual* 41).

57. Turner comments extensively on *communitas* in his research. In *On the Edge of the Bush: Anthropology of Experience*, he observes that "communitas is the implicit law of wholeness arising out of relations between totalities. But communitas is intrinsically dynamic, never quite being realized. It is not being realized precisely

liminal phenomenon, consisting of a blend of humility and comrade-ship" (Turner, *On the Edge* 173). It is important to bear in mind a point made by Eugene Anderson: that there is no better way to express sol-idarity and comradeship than sharing food (*Everyone Eats* 125).[58] As such, commensality encourages the convivial experience of friendship, good will and communion of individuals. *Communitas*, as "an undif-ferentiated, egalitarian, direct, extant, nonrational, existential relation-ship which may arise spontaneously among human beings," strives for human interrelatedness (Turner, *On the Edge* 286). If accepted and acted on, Sally's offer to share a pie with her customers might well release the full human capacity in them, which Turner identifies as characteristic of *communitas* (*From Ritual* 46). The relationship of *com-munitas* does not imply, however, that people forget hierarchies and differences; instead they simply mute or suspend them for the sake of human interrelatedness in order to work through whatever social drama in whose midst they find themselves.[59] The actors in this social drama have to engage in "the truly 'spontaneous' unit of human social perfor-mance . . . which results precisely from the suspension of normative role-playing . . . since in the social drama it becomes a matter of urgency to become reflexive about the cause and motive of action damaging to the social fabric" (Turner, *On the Edge* 196).

Before *communitas* among Mary, Annie, and Sally can even be established, let alone evolve from its spontaneous to normative form,[60]

---

because individuals and collectivities try to impose their cognitive schemata on one another" (190). Whereas in *From Ritual to Theatre* he claims that "the spontaneity and immediacy of communitas . . . can seldom be sustained for long. Communitas itself soon develops (protective social) structure" (47).

58. The religious implication of commensality expressed by Anderson—"the word 'companion' means 'bread sharer' (Latin *cum panis*)" (*Everyone Eats* 125)—is also reflected in Turner's assessment of spontaneous communitas, which "is more a matter of 'grace' than 'law.'" (*From Ritual* 49).

59. Turner observes that "communitas does not represent the erasure of structural norms from the consciousness of those participating in it; rather its own style, in a given community, might be said to depend on the way in which it symbolizes the abrogation, negation, or inversion of the normative structure in which its partici-pants are quotidianly involved" (*From Ritual* 47).

60. Turner posits that *communitas* consists of "three distinct and not necessarily sequential forms": spontaneous, ideological, and normative. *Communitas* can evolve from total personal reaction, through its description, toward "attempts to foster and maintain relationships or spontaneous communitas on a more or less permanent basis" (*From Ritual* 49).

Mr. May appears in the store and dispels the magic of the moment. The actors of the social drama retreat into their normative roles— "Mary [spins] around and pretend[s] to be interested in the bath soaps" (Grooms, "Food" 141), Sally resumes the role of waitress, and Annie emerges from behind the lunch counter. When confronted with the ultimate representative of Southern authority—a White man—they all individually "assign *meaning* to what has happened" (Turner, *On the Edge* 210). Their instant, instinctive assessment of the situation clearly bespeaks the women's retreat from the fleeting possibility of *communitas*, but also reveals reflexive commentary on society's general aversion to such relations. This antipathy is reflected in Mr. May's assessment of the situation: "Look at this place? What the hell happened here? Goddamnit, can't you control that freak?" (Grooms, "Food" 142), which interestingly enough brings his latent hostility to the Other, be it Black or "freak," out into the open.

Interrupted by Mr. May, the redressive phase appears to be left without resolution. The social drama at the lunch counter does not conclude, as Victor Turner hypothesizes, "either in the reconciliation of the contending parties or their agreement to differ" (*From Ritual* 10). On the surface, Annie and Mary, as representatives of the disturbed social group, are not openly reintegrated into their shared social system, nor do they have an opportunity to revert into crisis (*From Ritual* 71).[61] Even though from the perspective of the civil rights movement this is a relatively minor incident in the attempt to desegregate Southern eating places, which "often took place quietly with little advertisement or publicity to avoid counterdemonstrations and violence" (Cooley, *To Live* 235–36), for the actors in this social drama the incident offers a self-reflexive glimpse into the truths about themselves, which are often blurred by quotidian existence.

Annie and Mary's individual interpretations of and responses to the outcome of their demands for equal rights in May's Drugstore that they make on the way to their car demonstrate that there may not be a visible, definite resolution to this social drama, but this sit-in has offered them a chance to see their own true nature. Because Mary's rejection of nonviolence is so definite, as she sees no fault in

---

61. Turner also envisions a partial success in redressive procedures, leading to reconciliation that "may only seem to have been achieved in phase four, with real conflicts glossed over but not resolved" (*From Ritual* 71).

her behavior, she tends to blame everybody else for the outcome but herself: "That wasn't fair . . . How come that stupid gorilla had to be there? How come *she* had to be there in the first place? Ole lady May the one I wanted to be there. I could have said something if it hada been her" (Grooms, "Food" 141). Mary's lack of humility, which could potentially educate and transform her, prevents her from developing self-awareness or even considering the impact of her values and beliefs on her own actions and those of others. As an anti-epitome of nonviolence, Mary will not willingly accept the consequences of her actions. Her aggressive hate-mongering response, "Shit. . . . we won't ever get nothing, nothing—unless we, we . . . uggghhh! . . . *kill* them, or something" (142; emphasis in original), shows that her hidden intentions are not integrationist, but rather bellicose, if not downright gladiatorial. Mary's hatred of White people is reminiscent of Malcolm X's sentiment; it guides her decision-making process and actions.[62] Because of it, Mary is locked in a stalemate: she will never have a clear sense of self if she does not understand the other side of the conflict. The outcome of her actions verifies Martin Luther King Jr.'s claim that "we will not build a peaceful world by following a negative path" ("Peace and Justice").

Mary's and Annie's widely divergent motivations behind their protest against discriminatory exclusion of African Americans in public spaces resonate with the polarized opinions within the civil rights movement. On a broader canvas, Malcolm X's radicalism and acceptance of direct, aggressive action as a justifiable means of dealing with systemic oppression and abuse clashed with the nonviolent *agape* advocated by Dr. King. According to King, love[63] and empathy are necessary to resolve a racial stalemate: "Hatred paralyzes life; love releases it. Hatred confuses life; love harmonizes it. Hatred darkens life; love illuminates it" ("Strength to Love"). In contradistinction to Annie, who

---

62. In his autobiography, Malcolm X elucidated his belief that all White men are evil, justified violence in pursuing equality for African Americans, and encouraged his people to take matters into their own hands without expecting any help from Whites.

63. In his Nobel Prize lecture, King elucidated what he means by love: "When I speak of love I am not speaking of some sentimental and weak response which is little more than emotional bosh. I am speaking of that force which all of the great religions have seen as the supreme unifying principle of life. Love is somehow the key that unlocks the door which leads to ultimate reality" ("Peace and Justice").

is able to revise her views, Mary is still blinded by hatred and a desire for revenge after the incident at May's Drugstore: "'We never gone get our rights.' Mary clenched her teeth. 'Especially with you around pattin' that goddamn monster on the hand. . . . Some civil rights marcher you is. Bill Green will be 'shame' to know you'" (Grooms, "Food" 141–42). Mary wanted to prove her point and take a stance, and consequently she is unable to review her beliefs and motives when confronted with an unexpected turn of events. With such a low level of self-awareness, Mary lacks the capacity for reflexive and constructive self-analysis. Hence, Thomas Scott's observation in his interview with Anthony Grooms that "the young ladies actually learn a great deal about themselves, and about the complexities of life, when they try to hold their sit-in" (Grooms, "Interview") is only partially valid.

The social drama involving Annie and Mary seems to bear out Martin Luther King Jr.'s observation that "the ultimate measure of a man is not where he stands in moments of comfort and convenience, but where he stands in moments of challenge and controversy" ("Strength to Love"). The crisis in the store has the potential of revealing to Annie and Mary truths about themselves (truths obscured by quotidian existence), providing that the women are ready for self-audit—a prerequisite of self-transformation. Pattanaik perceptively observes that "in most of his stories Grooms places his characters in situations that test their worth as humans. His people are always in a state of flux, in a state of becoming and they grow or diminish as they come to terms with the broader life that confronts them" (194). While Mary's humanity is diminished by her aggression and retaliation, Annie's reactions, motivated by sensitivity and compassion, illustrate her moral growth. Love and empathy open her eyes: "She was beginning to tremble on the inside. The world seemed complex and uncertain. She remembered touching the man, her brown hand against his white one. . . . She remembered the look on the woman's face when she had patted the man's hand. She thought the woman had loved her for a moment" (Grooms, "Food" 141). Love and understanding have the potential to create a transient *communitas*, which, according to Turner, can release the full human capacity of actors in a social drama (*From Ritual* 46). Sally and Annie come close to achieving this human capacity in their shared understanding of the need for empathy and love beyond the constraints of color or shape.

Annie's assessment of Willie—"he couldn't help the way he was born" (141)—not only refers to Sally's earlier explanation of her son's condition, "just born thatta way, child. Just born like that" (140), but more importantly, offers a self-reflective interpretation of her own existence, which in turn may synecdochally refer to all human beings regardless of color or shape. Clearly, the issue of race is complicated by its relations to both class and able-bodiedness. Interestingly enough, Annie does not share her final epiphany with Mary, the very person who is on "her side" of the racial conflict. Annie knows that non-violence and love, as its correlative, however difficult to practice under given circumstances, are the only ways to resolve conflict. Thus, Annie is one of Grooms's characters who, according to Pattanaik, "[has] become human by discovering the gap between their own ideals and practices. A few, however, keep alive the hope of liberation by trying to bridge that gap. They make us aware that the limiting conditions are not metaphysical, unexplainable, but very human, identifiable and transparent, and therefore, all the more tragic. Our sense of worth depends on our decision to overcome these limitations" (195). Annie's thoughts and reactions reveal her newly acquired awareness that one cannot achieve human rights and equality at the expense of exercising one's humanity. It is this lack of awareness that precludes the possibility of Mary sharing Annie's epiphany that "things were very complicated, far more complicated than she had ever thought" (Grooms, "Food" 142).

In an interview with Thomas Scott and Dede Yow, Anthony Grooms claims that places where there is conflict, such as Mississippi or Ireland, produce great writers. Born in a society where overt and covert racial tensions are daily bread, Southern writers bare the patterns of social interaction and reveal social dramas both large and small in which, according to Victor Turner, social behaviors are assessed, and relations and cultural experiences are reconsidered (*From Ritual* 42). Unlike "happy stories [which] aren't interesting" (Grooms, "Interview"), "Food that Pleases, Food to Take Home" offers a fascinating glimpse of attempts to abrogate the normative system of racial segregation. The story about Annie and Mary's sit-in at May's Drugstore reveals the hypocrisy of the oppressive racial situation in the South that led to the civil rights protests. Annie and Mary, like their historical counterparts—the flesh-and-blood civil rights activists—demand at the lunch counters, to use Cooley's words, that "their interpretation of the appropriate use of southern space [be] respected and accepted.

Civil rights activists challenged the inferior status of African Americans in southern consumer culture as well as the representation of blacks as subservient in public spaces and images devoted to the preparation, consumption, and service of food" ("The Customer" 241).

More importantly, however, Grooms's short story focuses, as Pattanaik aptly remarks, on "heterogeneous political viewpoints that guide the struggle of African Americans to achieve equality and justice" (193). By contrasting Annie's *agape* and nonviolence with Mary's assaultive behavior as means of challenging Jim Crow segregation, Grooms manages to complicate the facile presentation of a homogeneous, peaceful group of demonstrators. Grooms avoids putting all civil rights protestors under one banner of noble people fighting for a noble cause with integrationist intent. By spotlighting different paths and the varying results of confronting the social injustice of segregation in public spaces, Anthony Grooms points to divergent communities of interests not simply across the obvious color line, but more interestingly, within one's own racial group.[64] The façade of a united front against discrimination and segregation is torn by conflicting motivations and disparate moral stances.[65] For Mary the South seems to be a zero-sum game when it comes to racial relations. Whereas hatred glares malignly in Mary's attempts to defeat the enemy, Annie nonviolently disturbs the status quo and intrudes on Sally's complacency behind the counter. However, Sally, as a gradualist, does not challenge the discriminatory laws out of her own volition. Her complicity in passively preserving the status quo comes at the expense of exercising her own humanity towards others. Even though Annie and Sally's personal epiphanies do not change the systemic racism, the seeds that might grow and puncture the oppressive system are there. After all, both Annie and Sally do demonstrate their humanity by

---

64. Grooms explains that "one of the things that I wanted to try to convey, is that people have different aspects to their problems, and they're driven by different reasons. And even though their positions might not be ones that ideally we would think of as morally right positions, their roots might not have evolved in locating evil . . . They get there by different means. That's part of the complexity of it" ("Interview").

65. I concur with Pattanaik, who makes a general observation about Grooms's characters, that "their private heroism and cowardice, commitments and betrayals, triumphs and failures show how hard it is to stereotype any group of people by their sole membership in any particular race, gender or nationality" (194).

reaching across the color line (contact with Willie) and negotiating commensality (attempts to share a pie).

■ ■ ■

The significance of the erosion of Jim Crow segregation in Southern places of public consumption is widely accepted (despite the aforementioned voices of segregationists who denied the symbolic meaning of commensality in public spaces). "The desegregation of lunch counters, libraries, [and] schools on a token basis may seem a small breach in the enormous fortress of injustice, but considering the strength of the fortress," Martin Luther King Jr. observed, "it was a towering achievement" (*Why We Can't Wait* 114). Against the opposition of Southern White supremacists, on July 2, 1964, President Lyndon B. Johnson signed the Civil Rights Bill, which legally ended "discrimination or segregation on the ground of race, color, religion, or national origin" in such establishments as "any restaurant, cafeteria, lunchroom, lunch counter, soda fountain, or other facility principally engaged in selling food for consumption on the premises, including, but not limited to, any such facility located on the premises of any retail establishment; or any gasoline station."[66]

Even though the breach in the wall of social injustice led to the social drama of the civil rights movement, it would be too idealistic to expect that after the 1964 Civil Rights Act, both de jure and de facto discrimination and segregation practices would cease forthwith. Ferris states that "the process of desegregation went on for years, again determined by the particular racial dynamics of communities throughout the South, often ending in lawsuits and covert orders that forced businesses and schools to integrate" (*The Edible South* 282). Jason Sokol brilliantly captures the immediate impact of "the Civil Rights Act, [which] like many other victories of the civil rights movement, changed everything and nothing in southern life . . . The law could not compel African-Americans to *desire* to integrate many places, much less compel whites to embrace them when they did" (213–14; qtd. in Ferris, *The*

---

66. Respectively: Civil Rights Act of 1964, Pub. L. No. 88–352, July 2, 1964, §201(a); and Civil Rights Act of 1964, Pub. L. No. 88–352, July 2, 1964, §201(b)(2). Retrieved from US Equal Employment Opportunity Commission, https://www.eeoc.gov/eeoc/history/35th/thelaw/civil_rights_act.html.

Edible South 282). Overt compliance with enforced desegregating policies could hide personal racist sentiments, mainly because "it is entirely possible to desegregate without integrating."[67] Not being served without incident constitutes "a difference between sitting in and being in."[68] In his Nobel Prize lecture, delivered just five months after Johnson signed the Civil Rights Bill into law, Dr. King expressed his skepticism about the efficacy of its results: "Let me not leave you with a false impression. The problem is far from solved. We still have a long, long way to go before the dream of freedom is a reality for the Negro in the United States" ("Peace and Justice").[69] Forty years later, Anthony Grooms shared a similar sentiment with his interviewers: "Now that we've gotten rid of the more obvious racism and sexism, we're dealing with even more complex issues; because it's really the subtle stuff that people have to think about" ("Interview").

"Food deserts" and "tableside racism" are emblematic of "the subtle stuff" Anthony Grooms mentioned. "Food deserts" are impoverished areas with a dearth of affordable, healthy, fresh food, but with a high concentration of convenience stores peddling fast food and other highly processed foodstuffs. Inequitable distribution of healthy foods visibly isolates Black and poor residents, thus making it both a race and class issue. Bold agricultural solutions to the problems of food deserts and other forms of "nutritional apartheid"[70] already had been

---

67. Leonard Steinhorn and Barbara Diggs-Brown reveal that "although desegregation is a necessary precondition for integration, it is entirely possible to desegregate without integrating. . . . Desegregation may unlock doors, but integration is supposed to open minds, which is why some say that integration makes desegregation look easy. Indeed, what makes racial integration so compelling is that it is about people, not laws" (5).

68. Williamson demonstrates that "Black people were finding that there was a difference between sitting in and being in. A legal and a physical revolution, putting black bodies among white bodies in either token or massive numbers, had not produced a revolution in white attitudes. Indeed, many blacks found that being close to whites was much more painful than being away from them. The closer they got, the greater the pain" (*The Crucible of Race* 505).

69. President Jimmy Carter seemed to share King's sentiment on that matter. On accepting the Martin Luther King Jr. Nonviolent Peace Prize bestowed on him by the King Center on January 14, 1979, Carter voiced the feeling of disfranchisement and frustration of all those African Americans who felt forgotten: "It's not enough to have a right to sit at a lunch counter if you can't afford to buy a meal" ("Georgia Remarks").

70. Slocum claims that "'nutritional apartheid' in availability of grocery stores (Garrett, 2008), the scarcity of unpolluted land for urban agriculture in non-white

introduced, as John Edge reveals, as early as in the late 1960s by Fannie Lou Hamer and other radical Southerners ("The Hidden Radicalism"). While food deserts, as a form of economic stratification and social exclusion, mark a visible social demarcation line, "tableside racism" is less tangible, but may still be equally present in the South. Even though the policies and practices of Jim Crow segregation—which affected the service, personal treatment, and length of wait in public eating facilities—was legally barred in 1964, African American customers have reported experiencing racial discrimination in Southern public eating establishments since then. "Tableside racism," or the racial bias of servers, as reported for instance by Denny's and Cracker Barrel patrons as late as the 1990s and 2000s (Shah 131),[71] are searing reminders that Dr. King's dream "that one day on the red hills of Georgia the sons of former slaves and the sons of former slaveowners will be able to sit down together at the table of brotherhood" has yet to be fully realized. So far it has been, to quote a Langston Hughes poem, "a dream deferred." The dream's hidden explosive potential, which Hughes envisioned in his poem, unveiled itself at the beginning of the twenty-first century. The future legacy of Hughes's and King's dreams endured and arose anew in 2013, in the form of Black Lives Matter.[72]

---

neighborhoods (McClintock, 2008) and zoning against urban gardening but for white hobby farms, among other forms of development (Barraclough, 2009), affect food sovereignty" (313).

71. In discussing the servers' racial bias, such as requiring Black patrons to pay up front, delaying seating and serving, or allowing White servers to refuse to wait on Black customers, Aarushi Shah makes use of Zachary Brewster and Sarah Rusche's research into tableside racism in full-service restaurants, published in the *Journal of Black Studies* (2012).

72. Joshua Adams convincingly argues that the legacy of James Baldwin, one of the most important voices to advocate for and document the civil rights movement, is espoused by the Black Lives Matter movement ("James Baldwin says #BlackLivesMatter"). As Martin Luther King Jr.'s devoted disciple, Baldwin unequivocally embraced King's nonviolence as the only sound and morally impeccable way to deal with racial injustice. In his later years, though, Baldwin also accepted Malcolm X's radical discourse, such as a belief in the need for reparative and restorative processes, and justified the use of direct action and confrontation as a response to systemic oppression and violence. Such documentaries as *I Am Not Your Negro* (2016), which uses James Baldwin's archival materials, show that the civil rights protests have great relevance to the contemporary sociopolitical scene. I thank Professor Dominika Ferens for reminding me of the evolution of James Baldwin's opinions regarding paths to a truly integrated United States.

Coda
Food for Thought

Eating grits . . . can mean something entirely different today from what it did then to the Mississippi sharecropper who ate them because that's what he had. Eating grits today can be manipulated as a sign of southernness: to eat grits is, in one sense, to identify oneself as a southerner.

—Scott Romine, *The Narrative Forms of Southern Community*

The connection between food and race is constantly being remade in America. This continuing dynamic was highlighted in 2013 as the media covered a lawsuit involving television celebrity and chef Paula Deen, who allegedly used the N-word and told racist jokes. Her derogatory remarks sparked heated debate, but few paid much attention to Deen's exploitation of African American cooks working in her Savannah, Georgia, restaurants.[1] The conflation of race and food also became evident in the social media fallout after Burger King's "crispy chicken snack wraps" commercial featuring Mary J. Blige (2012) and in commercials for Glory Foods (2012), which perpetuate racial stereotypes such as that of a helpless White housewife in need of help from an Aunt Jemima–type savior.[2] More recently the food–race debate was reheated after the premiere of the fourteenth season of *Top Chef*, shot during 2016 at Boone Hall Plantation in Charleston, South Carolina. Tom Colicchio was castigated on social media for selecting a former cotton plantation as the site of that season's culinary contest. It is

---

1. More about the controversy surrounding Paula Deen and her appropriation of racialized stereotypes of Black women and food can be found in Kimberly D. Nettles-Barcelón, "The Sassy Black Cook and the Return of the Magical Negress: Popular Representations of Black Women's Food Work," 107–20.
2. For a perceptive analysis of the Glory Foods commercials, see Karen L. Cox, "Black Domestic in a Can: A South Carolina Ad Agency 'Helps' Glory Foods."

unclear whether such a backlash against the historic residue connected with this particular setting would have been equally fierce if Gerald Sombright, a Black chef, had not lost to John Tesar, a White chef.

Denial of subjectivity, racial stereotyping, and the oppressive tactics of racial subordination that tainted the antebellum South have cast a long shadow on the twentieth and now the twenty-first century. The oppression of African Americans, which was institutionalized after Reconstruction was halted, in the Black codes or Jim Crow laws, turned into the more subtle, yet nonetheless highly discriminatory, practices of tableside racism and food deserts. Clearly the pervasiveness of racial inequality and injustice is not limited to the American South, but spans the whole United States. I do not intend my research into the connections between race and food to disturb people amid what Robin DiAngelo calls their "White fragility."[3] The sole purpose of my analyses has been to probe fictional accounts of racial encounters for the potential insights they might offer. To avoid critical accusations such as those raised by Zora Neale Hurston about the "'arrogance' of whites assuming that black lives are only defensive reactions to white actions" (Gates 199), I aimed to tease out how issues surrounding race are reconfigured and how changes in the performance of race relations in the South are embodied by and reflected in the social practices and material culture associated with the foodscape of the twentieth-century American South.

Barbara Kirshenblatt-Gimblett's observation that "food and performance converge conceptually at three junctures" captures the essence of performing identities through food: "First, *to perform is to do*, to execute, to carry out to completion . . . Second, *to perform is to behave*. This is what Erving Goffman calls the performance in everyday life . . . Third, *to perform is to show*" (1–2). The formation of various identities,

---

3. DiAngelo explains the dynamics of "White fragility" in the following terms: "White people in North America live in a social environment that protects and insulates them from race-based stress. This insulated environment of racial protection builds white expectations for racial comfort while at the same time lowering the ability to tolerate racial stress, leading to what I refer to as White Fragility. White Fragility is a state in which even a minimum amount of racial stress becomes intolerable, triggering a range of defensive moves. These moves include the outward display of emotions such as anger, fear, and guilt, and behaviors such as argumentation, silence, and leaving the stress-inducing situation. These behaviors, in turn, function to reinstate white racial equilibrium" (54).

be they racial, ethnic, or regional, reflects Kirshenblatt-Gimblett's conflation of food and performance: identities are developed and enacted (through the distribution of duties and practices connected with preparing, serving, and consuming food), they either abide by or contest normative identities (through customs, rituals, or codes of behavior), and last, they are displayed as markers of social differentiation (taste and distaste, Mary Douglas's purity and danger). Because social identities are performed, they are not reified but are rather always in the process of becoming. They are negotiated in relation to a specific culture that, according to historian T. H. Breen, is "a continuing series of reciprocal relationships, involving borrowing and resistance, conflict and cooperation, modification and invention" (qtd. in Ferris, "Studying Southern Food" 5). Hence, the meaning of foodways and foodscape, as instrumental ingredients of identity formation, evolves in tandem with changes in the sociohistorical context.

Over the years, the everyday practical experiences of racial ideology have evolved in the South. Food is an additional prism through which these changes in formulations and uses of racial ideology are refracted and reflected. Hence, *Race and Repast* has aimed to explore how, following Marcie Cohen Ferris's observation, some "white and black southerners waged a war against racial injustice, labor exploitation, and other causes that often found expression at the table" ("The Edible South" 15). It has been my intention to refrain from myopically "whitewashing" the racial history of the South and nostalgically embracing food's potential, as ascribed by Atkins-Sayre and Stokes, "to celebrate the South's history while temporarily setting aside the troubling memories of the segregated and poverty-ridden South" (79). Indeed, one of the aims of this work has been to tease out and trouble the connection between race and food in relation to Southern history and culture. Motivated by Anita Mannur's lament that "the looming figures within African-American literary and cultural critique had precious little to say about the politics of eating or the body and consumption" ("Edible Discourse" 393), my project draws on research by Psyche Williams-Forson, Doris Witt, Jessica Harris, Frederick Douglass Opie, Rebecca Sharpless, and Angela Cooley in order to reframe a perspective on Southern racial relations through the prism of literary and cultural food studies.

The selection of literary texts discussed in *Race and Repast* is not meant to be comprehensive or representative. Different contexts foster different areas for literary and cultural study of how food and race are instrumentally interconnected. Among other avenues of analysis that could be pursued is inquiry into "culinary passing," which Camille Cauti defines as "attempting to gain acceptance among an ethnic group to which one does not belong via the preparation and eating of certain foods" (10). Dori Sanders's *Clover* (1990) offers interesting material for an analysis of the culinary crossing of racial and cultural differences in a cross-racial family. Gloria Naylor's *Linden Hills* (1986) nicely illustrates how class and materialism have an impact on African American identity through the process of culinary signifying.[4] The rhetoric of *My Momma Throws Down* (2012), a short-lived cooking television series showcasing the amateur cooking abilities of Black mothers, can be interrogated with the "natural-born cooks" stereotype associated with Black women.[5] Likewise, contemporary uses of the Aunt Jemima image can be explored in the already mentioned Glory Foods campaign; in African American art by Faith Ringgold, Jeff Donaldson, Betye Saar, and Michael Ray Charles among others;[6] or in Dawolu Jabari Anderson's imaginary comic book series, *Gullah Sci-Fi Mysteries* (2008).

Although Du Bois's "color line" is now allegedly blurred according to the "race is over" thesis, the gastro-political debate about New Orleans, Louisiana, that occurred in the aftermath of Hurricane Katrina proves that race is not passé. The HBO drama series *Treme* (2010–13) depicts how residents of the historically Black neighborhood hit hardest by the hurricane have struggled to rebuild their homes, reclaim their lives, and maintain their unique culture. The analysis of New Orleans's culinary landscape might reveal the symbolical value of

---

4. For more about the process of culinary signifying in Gloria Naylor's *Linden Hills*, see Psyche Willliams-Forson, *Building Houses*, 142–44.

5. See Jessica Kenyatta Walker, "Mighty Matriarchs Kill It with a Skillet: Critically Reading Popular Representations of Black Womanhood and Food," 121–34.

6. Here I specifically refer to such works of art as Jeff Donaldson's *Aunt Jemima and the Pillsbury Doughboy* (1963), Joe Overstreet's pop art rendition of *Jemima* (1964), Murry N. DePillars' *Aunt Jemima* (1968), Jon Onye Lockard's *No More* (1972), Betye Saar's seminal *The Liberation of Aunt Jemima* (1972), Michael Ray Charles's politically ironic scenes that rework canonical images (such as Rockwell's nostalgic *Saturday Evening Post* style, which evokes and extends the realistic portraiture of Grant Wood's *American Gothic*), Faith Ringgold's quilts such as *Who's Afraid of Aunt Jemima?* (1983), and Renée Cox's large-format color photograph entitled *The Liberation of Lady J and U.B.* (1998).

eating out as a (self)-healing process in times of recovery from a natural disaster. By contrast, the "power dynamics whose unresolved tensions in terms of class, race, and cultural identity have dramatically come to light in the aftermath of Katrina" (Parasecoli 451) are erased in *The Princess and the Frog*, a 2009 American animated comedy-drama, which offers another culinary disclosure of Louisiana. In this romantic fantasy, cinematic representation of the culinary reproduction of Blackness shifts interpretative weight from racial injustice and cultural uniqueness (as evidenced in *Treme*) to gender stereotyping as intraracial politics.

Moreover, the analytical framework in the third chapter of the present study can be used to mine social landscapes depicted in other civil rights fictions. Thulani Davis's novel *1959* (1992) dramatizes the protests by African American college students who organized sit-ins at the lunch counter of the local Woolworth's. Davis skillfully portrays how White supremacists' reactions to the nonviolent protest (including severely beating and jailing protestors) served to galvanize the African American community. Apart from the texts that adopt a Black voice/perspective, such as Davis's *1959* or ZZ Packer's "Doris Is Coming" (2003), which depicts the segregationist politics of the United States as confronted by a small girl during a sit-in at a five-and-dime, there are the stories written by Joanne Leedom-Ackerman and Lee Martin that trouble the 1960s critical consensus about "protest" versus "moral" fictions, penned respectively by African American and White authors.[7] For instance, in Leedom-Ackerman's "The Beginning of Violence" (1985), one White student's compassion, which masks her benign paternalism and inherent insensitivity to African American lives, leads to a tragedy in a Black family. In Martin's "The Welcome Table" (1996), a New Hampshire family, relocated to Nashville, participates in training sessions that include role playing. Ostensibly benign White involvement in nonviolent demonstrations, such as aiding lunch counter protestors in mastering nonviolence, accidentally brings to life the son's true racial sentiments. Last, James Alan McPherson's "A Loaf of Bread" (1977) offers a broad commentary on race relations after the

---

7. Sharon Monteith explains that "by the 1960s, another assumption had come close to critical consensus: that when Black writers portrayed race relations, it was in the form of 'protest' fictions or 'problem' novels, and that 'moral' fictions about the civil rights–era South were written by whites coming to consciousness of the movement's destabilizing of the racial status quo" ("Civil Rights Fiction" 161).

civil rights movement. The short story depicts race relations as a zero-sum game in which socialism (hiding behind Christianity) competes with Ayn Rand's objectivism and moralism (hiding behind capitalism) for predominance. In McPherson's story, Whites tend to underestimate the prevalence and severity of the structural differences that disfranchise Blacks, whereas African Americans do not seem to strive for the agency needed to start grocery stores or urban farms in their impoverished neighborhood, which could just as well be any typical food desert in America. The sheer number of references to intersections of food and race in the fictions of the civil rights era and beyond suggests the potency of that particular social drama as a source of creative inspiration for imaginative narrative renditions. The need to revisit old battlefields is suggestive of their enduring importance on the contemporary social scene; thus, as Sharon Monteith claims, "their continuing relevance carries them into the twenty-first century" ("Civil Rights Fiction" 171).

The choice of Du Bois's color line as a defining feature behind the selection of material for the analysis at hand does not assume a single "grand narrative" about Southern identities. Monocausal explanations generally present difficulties as they are reductive in nature. However, in the context of the American South as examined in this study, the biracial prism does not necessarily impose interpretative limitations. John Howard Griffin's assertion about the universality of racism opens the possibility of including other ethnic groups in research projects like this one:

> The Negro. The South. These are details. The real story is the universal one of men who destroy the souls of other men (and in the process destroy themselves) for reasons neither really understands. It is the story of the persecuted, the defrauded, the feared and detested. I could have been a Jew in Germany, a Mexican in a number of states, or a member of any "inferior" group. Only the details would have differed. The story would be the same. (Griffin, *Black Like Me*)[8]

The inclusion of ethnic groups, racial in-betweenness and other forms of racial negotiation will reframe the nature and tenor of the analysis of Southern identities reflected through foodways and foodscape. The

---

8. Qtd. in Sharon Monteith, "Southern Like Us?" 69–70.

current research can be expanded in the future to follow the recent ethnic turn in Southern studies and decenter that discipline's focus on race as the prime focus of analysis.

The current project also opens up the spectrum of interrelations between race and food and suggests directions for future research that might offer an even wider array of their correlations in literary and cultural studies. Although the connection of food to ethnicity has not been pursued in this project, applications of identity negotiations analogous to this study's exploration of racial identity in relation to foodscapes and foodways suggest productive venues for further research. The presence of Asian Americans and those of Hispanic and Latinx descent, the two most culturally visible minorities not just in the South, but throughout the United States, complicate the neat White–Black boundaries. Such a discussion of ethnic groups can be instructive while reimagining the South at the end of the twentieth century. It would add "color" to the conventional White–Black binary and expand research possibilities regarding the rich panoply of the contemporary South's ethnic diversity, which would reposition the South within the larger narrative of multicultural America. Hence, the shift toward ethnicity might add to, and possibly "dethrone," race and class as major categories differentiating Southerners. This conflation of race and ethnicity is illustrated by "the racial middle," the term Eileen O'Brien coined to encompass other racial and ethnic groups in America, or Leslie Bow's "partly colored" category, the term the critic used to describe Asian Americans in the South. Novels such as Lan Cao's *Monkey Bridge* (1997) depict how diasporic groups negotiate their identities in the process of cultural assimilation through foodways and foodscape. Other works such as Monique Truong's *Bitter in the Mouth* (2010) and *Daughter from Đà Nẵng*, a 2002 documentary by Gail Dolgin and Vicente Franco, depict how Vietnamese Americans, being "partly colored," experience the Du Boisian "double consciousness" below the Mason-Dixon line. New immigration patterns and ethnic diasporas with markedly different histories and cultural influences that have shaped the social landscape in the American South in the second half of the twentieth century emphasize the need for the renegotiation of Whiteness[9]

9. Susan Koshy even claims that "a crucial effect of this renegotiation was the morphing of race into ethnicity in public discourses about national belonging, social difference, economic inequality, and global competitiveness" (156).

and the reconstruction of the rich racial and ethnic diversity that exists beyond the Du Boisian color line. Although the present study has focused on race—and for good reason—it does provide a template for future scholarship focusing on foodways and foodscapes depicted in media texts as a means of understanding ethnicity within the increasingly complex and shifting demographics of the American South.

WORKS CITED

Primary Sources

Douglas, Ellen. *Can't Quit You, Baby*. Penguin, 1989.

Driving Miss Daisy. Directed by Bruce Beresford. Performances by Jessica Tandy, Morgan Freeman, and Dan Aykroyd. Warner Brothers, the Zanuck Company, 1989.

Flagg, Fannie. *Fried Green Tomatoes at the Whistle Stop Cafe*. 1987. McGraw-Hill, 1988.

Gaines, Ernest. "The Sky Is Gray." 1963. *The Oxford Book of the American South: Testimony, Memory, and Fiction*, edited by Edward L. Ayers and Bradley C. Mittendorf. Oxford, 1997, pp. 492–516.

Grooms, Anthony. "Food that Pleases, Food to Take Home." 1995. *Crossing the Color Line: Readings in Black and White*, edited by Suzanne W. Jones. University of South Carolina Press, 2000, pp. 133–42.

O'Connor, Flannery. "The Artificial Nigger." *The Complete Stories*. Farrar, Straus and Giroux, 1971, pp. 249–70.

Percy, Walker. *The Last Gentleman*. 1966. Picador, 1999.

Stockett, Kathryn. *The Help*. G. P. Putnam's Sons, 2009.

Uhry, Alfred. *Driving Miss Daisy*. 1986. Theatre Communications Group, 2008.

Secondary Sources

Abel, Elizabeth. *Signs of the Times: The Visual Politics of Jim Crow*. University of California Press, 2010.

Adams, Joshua. "James Baldwin Says #BlackLivesMatter." *HuffPost* August 2, 2016. Essay originally presented at the 2016 International James Baldwin Conference at the American University of Paris. http://www.huffingtonpost.com/entry/james-baldwin-says-blacklivesmatter_us_57a0c7a8e4b07066ba1fba48. Accessed May 2, 2017.

Adema, Pauline. *Garlic Capital of the World: Gilroy, Garlic, and the Making of a Festive Foodscape*. University Press of Mississippi, 2009.

Alexander, Michelle. *The New Jim Crow: Mass Incarceration in the Age of Colorblindness*. The New Press, 2010.

Anderson, Dawolu Jabari. *Gullah Sci-Fi Mysteries*. 2008–10. http://gullah-sci-fi-mysteries.blogspot.nl. Accessed February 14, 2013.

Anderson, Eugene N. *Everyone Eats: Understanding Food and Culture*. New York University Press, 2005.

Armstrong, Julie Buckner. "Civil Rights Movement Fiction." *The Cambridge Companion to American Civil Rights Literature*, edited by Julie Buckner. Cambridge University Press, 2015, pp. 85–103.

Atkins-Sayre, Wendy, and Ashli Quesinberry Stokes. "Crafting the Cornbread Nation: The Southern Foodways Alliance and Southern Identity." *Southern*

Communication Journal, vol. 79, no. 2, 2014, pp. 77–93. DOI:
10.1080/1041794X.2013.861010.

Babb, Valerie. *Ernest Gaines: A Critical Companion*. Twayne Publishers, 1991.

Baker, Ella. "Bigger Than a Hamburger." 1960. *Let Nobody Turn Us Around: Voices
of Resistance, Reform, and Renewal*, edited by Manning Marable and Leith
Mullings. Rowman and Littlefield, 2009, pp. 375–76.

Baldwin, James. *Nobody Knows My Name: More Notes of a Native Son*. 1961.
Vintage, 1993.

Barbas, Samantha. "Just Like Home: 'Home Cooking' and the Domestication of the
American Restaurant." *Gastronomica: The Journal of Food and Culture*, vol. 2,
no. 4, 2002, pp. 43–52.

Barthes, Roland. "Toward a Psychosociology of Contemporary Food Consumption."
1961. *Food and Culture: A Reader*, 3rd edition, edited by Carol Counihan and
Penny Van Esterik. Routledge, 2013, pp. 23–30.

Beardsworth, Alan, and Teresa Keil. *Sociology on the Menu: An Invitation to the
Study of Food and Society*. Routledge, 1997.

Bell, David, and Gill Valentine. *Consuming Geographies: We Are Where We Eat*.
Routledge, 1997.

Benson, Melanie. *Disturbing Calculations: The Economics of Identity in Postcolonial
Southern Literature, 1912–2002*. University of Georgia Press, 2008.

Berg, Jennifer, et al. "Food Studies." *Encyclopedia of Food and Culture*. Vol. 2. *Food
Production to Nuts*, edited by H. Katz. Charles Scribner's Sons, 2003, pp. 16–18.

Bilyeu, Suzanne. "1960: Sitting Down to Take a Stand." *New York Times Upfront*,
January 18, 2010, pp. 24–27.

Block, Mary. "African American Responses to Early Jim Crow." *African Americans
in the Nineteenth Century: People and Perspectives*, edited by Dixie Ray
Haggard. ABC-CLIO, 2010, pp. 111–32.

Boatswain, Sharon, and Richard Lalonde. "Social Identity and Preferred Ethnic/
Racial Labels for Blacks in Canada." *Journal of Black Psychology*, vol. 26,
no. 2, May 2000, pp. 216–34.

Bomberger, Ann. "The Servant and the Served: Ellen Douglas's *Can't Quit You,
Baby*." *Southern Literary Journal*, vol. 31, 1998, pp. 17–34. Ebscohost,
Academic premier. http://search.ebscohost.com. Accessed July 10, 2011.

Bonilla-Silva, Eduardo. *Racism without Racists: Color-Blind Racism and the
Persistence of Racial Inequality in America*. Littlefield Publishers, 2003.

Bourdain, Anthony. *A Cook's Tour: Global Adventures in Extreme Cuisines*.
Bloomsbury Press, 2001.

Brewster, Zachary, and Sarah Rusche. "Quantitative Evidence of the Continuing
Significance of Race: Tableside Racism in Full-Service Restaurants." *Journal
of Black Studies*, vol. 43, no. 4, May 2012, pp. 359–84.

Brown, David, and Clive Webb. *Race in the American South: From Slavery to Civil
Rights*. Edinburgh University Press, 2007.

Brown, Nikki, and Barry Stentiford. "Introduction." *The Jim Crow Encyclopedia*,
edited by Nikki Brown and Barry Stentiford. Greenwood Press, 2008,
pp. xvii–xxii.

Burke, William. "*Bloodline*: A Black Man's South." *College Language Association
Journal*, vol. 19, 1976, pp. 545–58.

Callahan, John F. "Hearing Is Believing: The Landscape of Voice in Ernest Gaines's *Bloodline.*" *Callaloo*, vol. 20, Winter 1984, pp. 86–112.

Camp, Charles. "Foodways." *American Folklore: An Encyclopedia*, edited by Jan Harold Brunvand. Garland, 1996, pp. 622–28.

———. "Foodways." *Encyclopedia of Food and Culture*. Vol. 2. *Food Production to Nuts*, edited by H. Katz. Charles Scribner's Sons, 2003, pp. 29–31.

Carey, James. *Communication as Culture*. 1989. Routledge, 2009.

Carter, Jimmy. "Atlanta, Georgia Remarks Accepting the Martin Luther King, Jr. Nonviolent Peace Prize. Jan. 14, 1979." *Public Papers of the Presidency of the United States: Jimmy Carter, January 1 to June 22, 1979*. The American Presidency Project. https://www.presidency.ucsb.edu/documents/atlanta-georgia-remarks-accepting-the-martin-luther-king-jr-nonviolent-peace-prize. Accessed November 13, 2016.

Cauti, Camille. "'Pass the Identity Please': Culinary Passing in America." *A Tavola: Food, Tradition, and Community Among Italian Americans*, edited by Edvige Giunta and Samuel J. Patti. American Italian Historical Association, 1998, pp. 10–19.

Certeau, Michel de. *The Practice of Everyday Life*. Translated by Steven Rendall. University of California Press, 1984.

Chee-Beng, Tan. "Commensality and the Organization of Social Relations." *Commensality: From Everyday Food to Feast*, edited by Susanne Kerner et al. Bloomsbury, 2015, pp. 13–29.

Childress, Alice. *Like One of the Family: Conversations from a Domestic's Life*. 1956. Beacon Press, 1986.

"Civil Rights Act of 1964." Pub. L. 88-532. 78 Stat. 241. July 2, 1964.

Clark, Clifford E. "The Vision of the Dining Room: Plan Book Dreams and Middle-Class Realities." *Dining in America, 1850–1900*, edited by Kathryn Grove. University of Massachusetts Press, 1987, pp. 142–72.

Clark-Lewis, Elizabeth. "'This Work Had a' End': The Transition from Live-In to Day Work. Southern Women: The Intersection of Race, Class and Gender. Working Paper #2." Center for Research on Women, Memphis State University, 1985. https://archive.org/details/ERIC_ED287744. Accessed May 15, 2017.

Connerly, Charles. *"The Most Segregated City in America": City Planning and Civil Rights in Birmingham, 1920–1980*. University of Virginia Press, 2005.

Cooley, Angela Jill. "'The Customer Is Always White': Food, Race, and Contested Eating Space in the South." *The Larder: Food Studies Methods from the American South*, edited by John Edge et al. University of Georgia Press, 2013, pp. 240–72.

———. "'Eating with Negroes': Food and Racial Taboo in the Twentieth-Century South." *Southern Quarterly*, vol. 52, no. 2, Winter 2015, pp. 69–89.

———. *To Live and Dine in Dixie: Foodways and Culture in the Twentieth-Century South*. Dissertation, Tuscaloosa, Ala., University of Alabama Libraries, 2011. http://purl.lib.ua.edu/41216. Accessed September 10, 2015.

Costello, Brannon. "Hybridity and Racial Identity in Walker Percy's *The Last Gentleman.*" *Mississippi Quarterly*, vol. 55, no. 1, Winter 2001/2002, pp. 3–41.

Counihan, Carole M. "Food Rules in the United States: Individualism, Control, and Hierarchy." *Anthropological Quarterly*, vol. 65, no. 2, April 1992, pp. 55–66.

Cox, Karen L. "Black Domestic in a Can: A South Carolina Ad Agency 'Helps' Glory Foods." *University of North Carolina Press Blog*. Posted April 19, 2012. http://uncpressblog.com/2012/04/19/karen-l-cox-black-domestic-in-a-can-a -south-carolina-ad-agency-helps-glory-foods/. Accessed January 11, 2017.

Cuthbert-Kerr, Simon T. "Sit-Ins." *The Jim Crow Encyclopedia*, edited by Nikki Brown and Barry Stentiford. Greenwood Press, 2008, pp. 732–37.

Davie, Maurice R. *Negroes in American Society*. Whittlesey House, 1950.

Davis, David. "Invisible in the Kitchen: Racial Intimacy, Domestic Labor, and Civil Rights." *Writing in the Kitchen: Essays on Southern Literature and Foodways*, edited by David A. Davis and Tara Powell. University Press of Mississippi, 2014, pp. 143–58.

Davis, Thulani. *1959*. Grove Press, 1992.

DeVault, Marjorie. *Feeding the Family: The Social Organization of Caring as Gendered Work*. University of Chicago Press, 1991.

DiAngelo, Robin. "White Fragility." *International Journal of Critical Pedagogy*, vol. 3, no. 3, 2011, pp. 54–70.

Dickson-Carr, Darryl. "Grooms, Anthony." *The Columbia Guide to Contemporary African American Fiction*, edited by Dickson-Carr. Columbia University Press, 2005, pp. 113.

Diner, Hasia. *Hungering for America: Italian, Irish, and Jewish Foodways in the Age of Migration*. Harvard University Press, 2001.

Dollard, John. *Caste and Class in a Southern Town*. Doubleday Anchor Books, 1949.

Donaldson, Susan. "'A Stake in the Story': Kathryn Stockett's *The Help*, Ellen Douglas's *Can't Quit You, Baby*, and the Politics of Southern Storytelling." *Southern Cultures*, vol. 20, no. 1, Spring 2014, pp. 38–50.

Douglas, Mary. "Deciphering a Meal." *Daedalus*, vol. 101, no. 1, Winter 1972, pp. 61–81.

———. *Natural Symbols: Explorations in Cosmology*. 1970. Routledge, 1996.

———. *Purity and Danger*. Routledge, 1966.

Douglass, Frederick. *My Bondage and My Freedom*. Miller, Orton, and Mulligan, 1855. Documenting the American South. http://docsouth.unc.edu/neh /douglass55/douglass55.html. Accessed May 10, 2017.

Draaisma, Douwe. *Forgetting: Myths, Perils, and Compensations*. 2010. Translated by Liz Waters. Yale University Press, 2015.

Du Bois, W. E. B. "The Position of the Negro in the American Social Order: Where Do We Go from Here?" *Journal of Negro Education*, vol. 8, no. 3, July 1939, pp. 551–70.

———. "Reconstruction and Its Benefits." *The American Historical Review*, vol. 15, no. 4, July 1910, pp. 781–99.

———. *The Souls of Black Folk*. 1903. With an Introduction and Chronology by Jonathan Scott Holloway. Yale University Press, 2015.

———. "The Souls of White Folk." 1921. *The Oxford W. E. B. Du Bois Reader*, edited by Eric J. Sundquist. Oxford University Press, 1996, pp. 497–511.

Dunbar, Paul Laurence. "We Wear the Mask" (1896). *The Lyrics of Lowly Life*. University of Michigan Humanities Text Initiative, 1995. http://name.umdl .umich.edu/BAC5659.0001.001. Accessed December 15, 2015.

Durr, Virginia Foster. *Outside the Magic Circle: The Autobiography of Virginia Foster Durr*, edited by Hollinger F. Barnard. University of Alabama Press, 1985.

Edge, John. *A Gracious Plenty*. Putnam, 1999.

———. "The Hidden Radicalism of Southern Food." *New York Times*, May 6, 2017. https://www.nytimes.com/2017/05/06/opinion/sunday/the-hidden -radicalism-of-southern-food.html. Accessed May 10, 2017.

———. *The Potlikker Papers: A Food History of the Modern South*. Penguin Press, 2017.

Egerton, John. "Fried Chicken." *The New Encyclopedia of Southern Culture: Foodways*. Vol. 7, edited by John Edge. University of North Carolina Press, 2007, pp. 141–43.

———. *Southern Food: At Home, on the Road, in History*. Knopf, 1987.

Ellison, Ralph. *Invisible Man*. 1952. Vintage, 1972.

Entman, Robert. "Framing: Toward Clarification of a Fractured Paradigm." *Journal of Communication*, vol. 43, 1993, pp. 51–58.

Essien, Kwame. "Greensboro Four." *The Jim Crow Encyclopedia*, edited by Nikki Brown and Barry Stentiford. Greenwood Press, 2008, pp. 348–49.

Faulkner, William. *Intruder in the Dust*. 1948. Signet, 1958.

Ferris, Marcie Cohen. "The Edible South: Introduction." *Southern Cultures*, vol. 15, no. 4, Winter 2009, pp. 3–27.

———. *The Edible South: The Power of Food and the Making of an American Region*. University of North Carolina Press, 2014.

———. "Feeding the Jewish Soul in the Delta Diaspora." *Southern Cultures*, vol. 10, no. 3, 2004, pp. 52–85.

———. "History, Place, and Power: Studying Southern Food." *Southern Cultures*, vol. 21, no. 1, Spring 2015, pp. 2–7.

Fischer, Roger. "Hollywood and the Mythic Land Apart, 1988–1991." *A Mythic Land Apart: Reassessing Southerners and Their History*, edited by John Smith and Thomas H. Appleton Jr. Greenwood Press, 1997, pp. 177–90.

Fischler, Claude. "Food, Self, Identity." *Social Science Information*, vol. 27, no. 2, 1988, pp. 275–92.

Fleming, Walter. "The Servant Problem in a Black Belt Village." *Sewanee Review*, vol. 13, no. 1, January 1905, pp. 1–17.

Franklin, John. "Martin Luther King, Jr. and the Afro-American Protest Tradition." *We Shall Overcome: Martin Luther King, Jr. and the Black Freedom Struggle*, edited by Peter Albert and Ronald Hoffman. Pantheon Books, 1990, pp. 95–112.

Freidberg, Susanne. "Editorial: Not All Sweetness and Light; New Cultural Geographies of Food." *Social and Cultural Geography*, vol. 4, no. 1, 2003, pp. 3–6.

Freud, Sigmund. *Totem and Taboo*. Vintage, 1918.

Foucault, Michel. "Afterword: The Subject and Power." *Michel Foucault: Beyond Structuralism and Hermeneutics*, edited by H. L. Dreyfus and P. Rabinow. University of Chicago Press, 1982, pp. 208–26.

———. *The Will to Knowledge: The History of Sexuality*. Vol. 1. 1978. Translated by Robert Hurley. Penguin, 1998.

Gabaccia, Donna R. *We Are What We Eat: Ethnic Food and the Making of Americans*. Harvard University Press, 1998.

Gates, Henry Louis, Jr. "Afterword—Zora Neale Hurston: A Negro Way of Saying." *Their Eyes Were Watching God*, by Zora Neale Hurston, 1937. Harper Perennial Modern Classics, 2006, pp. 195–205.

Gatewood, Willard B. *Aristocrats of Color: The Black Elite, 1880–1920.* Indiana University Press, 1990.

Gaudet, Marcia, and Carl Wooton. *Porch Talk with Ernest Gaines: Conversations on the Writer's Craft.* Louisiana State University Press, 1990.

Genovese, Eugene. *Roll, Jordan, Roll: The World the Slaves Made.* Vintage Books, 1976.

George, Rosemary. *The Politics of Home: Postcolonial Relocations and Twentieth-Century Fiction.* Cambridge University Press, 1996.

Goffman, Erving. *The Presentation of Self in Everyday Life.* Doubleday, 1959.

Golden, Harry. *Only in America.* 1958. PermaBook, 1959.

Goldman, Anne E. " 'I Yam What I Yam': Cooking, Culture, and Colonialism." *De/Colonizing the Subject: The Politics of Gender in Women's Autobiography,* edited by Sidonie Smith and Julia Watson. University of Minnesota Press, 1992, pp. 169–95.

Green, Victor, editor. *The Negro Motorist Green Book: An International Travel Guide.* Victor H. Green, 1936–66.

"The Greensboro Chronology." *International Civil Rights Center and Museum.* http://www.sitinmovement.org/history/greensboro-chronology.asp. Accessed June 10, 2015.

Grier, William, and Price M. Cobbs. *Black Rage.* BasicBooks, 1992.

Griffin, John Howard. *Black Like Me.* Signet, 1996.

Grooms, Anthony. "Interview with Tony M. Grooms." Interview by Thomas Scott and Dede Yow. Edited and indexed by Susan F. Batungbacal. Conducted at Kennesaw State University, January 18, 2006. "Kennesaw State U Oral History Project," KSU Oral History Series, no. 44. https://soar.kennesaw.edu/bitstream/handle/11360/351/ksu-45-05-001-03044.pdf?sequence=1. Accessed December 12, 2014.

Grubb, Alan. "House and Home in the Victorian South: The Cookbook as Guide." *Joy and In Sorrow: Women, Family, and Marriage in the Victorian South, 1830–1900,* edited by Carol Bleser. Oxford University Press, 1991, pp. 154–75.

Gwin, Minrose. *Black and White Women of the Old South: The Peculiar Sisterhood in American Literature.* University of Tennessee Press, 1985.

———. "Sweeping the Kitchen: Revelation and Revolution in Contemporary Southern Women's Writing." *Southern Quarterly,* vol. 30, no. 2–3, Winter–Spring 1992, pp. 54–62.

Hampton, Henry, and Steve Fayer. *Voices of Freedom: An Oral History of the Civil Rights Movement from the 1950s through the 1960s.* Bantam Books, 1990.

Hale, Grace Elizabeth. *Making Whiteness: The Culture of Segregation in the South, 1890–1940.* Pantheon, 1998.

Hall, Stuart. "Cultural Identity and Diaspora." *Identity: Community, Culture, Difference,* edited by Jonathan Rutherford. Lawrence and Wishart Ltd, 1990, pp. 222–37.

Harré, Rom. "Positioning Theory: Moral Dimensions of Social-Cultural Psychology." *The Oxford Handbook of Culture and Psychology,* edited by Jaan Valsiner. Oxford University Press, 2012, pp. 191–206.

Harris, Jessica B. *High on the Hog: A Culinary Journey from Africa to America.* Kindle edition. Bloomsbury, 2001.

Harris, Trudier. *From Mammies to Militants: Domestics in Black American Literature.* Temple University Press, 1982.

Hauck-Lawson, Annie. "Hearing the Food Voice: An Epiphany for a Researcher." *Digest: An Interdisciplinary Study of Food and Foodways*, vol. 12, no. 1–2, 1992, pp. 26–7.

Higginbotham, Evelyn Brooks. "African-American Women's History and the Metalanguage of Race." *Signs*, vol. 17, no. 2, Winter 1992, pp. 251–74.

Hillard, Kathleen. *Masters, Slaves, and Exchange: Power's Purchase in the Old South.* Cambridge University Press, 2014.

Hoelscher, Steven. "Making Place, Making Race: Performances of Whiteness in the Jim Crow South." *Annals of the Association of American Geographers*, vol. 93, no. 3, 2003, pp. 657–86.

Holland, Sharon. *Erotic Life of Racism.* Duke University Press, 2012.

hooks, bell. *Black Looks: Race and Representation.* 1992. Routledge, 2015.

———. *Yearning: Race, Gender, and Cultural Politics.* South End Press, 1990.

Horowitz, David. *Inside the Klavern: The Secret History of a Ku Klux Klan of the 1920s.* Southern Illinois University Press, 1999.

Hughes, Langston. *Not Without Laughter.* In *The Collected Works of Langston Hughes.* Vol. 4, edited by Dolan Hubbard. University of Missouri Press, 2001, pp. 13–210.

———. "What Shall We Do about the South?" *Common Ground*, vol. 3, Winter 1943, pp. 3–6.

Hurston, Zora Neale. *Dust Tracks on a Road: An Autobiography.* Virago, 1986.

Huxley, Julian. "Clines: An Auxiliary Taxonomic Principle." *Nature*, vol. 142, 1938, pp. 219–20.

Jacobsen, Karen. "Disrupting the Legacy of Silence: Ellen Douglas's *Can't Quit You, Baby*." *Southern Literary Journal*, vol. 32, 2000, pp. 15–27. Ebscohost, Academic premier. http://search.ebscohost.com. Accessed July 10, 2011.

James, Theresa. "Race in the Kitchen: Domesticity and the Growth of Racial Harmony in Ellen Douglas's *Can't Quit You, Baby* and Christine Wiltz's *Glass House*." *South Atlantic Review*, vol. 65, no. 1, Winter 2000, pp. 78–97.

Janeway, Elizabeth. *Powers of the Weak.* William Morrow, 1981.

Johnson, Charles S. *Growing Up in the Black Belt: Negro Youth in the Rural South.* 1941. Schocken Books, 1967.

Johnson, James Weldon. *Along This Way: The Autobiography of James Weldon Johnson.* Viking, 1933.

Kalcik, Susan. "Ethnic Foodways in America: Symbol and the Performance of Identity." *Ethnic and Regional Foodways in the United States: The Performance of Group Identity*, edited by Linda Keller Brown and Kay Mussell. University of Tennessee Press, 1984, pp. 37–65.

Katzman, David. *Seven Days a Week: Women and Domestic Service in Industrializing America.* Oxford University Press, 1978.

Kelley, Robin. *Race Rebels: Culture, Politics, and the Black Working Class.* Free Press, 1996.

Kerner, Susanne and Cynthia Chou. "Introduction." *Commensality: From Everyday Food to Feast*, edited by Susanne Kerner et al. Bloomsbury, 2015, pp. 1–12.

King, Martin Luther, Jr. "I Have a Dream." Speech at March on Washington for Jobs and Freedom, Washington, DC, August 28, 1963. The Martin Luther King, Jr. Center for Nonviolent Social Change. http://www.thekingcenter.org/archive/document/i-have-dream-2#. Accessed May 20, 2015.

———. "Letter from Birmingham Jail." April 16, 1963. The Martin Luther King, Jr. Research and Education Institute, Stanford University. https://kinginstitute.stanford.edu/king-papers/documents/letter-birmingham-jail. Accessed March 26, 2015.

———. "The Quest for Peace and Justice." Nobel Lecture. December 11, 1964. The Nobel Foundation: http://www.nobelprize.org/nobel_prizes/peace/laureates/1964/king-lecture.html. Accessed November 11, 2015. Also published in *Nobel Lectures—Peace 1951–1970*, vol. 3, edited by Frederick W. Haberman. Elsevier Publishing Company, 1972.

———. "Strength to Love." 1963. The Martin Luther King, Jr. Center for Nonviolent Social Change. http://www.thekingcenter.org/archive/document/strength-love. Accessed May 17, 2015.

———. *Where Do We Go from Here. Chaos or Community?* 1968. Foreword by Coretta Scott King. Introduction by Vincent Harding. Beacon Press, 1986.

———. *Why We Can't Wait*. New American Library, 1964.

"The King Philosophy." The Martin Luther King, Jr. Center for Nonviolent Social Change. http://www.thekingcenter.org/king-philosophy. Accessed May 17, 2015.

Kirshenblatt-Gimblett, Barbara. "Playing to the Senses: Food as a Performance Medium." *Performance Research*, vol. 4, no. 1, 1999, pp. 1–30.

Kissel, Susan. *Moving On: The Heroines of Shirley Ann Grau, Anne Tyler, and Gail Godwin*. Bowling Green State University Popular Press, 1996.

Klarman, Michael. *From Jim Crow to Civil Rights: The Supreme Court and the Struggle for Racial Equality*. Oxford University Press, 2004.

Koshy, Susan. "Morphing Race into Ethnicity: Asian Americans and Critical Transformations of Whiteness." *Boundary* 2, vol. 28, no. 1, 2001, pp. 153–94.

Kossie-Chernyshev, Karen. "Racial Customs and Etiquette." *The Jim Crow Encyclopedia*, edited by Nikki Brown and Barry Stentiford. Greenwood Press, 2008, pp. 643–50.

Kovacik, Charles, and John Winberry. *South Carolina: A Geography*. Westview Press, 1987.

Kowal, Rebekah J. "Staging the Greensboro Sit-Ins." *Drama Review*, vol. 48, no. 4, Winter 2004, pp. 135–54.

Krissoff Boehm, Lisa. *Making a Way out of No Way: African American Women and the Second Great Migration*. University Press of Mississippi, 2009.

Kristeva, Julia. *Powers of Horror: An Essay on Abjection*. Columbia University Press, 1982.

Latshaw, Beth. "The Soul of the South: Race, Food, and Identity in the American South." *The Larder: Food Studies Methods from the American South*, edited by John T. Edge et al. University of Georgia Press, 2013, pp. 99–127.

Lee, Harper. *To Kill a Mockingbird*. Lippincott, 1960.

Leedom-Ackerman, Joanne. "The Beginning of Violence." 1985. *Short Stories of the Civil Rights Movement: An Anthology*, edited by Margaret Earley Whitt. University of Georgia Press, 2006, pp. 53–63.

Levenstein, Harvey. *The Paradox of Plenty: A Social History of Eating in Modern America.* Oxford University Press, 1993.

Lévi-Strauss, Claude. "The Culinary Triangle." 1966. *Food and Culture Reader.* Third edition, edited by Carole Counihan and Penny Van Esterik. Routledge, 2013, pp. 40–47.

Lewis, Anthony. *Portrait of a Decade: The Second American Revolution.* Random House, 1964.

Lindenfeld, Laura. "Women Who Eat Too Much: Femininity and Food in *Fried Green Tomatoes.*" *From Betty Crocker to Feminist Food Studies: Critical Perspectives on Women and Food,* edited by Arlene Voski Avakian and Barbara Haber. University of Massachusetts Press, 2005, pp. 221–45.

Lipsitz, George. *The Possessive Investment of Whiteness: How White People Profit from Identity Politics.* Temple University Press, 1998.

Livingstone, Frank B. "On the Non-existence of Human Races." *Current Anthropology,* vol. 3, 1962, pp. 279–81.

Lumpkin, Katharine Du Pre. Fragment from *The Making of a Southerner.* In *Southern Selves: From Mark Twain and Eudora Welty to Maya Angelou and Kaye Gibbons; A Collection of Autobiographical Writing,* edited by James H. Watkins. Vintage Books, 1998, pp. 145–58.

Madison, Soyini. *Critical Ethnography: Method, Ethics, and Performance.* Sage, 2005.

Mannur, Anita. "Edible Discourse: Thinking through Food and Its Archives." *American Literary History,* vol. 27, no. 2, Summer 2015, pp. 392–403.

Martin, Ben. "From Negro to Black to African American: The Power of Names and Naming." *Political Science Quarterly,* vol. 106, 1991, pp. 83–107.

Martin, Katrina. "'Let's All Sit Together:' Greensboro Citizens Respond to the 1960 Sit-Ins in the Edward R. Zane Papers." *The Devil's Tale* (blog), Duke University Libraries, posted February 11, 2016. https://blogs.library.duke.edu/rubenstein/2016/02/11/greensboro-sit-ins/. Accessed June 10, 2022.

Martin, Lee. "The Welcome Table." 1996. *Short Stories of the Civil Rights Movement: An Anthology,* edited by Margaret Earley Whitt. University of Georgia Press, 2006, pp. 64–80.

Massey, Doreen. "A Place Called Home?" *New Formations,* vol. 17, 1992, pp. 3–15.

McIntosh, William Alex, and Mary Zey. "Women as Gatekeepers of Food Consumption: A Sociological Critique." *Food and Foodways,* vol. 3, 1989, pp. 317–32.

McMurry, Linda O. *To Keep the Waters Troubled: The Life of Ida Wells.* Oxford University Press, 1998.

McPherson, James Alan. "A Loaf of Bread." 1977. *Crossing the Color Line: Readings in Black and White,* edited by Suzanne W. Jones. University of South Carolina Press, 2000, pp. 81–96.

Meier, August, and Elliott M. Rudwick. *CORE: A Study in the Civil Rights Movement, 1942–1968.* Oxford University Press, 1973.

Mennell, Stephen, et al. *The Sociology of Food: Eating, Diet, and Culture.* Sage, 1992.

Metress, Christopher. "Making Civil Rights Harder: Literature, Memory, and the Black Freedom Struggle." *Southern Literary Journal,* vol. 40, no. 2, Spring 2008, pp. 138–50.

Miller, Adrian. *Soul Food: The Surprising Story of an American Cuisine, One Plate at a Time*. University of North Carolina Press, 2013.

Miller, William. *The Anatomy of Disgust*. Harvard University Press, 1997.

Mintz, Sidney. "Food Enigmas, Colonial and Postcolonial." *Gastronomica: The Journal of Food and Culture*, vol. 10, no. 1, 2010, pp. 149–54.

Mirzoeff, Nicholas. "The Right to Look." *Critical Inquiry*, vol. 37, no. 3, Spring 2011, pp. 473–96. www.jstor.org. Accessed May 14, 2012.

Mitchell, Koritha. "Mamie Bradley's Unbearable Burden: Sexual and Aesthetic Politics in Bebe Moore Campbell's *Your Blues Ain't Like Mine*." *Callaloo*, vol. 31, no. 4, 2008, pp. 1048–67.

Montanari, Massimo. *Food Is Culture*. Translated by Albert Sonnenfeld. Columbia University Press, 2006.

Monteith, Sharon. "Civil Rights Fiction." *The Cambridge Companion to the Literature of the American South*, edited by Sharon Monteith. Cambridge University Press, 2013, pp. 159–73.

———. "Southern Like Us?" *The Global South*, vol. 1, nos. 1 and 2, 2007, pp. 66–74.

Moody, Anne. *Coming of Age in Mississippi*. 1968. Kindle edition. Bantam Dell, 2011.

Morgan, Iwan, and Philip Davies, eds. *From Sit-Ins to SNCC: The Student Civil Rights Movement in the 1960s*. University Press of Florida, 2012.

Morrison, Toni. *Jazz*. 1992. Vintage, 2004.

———. *Sula*. 1973. Vintage, 2004.

Moss, Thylias. "Lunchcounter Freedom." *Small Congregations: New and Selected Poems*. Ecco Press, 1993.

Muir, Diana. "Proclaiming Thanksgiving Throughout the Land: From Local to National Holiday." *We Are What We Celebrate: Understanding Holidays and Rituals*, edited by Amitai Etizoni and Jared Bloom. New York University Press, 2004, pp. 194–212.

Naylor, Gloria. *Linden Hills*. Penguin Books, 1986.

Nettles-Barcelón, Kimberly. "The Sassy Black Cook and the Return of the Magical Negress: Popular Representations of Black Women's Food Work." *Dethroning the Deceitful Pork Chop: Rethinking African American Foodways from Slavery to Obama*, edited by Jennifer Jensen Wallach. University of Arkansas Press, 2015, pp. 107–20.

Niewiadomska-Flis, Urszula. "Come Dine with Me, or Not: Performing Racial Relations in the Domestic Sphere in Alfred Uhry's *Driving Miss Daisy*." *Performing South: The U.S. South as Medium/Message*, edited by Beata Zawadka. Wydawnictwo Naukowe Uniwersytetu Szczecińskiego, 2015, pp. 185–203.

———. "Consuming Racial Expectations in Flannery O'Connor's 'The Artificial Nigger.'" *Southern Exposure: Essays Presented to Jan Nordby Gretlund*, edited by Thomas Ærvold Bjerre et al. Department for the Study of Culture, University of Southern Denmark, 2017, pp. 153–66.

———. "A Culinary Journey across the Color Line: Foodways and Race in Southern Literature and Motion Pictures." *Unsteadily Marching On: The US South in Motion*, edited by Constante Gonzáles Groba. Publicacions de la Universitat de València, 2013, pp. 101–10.

———. "From a White Woman's Kitchen into a Black Woman's Living Room: A

Reconfiguration of the Servant/Served Paradigm in Ellen Douglas's *Can't Quit You, Baby.*" *Annales Universitatis Mariae Curie-Skłodowska*, Sec. FF, vol. 34, 2016, pp. 95–106.

———. *Live and Let Di(n)e: Food and Race in the Texts of the American South*. KUL Publishing House, 2017.

———. "The Whistle Stop Cafe as a Challenge to the Jim Crow Bipartition of Society in Fannie Flagg's *Fried Green Tomatoes at the Whistle Stop Cafe.*" *Roczniki Humanistyczne*, vol. 64/11, 2016, pp. 169–84.

———. "Zapisy na stole, wywrotowe jedzenie: heteronormatywność i pomidory, *Smażone zielone pomidory*" ("Table Inscriptions, Subversive Foodways: Heteronormativity and Tomatoes, *Fried Green Tomatoes*"). *Inne Bębny. Różnica i Niezgoda w Literaturze i Kulturze Amerykańskiej* (*Different Drums: Difference and Dissent in American Literature and Culture*), edited by Izabella Kimak et al. Wydawnictwo UMCS, 2013, pp. 28–46.

"The Niagara Movement Declaration of Principles." 1905. Special Collections and University Archives. W. E. B. Du Bois Library. University of Massachusetts, Amherst, December 18, 2013. http://scua.library.umass.edu/collections/etext/dubois/niagara.pdf. Accessed July 20, 2016.

Oppenheimer, Gerald. "Paradigm Lost: Race, Ethnicity, and the Search for a New Population Taxonomy." *American Journal of Public Health*, vol. 91, 2001, pp. 1049–55.

Oates, Joyce Carol. "The Action of Mercy." *Flannery O'Connor*, edited by Harold Bloom. Bloom's Literary Criticism, 2009, pp. 43–48.

O'Connor, Flannery. *Mystery and Manners: Occasional Prose*, edited by Sally and Robert Fitzgerald. Farrar, Straus and Giroux, 1979.

Oldenburg, Ray. *The Great Good Place: Cafés, Coffee Shops, Bookstores, Bars, Hair Salons, and Other Hangouts at the Heart of a Community*. Marlowe and Company, 1999.

Opie, Frederick Douglass. *Hog and Hominy: Soul Food from Africa to America*. Kindle edition. Columbia University Press, 2008.

———. *Southern Food and Civil Rights: Feeding the Revolution*. The History Press, 2017.

Packer, ZZ. "Doris Is Coming." 2003. *Short Stories of the Civil Rights Movement: An Anthology*, edited by Margaret Earley Whitt. University of Georgia Press, 2006, pp. 102–25.

Palmer, Phyllis. *Domesticity and Dirt: Housewives and Domestic Servants in the United States, 1920–1945*. Temple University Press, 1989.

Parasecoli, Fabio. "A Taste of Louisiana: Mainstreaming Blackness through Food in *The Princess and the Frog.*" *Journal of African American Studies*, vol. 14, no. 4, December 2010, pp. 450–68. DOI: 10.1007/s12111-010-9137-y.

Parker, Idella, and Marjorie Keating. *Idella: Marjorie Rawlings' "Perfect Maid."* University Press of Florida, 1992.

Pascoe, Peggy. "Miscegenation Law, Court Cases, and Ideologies of 'Race' in Twentieth-Century America." *Journal of American History*, vol. 83, no. 1, June 1996, pp. 44–69.

Pattanaik, Diptiranjan. Review of *Trouble No More* by Anthony Grooms. *Melus*, vol. 24, no. 3, Fall 1999, pp. 193–95.

Peck, James. *Cracking the Color Line: Nonviolent Direct Action Methods of Eliminating Racial Discrimination*. CORE, 1960.

Pegram, Thomas. *One Hundred Percent American: The Rebirth and Decline of the Ku Klux Klan in the 1920s*. Ivan R. Dee, 2011.

Percy, William Alexander. *Lanterns on the Levee: Recollections of a Planter's Son*. Louisiana State University Press, 1941.

Piacentino, Edward. "Ku Klux Klan." *Companion to Southern Literature*, edited by Joseph M. Flora and Lucinda H. MacKethan. Louisiana State University Press, 2002, pp. 410–12.

Piatti-Farnell, Lorna. *Food and Culture in Contemporary American Fiction*. Routledge, 2011.

Pinkney, Andrea Davis. *Sit-In: How Four Friends Stood Up by Sitting Down*. Illustrated by Brian Pinkney. Little, Brown Books for Young Readers, 2010.

Pond, Catherine Seiberling. "Brief History of Pantries." *In the Pantry* (blog). http://www.inthepantry.blogspot.com/p/pantry-timeline.html. Accessed January 30, 2012.

———. *The Pantry: Its History and Modern Uses*. Gibbs Smith, 2007.

———. "Storage and Nostalgia: Pantry Design Ideas for Every Era." *Old House Journal*, October 4, 2011, http://www.oldhouseonline.com/pantry-design-ideas/. Accessed December 12, 2011.

Pratt, Mary Louise. *Imperial Eyes: Travel, Writing, and Transculturation*. Routledge, 1992.

Probyn, Elsepth. *Carnal Appetites: FoodSexIdentities*. Routledge, 2000.

Reed, John Shelton. *Kicking Back: Further Dispatches from the South*. University of Missouri Press, 1995.

Ring, Natalie J. "Jim Crow." *The Jim Crow Encyclopedia*, edited by Nikki Brown and Barry Stentiford. Greenwood Press, 2008, pp. 416–19.

Ritterhouse, Jennifer. *Growing Up Jim Crow: How Black and White Southern Children Learned Race*. University of North Carolina Press, 2006.

Roberts, John W. "The Individual and the Community in Two Short Stories by Ernest J. Gaines." *Black American Literature Forum*, vol. 18, no. 3, Fall 1984, pp. 110–13.

Rollins, Judith. *Between Women: Domestics and Their Employers*. Temple University Press, 1985.

Romine, Scott. *The Narrative Forms of Southern Community*. Louisiana State University Press, 1999.

Rosenblatt, Paul. *The Impact of Racism on African American Families: Literature as Social Science*. Ashgate, 2014.

Rudwick, Elliott M. *CORE: A Study in the Civil Rights Movement, 1942–1968*. Oxford University Press, 1973.

Rustin, Bayard. *Strategies for Freedom: The Changing Patterns of Black Protest*. Columbia University Press, 1976.

Sanders, Dori. *Clover*. Algonquin Books, 1990.

Sartisky, Michael. "Writing about Race in Difficult Times: An Interview with Ernest J. Gaines." *Conversations with Ernest J. Gaines*, edited by John Lowe. University Press of Mississippi, 1995, pp. 253–75.

Scharnhorst, Gary. "A Glimpse of Dickinson at Work." *American Literature*, vol. 57, no. 3, 1985, pp. 483–5. http://www.emilydickinsonmuseum.org/poet_at_work. Accessed August 15, 2014.

Scheper-Hughes, Nancy, and Margaret M. Lock. "The Mindful Body: A Prolegomenon to Future Work in Medical Anthropology." *Medical Anthropology Quarterly*, vol. 1, no. 1, March 1987, pp. 6–41.

Scott, James. *Weapons of the Weak: Everyday Forms of Peasant Resistance*. Yale University Press, 1985.

Scott, Joan. "Multiculturalism and the Politics of Identity." *The Identity in Question*, edited by John Rajchman. Routledge, 1995, pp. 3–14.

Shah, Aarushi. "All of Africa Will Be Free before We Can Get a Lousy Cup of Coffee: The Impact of the 1943 Lunch Counter Sit-Ins on the Civil Rights Movement." *The History Teacher*, vol. 46, no. 1, November 2012, pp. 127–47. Ebscohost, Academic premier. http://search.ebscohost.com. Accessed December 12, 2016.

Sharpless, Rebecca. *Cooking in Other Women's Kitchens: Domestic Workers in the South, 1865–1960*. University of North Carolina Press, 2010.

Silkey, Sarah. *Black Woman Reformer: Ida B. Wells, Lynching, and Transatlantic Activism*. University of Georgia Press, 2015.

Singer, Milton. *Man's Glossy Essence: Explorations in Semiotic Anthropology*. Indiana University Press, 1984.

Slocum, Rachel. "Race in the Study of Food." *Progress in Human Geography*, vol. 35, no. 3, 2010, pp. 303–27.

Smith, Lillian. *Killers of the Dream*. 1949. W. W. Norton, 1994.

———. "The Walls of Segregation Are Crumbling." *New York Times Magazine*, July 15, 1951, p. 32. http://www.nytimes.com/1951/07/15/archives/the-walls-of -segregation-are-crumbling-in-ten-years-dixie-race.html.

Smith, Tom. "Changing Racial Labels: From 'Colored' to 'Negro' to 'Black' to 'African American.'" *Public Opinion Quarterly*, vol. 56, no. 4, 1992, pp. 496–514.

Smith-Marzec, Marcia. "Mr. Head's Journey to the Cross: Character, Structure, and Meaning in O'Connor's 'The Artificial Nigger.'" *Logos: A Journal of Catholic Thought and Culture*, vol. 1, no. 3, Fall 1997, pp. 51–70.

Spivey, Diane. *The Peppers, Crackling, and Knots of Wool Cookbook: The Global Migration of African Cuisine*. State University of New York Press, 1999.

Steinhorn, Leonard, and Barbara Diggs-Brown. *By the Color of Our Skin: The Illusion of Integration and the Reality of Race*. Plume Books, 2000.

Stentiford, Barry. "North Carolina." *The Jim Crow Encyclopedia*, edited by Nikki Brown and Barry Stentiford. Greenwood Press, 2008, pp. 603–5.

Taylor, Joe Gray, and John Edge. "Southern Foodways." *The New Encyclopedia of Southern Culture: Foodways*. Vol. 7, edited by John Edge. University of North Carolina Press, 2007, pp. 1–14.

Titus, Mary. "The Dining Room Door Swings Both Ways: Food, Race, and Domestic Space in the Nineteenth-Century South." *Haunted Bodies: Gender and Southern Texts*, edited by Anne Goodwyn Jones and Susan V. Donaldson. University of Virginia Press, 1997, pp. 243–57.

Tompkins, Kyla Wazana. *Racial Indigestion: Eating Bodies in the 19th Century*. New York University Press, 2012.

Turner, Victor. *Dramas, Fields, and Metaphors: Symbolic Action in Human Society.* Cornell University Press, 1974.

———. *From Ritual to Theatre: The Human Seriousness of Play.* PAJ Publications, 1992.

———. *On the Edge of the Bush: Anthropology of Experience.* University of Arizona Press, 1985.

Twain, Mark. *The Adventures of Tom Sawyer.* 1876. Edited by Peter Stoneley. Oxford University Press, 2007.

Valentine, Gill. "Eating In: Home, Consumption and Identity." *Sociological Review*, vol. 47, no. 3, 1999, pp. 491–524.

Vann, Helene, and Jane Caputi. "Driving Miss Daisy: A New 'Song of the South.'" *Journal of Popular Film and Television*, vol. 18, no. 2, Summer 1990, pp. 80–82. Ebscohost, Academic premier. http://search.ebscohost.com. DOI: 10.1080/01956051.1990.9943658.

Visser, Margaret. *Much Depends on Dinner.* McClelland and Stewart Weidenfeld, 1986.

Walker, Jessica Kenyatta. "Mighty Matriarchs Kill It with a Skillet: Critically Reading Popular Representations of Black Womanhood and Food." *Dethroning the Deceitful Pork Chop: Rethinking African American Foodways from Slavery to Obama*, edited by Jennifer Jensen Wallach. University of Arkansas Press, 2015, pp. 121–34.

Wallach, Jennifer Jensen. "Civil Rights Movement." *The Jim Crow Encyclopedia*, edited by Nikki Brown and Barry Stentiford. Greenwood Press, 2008, pp. 151–62.

———, ed. *Dethroning the Deceitful Pork Chop: Rethinking African American Foodways from Slavery to Obama.* University of Arkansas Press, 2015.

Warnes, Andrew. *Hunger Overcome? Food and Resistance in Twentieth-Century African American Literature.* University of Georgia Press, 2004.

———. *Savage Barbecue: Race, Culture, and the Invention of America's First Food.* University of Georgia Press, 2008.

Waters, Mary. *Ethnic Options: Choosing Identities in America.* University of California Press, 1990.

Weatherford, Carole Boston. *Freedom on the Menu: The Greensboro Sit-Ins.* Dial Books for Young Readers, 2005.

Webb, Clive. "Breaching the Wall of Resistance: White Southern Reactions to the Sit-Ins." *From Sit-Ins to SNCC: The Student Civil Rights Movement in the 1960s*, edited by Iwan Morgan and Philip Davies. University Press of Florida, 2012, pp. 58–80.

Welter, Barbara. "The Cult of True Womanhood: 1820–1860." *American Quarterly*, vol. 18, no. 2, Summer 1966, pp. 151–74.

West, Cornel. *Race Matters.* Beacon Press, 1993.

Whitaker, Jan. "Domesticating the Restaurant: Marketing the Anglo-American Home." *From Betty Crocker to Feminist Food Studies: Critical Perspectives on Women and Food*, edited by Arlene Voski Avakian and Barbara Haber. University of Massachusetts Press, 2005, pp. 89–105.

Williams, David. "African-American Health: The Role of The Social Environment."

Journal of Urban Health: Bulletin of the New York Academy of Medicine, vol. 75, no. 2, June 1998, pp. 300–321.

Williams, Juan. *Eyes on the Prize: America's Civil Rights Years, 1954–1965*. Viking Penguin, 1987.

Williams, Patricia. *Seeing a Color-Blind Future: The Paradox of Race*. The Noonday Press, 1997.

Williams-Forson, Psyche. *Building Houses out of Chicken Legs: Black Women, Food, and Power*. University of North Carolina Press, 2006.

———. "More than Just the 'Big Piece of Chicken': The Power of Race, Class, and Food in American Consciousness." *Food and Culture: A Reader*. Third edition, edited by Carol Counihan and Penny Van Esterik. Routledge, 2013, pp. 107–18.

———. "Other Women Cooked for My Husband: Negotiating Gender, Food, and Identities in an African American / Ghanaian Household." *Feminist Studies*, vol. 36, no. 2, Summer 2010, pp. 435–61.

Williamson, Joel. *The Crucible of Race: Black-White Relations in the American South since Emancipation*. Oxford University Press, 1984.

Wilson, Charles Reagan. "Biscuits." *The New Encyclopedia of Southern Culture: Foodways*. Vol. 7, edited by John Edge. University of North Carolina Press, 2007, pp. 122–25.

Wilson, William Julius. *The Declining Significance of Race: Blacks and Changing American Institutions*. University of Chicago Press, 1978.

Witt, Doris. *Black Hunger: Food and the Politics of U.S. Identity*. Oxford University Press, 1999.

———. *Black Hunger: Soul Food and America*. University of Minnesota Press, 2004.

Wolff, Miles. *Lunch at the 5 & 10*. Ivan R. Dee, 1990.

Wood, Ralph C. "Where Is the Voice Coming From? Flannery O'Connor on Race." *Flannery O'Connor Bulletin*, vol. 22, 1993–94, pp. 90–118.

Woodward, C. Vann. *The Strange Career of Jim Crow*. Oxford University Press, 1955.

Wright, Gavin. *Sharing the Prize: The Economics of the Civil Rights Revolution in the American South*. Harvard University Press, 2013.

Wynes, Charles E. "The Evolution of Jim Crow Laws in Twentieth Century Virginia." *Phylon*, vol. 28, no. 4, Winter 1967, pp. 416–25.

X, Malcolm. *The Autobiography of Malcolm X: With the Assistance of Alex Haley*. Grove Press, 1965.

Yaeger, Patricia. *Dirt and Desire: Reconstructing Southern Women's Writing, 1930–1990*. University of Chicago Press, 2000.

Yentsch, Anne. "Excavating the South's African American Food History." *African Diaspora Archeology Network Newsletter*, 2008. http://www.diaspora.uiuc.edu/news0608/news0608.html. Accessed September 27, 2016.

Zeck, Shari. "Laughter, Loss, and Transformation in *Fried Green Tomatoes*." *Performing Gender and Comedy: Theories, Texts, and Contexts*, edited by Shannon Hengen. Gordon and Breach, 1998, pp. 219–29.

Zilber, Jeremy, and David Niven. "'Black' versus 'African American': Are Whites' Political Attitudes Influenced by the Choice of Racial Labels?" *Social Science Quarterly*, vol. 76, no. 3, 1995, pp. 655–64.

Audiovisual Materials

Baldwin, James. *I Am Not Your Negro*. Directed by Raul Peck. Narrated by Samuel L. Jackson. Velvet Film, 2016.

The Birth of a Nation. Directed by David Wark Griffith. Performance by Lillian Gish. Epoch Producing Corporation, 1915.

"Crispy Chicken Snack Wraps," *Burger King* commercial featuring Mary J. Blige. April 2012. https://www.youtube.com/watch?v=XukHU8y5GRQ. Accessed May 14, 2016.

Glory Foods. http://www.gloryfoods.com/. Accessed April 16, 2015.

The Long Walk Home. Directed by Richard Pearce. Performances by Whoopi Goldberg and Sissy Spacek. Miramax Films, 1990.

Mississippi Masala. Directed by Mira Nair. Performances by Denzel Washington and Sarita Choudhury. Black River Productions, 1991.

My Momma Throws Down. Host: Ralph Harris. Triage Entertainment. TV One, 2012/2013.

The Princess and the Frog. Directed by Ron Clements and John Musker. Performances by Anika Noni Rose and Bruno Campos. Walt Disney Animation Studios, 2009.

Treme. Created by David Simon and Eric Overmyer. HBO, 2010–13.

INDEX

signs: 88, 120, 141–42. *See also* visual politics of Jim Crow

silence: code of silence, 62, 157; Cornelia's (in *Can't Quit*), 58

Sit-In: How Four Friends Stood Up by Sitting Down (Andrea Davis Pinkney), 133n

sit-ins: in Greensboro, 125–26, 125n–26n, 137, 139, 147, 152; in Jack Spratt's Coffee House, 126; in Stoner's Restaurant, 126

"The Sky Is Gray" (Ernest Gaines), 23, 68, 88–100, 88n

slogans, 131, 136, 141n

Smith, Lillian, 84n, 86n, 121, 122, 132

social drama (Victor Turner's concept), 7, 24, 25n, 118, 133–34, 138, 143–44, 154, 157–60, 162, 163, 165, 174. *See also* breach; crisis; redressive action; resolution

social exclusion, 140, 144, 150, 167

social identity, 171

social mission, 108

social performance: cultural scripts of, 158, 159; in third places, 106

the South: affiliation, 57, 79, 80n, 128; "the cultural South," 5, 7–8, 14, 29n, 37, 37n, 46n, 48n, 56n, 64, 69–70, 73, 92, 112, 112n, 143, 151, 151n, 157n, 165, 167, 171, 175; "the figurative South," 5, 30, 31, 38, 48, 68, 91, 120, 121, 130, 134, 144, 164, 170, 171, 173n, 174; "the imagined South," 7, 37, 73, 114, 118, 127, 170, 171; as a region, 18, 18n, 21–24, 25, 32, 39, 55, 72, 75, 77–78, 77n, 98n, 100, 101, 119, 123, 126, 126n, 129n, 131, 132, 136, 137, 140, 150–51, 163, 175

Southern Christian Leadership Conference (SCLC), 127, 133

Southern food studies, 5

Southern studies, viii–x, 175

Student Nonviolent Coordinating Committee (SNCC), 127–28, 127n

subjectivity, 6n, 29, 30, 30n, 92, 140, 140n, 170

subservience, 41, 41n, 55, 99, 128, 142, 145

Sula (Toni Morrison), 74n

"table of brotherhood," 167

takeaway food, 142, 157

Thanksgiving Day (in *Driving Miss Daisy*), 53

theft, 48 n, 48–49, 50, 51, 91n

third place, 105–6

"throwaway bodies" (Patricia Yaeger), 156

To Kill a Mockingbird (Harper Lee), 28n

Top Chef, 169

train, 73, 74, 77, 82, 84n, 86. *See also* diner

Treme (David Simon and Eric Overmyer), 172–73

Turner, Victor, 87, 118, 133, 143, 144n, 160, 163

uppitiness, 91, 92, 138

Vaughts' castle (in *The Last Gentleman*), 32, 34

"vertical Negro," 150–51

violence, 6, 24, 69, 91n, 114, 143n, 152–53, 153n, 156, 160, 161, 161n, 167n

visual politics of Jim Crow, 110, 111. *See also* curtain; signs; wall

waiters, 82, 84n, 86, 87, 87n

wall: 88, 104; walls of segregation, 86n

watermelon, 45, 87

"We Wear the Mask" (Paul Laurence Dunbar), 94, 94n

"The Welcome Table" (Lee Martin), 173

Wells, Ida, 74, 74n

Whistle Stop Cafe, 23, 68, 82, 100, 100n, 105–6, 109, 111

White domination, 36, 57

White fragility, 170, 170n

White privilege, 82, 100–1

White supremacy, 32, 42n, 68, 69, 72, 78, 82–84, 84n, 87, 100, 104, 108, 112, 119, 122, 122, 124, 131, 141, 165, 173; White supremacist ideology, 124, 135, 135n, 141

Whiteness, 14, 18, 18n, 49n, 61, 67, 68, 79, 86, 120, 121n, 121–22, 135n, 140, 140n, 155, 175

Willie (of "Food that Pleases, Food to Take Home"), 155–56, 156n–57n, 157, 160, 162

Williston Barrett (of *The Last Gentleman*), 30, 31

Woolworth's, 124, 125, 127, 129, 133n, 136–37, 137n, 139n, 143, 146n, 151